INVASION
WITHIN

INVASION WITHIN

Overcoming the Elitists' Attack on
Moral Values and the American Way

DOMENICK J. MAGLIO, Ph.D.

Since 1947
REGNERY
PUBLISHING, INC.
An Eagle Publishing Company • Washington, DC

Cataloging-in-Publication Data on file with the Library of Congress

ISBN 0-89526-044-1

Published in the United States by
Regnery Publishing, Inc.
An Eagle Publishing Company
One Massachusetts Avenue, NW
Washington, DC 20001

Visit us at www.regnery.com

Distributed to the trade by
National Book Network
4720-A Boston Way
Lanham, MD 20706

Printed on acid-free paper

Manufactured in the United States of America

10 9 8 7 6 5 4 3 2 1

Books are available in quantity for promotional or premium use. Write to Director of Special Sales, Regnery Publishing, Inc., One Massachusetts Avenue, NW, Washington, DC 20001, for information on discounts and terms, or call (202) 216-0600.

Dedication

This book is dedicated to the Franks, Lindas, Joes, Pauls, Tinas, Hectors, Gladyses, Lucindas, Robertos, Nicks, Lesters, and Dorises of our nation who, by their courageous moral choices, are revitalizing the best of our traditional culture. Through them we will achieve success in the Culture War for the benefit of our children and future generations.

They are the moral, responsible, God-fearing, family-oriented Americans—our everyday heroes. Through their daily deeds of doing the right thing these people are "taking care of business." This is the sustaining force of our nation's greatness. Our victory will be borne on the broad shoulders of these cultural warriors.

Contents

Preface

My loving wife and I have been married since 1965. We have sculpted a positive world for ourselves as the parents of four successful young adults and have recently been blessed by a healthy grandson and are looking forward to the addition of three more grandchildren. We are blessed to have developed a wonderful sanctuary where we live, with five acres of huge oak and magnolia trees, a grape arbor, and eighty citrus trees. Here we have many kinds of flowers, birds, and butterflies to warm the soul.

Every day we return to this sanctuary from another sanctuary we have created on a different five acres twenty miles away—a private school for children from ages three to eighteen. Thousands of students who have passed through this school, run by my wife and me since 1983, have been prepared for college and life. We get to know the children and their parents very well, watching them grow not only academically, but in character as well, through the support of their parents and our teachers.

My forty years of professional life, serving in the trenches of the Culture War, have been spiritually gratifying to me. I have been on the front lines as a clinical psychologist in the Florida prison system; a public school teacher; the director of the Hernando County Domestic Violence program for ten years; and the director of Open Door for

Mental Health, a program helping mentally ill patients transition from state mental hospitals to the community. I taught for a decade in higher education and serve as a board member with the National Independent Private Schools Association. For over a quarter of a century I have dealt with all types of people having difficulty functioning in life while running my private counseling practice and working at community mental health centers.

At the end of the day, I probably have gained more from my clients, students, and their parents than I have taught them. But I live what I preach to my children, students, and clients. I believe in God, though I am not a churchgoer, and I believe we create our own destiny by our choices. My wife and I have gladly sacrificed to gain what we wanted. We saw that the more we gave of what was right—not in a material sense—the more we received. We spent all of our time with our own children never feeling the need to get away. We worked on weekends with our children to build our dream of a school and homestead. The entire family pitched in to make our lives spiritually right. My children appreciate the results even though they have great stories to share about their hardships.

I am not a journalist researching the topic of peace. I am not a religious zealot writing from a biblical reference point. I do not come from a privileged conservative background. It was not until I traveled overseas as a Peace Corps volunteer that I began to question the anti-American sentiments I had learned on college campuses. The greater my exposure to other nations, the more I understood that even with its faults I lived in the best nation on earth. I have learned to appreciate the wisdom of our ancestors. I am proud to be an American traditionalist. I have learned what works and I want to share it with as many people as possible.

After writing my first book, *Essential Parenting,* I realized the significance of the Culture War. Even when parents saw the effective results of using the procedures of managing children outlined in the book, they reverted back to the ineffectual modern child-rearing advice. I realized the counterculture had co-opted the way young people are supposed to raise their children. Effective traditional, commonsense methods of child rearing would have a difficult time taking root without tilling under the wild utopian nonsense. The counterculture's nonfunctioning concepts have become entrenched.

America Is Out of Balance

It is difficult to be an adult. Too many parents are wasting the finite eighteen years of childhood instead of cultivating their children to take over as our future leaders. It is affecting every aspect of America. There are fewer young people prepared in skills, values, and morals to assume the reins of power—like a job, a family, and especially the responsibility of leadership. Our civic irresponsibility in teaching children is weakening every aspect of our nation. It is impossible for anyone to deny that we reap what we sow. We no longer can avoid the reality that taking shortcuts instead of doing the right thing is eroding the legacy of our nation.

Our founding fathers did not shirk responsibility. They heavily sacrificed for future generations to taste the fruit of their good works. They confronted the oppressive rule of the British Empire. They courageously fought and lost everything they possessed—including their lives—for our freedom. The heroes of the revolution were spiritual men.

These men created a culture of exceptionalism, a culture based on freedoms with accompanying responsibilities for those freedoms. They borrowed from the Greeks and the Romans to erect a society based on nature and God. Our culture of exceptionalism has nurtured our traditions that have directed the USA as a beacon of freedom throughout the world.

America's war on terrorism is based on the premise that repressed people given a taste of freedom will choose to fight to maintain their liberation. We believe all people have a right to be free and attempt to spread these traditions and beliefs to all corners of the world.

In order to effectively get nations to adopt our ways, we must live them. The Culture War will determine the war on terrorism. Victory over terrorism will happen only if we make the correct choice in the Culture War. If we follow the moral traditions of our founding fathers we will have the strength to prevail. If we choose the easier, modern path of self-centeredness—spoiling and drugging our children, engaging in sexual promiscuity, coddling weakness, and excusing irresponsibility—we will lose the war on terrorism and lose our nation.

There are two distinct ways of thinking that permeate each and every aspect of our culture. The strategy of approaching the issues of mental health, abortion, self-defense, criminality, alcoholism, obesity, homosexuality, and even one's view on getting a flu shot are radically different depending on one's cultural perspective. The modern elite-leaning people have adopted pseudo science as their religion and the proclamations of the Marxist intellectuals as their values. To these elites, human behavior is not due to individual choice, it is determined by forces outside the individual's control such as genetics, chemical balance, sociological, and psychological factors.

In contrast, the traditional perspective has been formulated by the belief in God, truth found in the Bible, history, and the wisdom obtained from learning what works in overcoming life's challenges. Traditional values are handed down from family members, from parents to children. Personal accountability, willpower, courage, and faith in God are characteristics of the traditionalists. In fact, 80 percent of our population believes in our American traditions. The problem is most Americans are not living their beliefs. It is up to the moral leadership of this country to convince our citizens of the concrete benefits to the individual, family, community, and nation of being a strong American.

Returning to the guiding light of our forefathers will empower all of us to follow a more difficult though far more beneficial journey. This spiritual path will lead to emotional and spiritual fulfillment. Following this path will require learning the moral lessons of life such as tolerating pain, persevering, and living with courage to establish and pursue the honorable goal of peace. There will be evil to conquer within and outside of ourselves. Yet we will realize that each step placed correctly will strengthen us on this courageous march to our destiny. The process of Americanization is a difficult process as well as an opportunity. My father was born in Italy in 1910 and, like all new arrivals in America, he paid his dues. He learned English, worked menial jobs to climb up the American ladder, and fought in six major battles in the Pacific front in World War II, winning five bronze stars for valor and gaining his citizenship. He earned his privileges as an American. He was given freedom and opportunity, not entitlements. It is not the easy path, though it paves the way for future generations to be productive citizens. It is the American way.

My parents showed me that doing the right things in life increase one's inner strength. My father was an honest, hardworking plumber-laborer who unfortunately chose to be an alcoholic. Even with my father's shortcomings, he and my mother taught me right from wrong. He was the most highly paid and respected plumber in a company of five hundred employees. Along with my mother, he raised three healthy, educated children. As the oldest son, I was the natural target of his displaced anger. His badgering started when I was very young. Night after night, he told me I was worthless or accused me of eating his food. His alcoholism progressed and his fits of anger became more abusive.

As a youngster of nine, I had a decision to make. I could be resentful and unappreciative of my blessings and accomplishments like my father. This would lead to depression, some form of addiction, and abuse of others. I knew the results of going down this path. Instead, I chose to learn from my father's mistakes and vowed to myself to live a disciplined life to avoid abusing others or myself. I became a defender for those who were treated unfairly.

My interest in politics started as a young boy coming home from elementary school and sitting down with my mother to watch the McCarthy hearings. My mother made me aware that times were changing though not always for the better. When I was growing up, the American culture of the 1950s promoted traditional families, values, and morals. It was the period after World War II that echoed my family's moral teaching. Absolute values still existed. Things were good or bad. One had to stand up regardless of the risk and say or do the right thing. The message was clear: There was no tolerance for bad behavior. I was convinced at an early age that the moral road was the right road and I became dedicated to the concept of justice.

There was no way my parents were going to allow me not to go to college. I was the first person in my family and my working class Bensonhurst, Brooklyn, neighborhood to go to college. I challenged my instructor's illogical statements and false assumptions. I was intrigued by the moxie of the suburban students who wore expensive clothes, received money from their affluent parents, and attacked everything that allowed them to have an opportunity to have a college education. I was confused. I accepted many of the Marxist concepts taught but knew things were not that simple. It sounded too good to be true.

In the 1960s I was in the middle of the elite Smuggers heyday at one of the most radical state universities of New York at New Paltz. Many of my professors were committed communists who traveled the seventy miles from New York City to teach courses. The head of the communist party at that time, Gus Hall, spoke at our campus. The Student Action Movement, SAM, was in full force taking over administration offices while in direct communication with Berkeley.

I graduated from the University of Connecticut with a master's degree and received a PhD from Union Institute and University advancing my indoctrination into the Marxist-Smugger world. I learned how to play the game. I knew what they wanted me to think and say but was never sure if it was true.

My Peace Corps and professional experiences taught me that much of what I learned was indeed useless and often downright destructive.

Even so, I am not writing to convert these counterculture Smugger activists. We just need to recognize and ignore them.

This book is written for people who want to preserve for their children the spiritual heritage of America. I am writing this book as an inspiration to all the families who are living their lives by making the decisions to live right. These are the people who reject self-centeredness, knocking down others to get ahead, breaking the Ten Commandments, and disregarding moral lessons from everyday life. These are the people who develop a zone of goodness to protect themselves from being seduced by negative, evil forces. I hope it brings into focus the culture war that mushroomed back in the 1960s and is presently raging around all of us. I hope to be a voice to others who are doing the everyday little things to live right.

I was given a special invitation to a seminar by one of the nation's renowned psychiatrists in May of 2004. He made the customary jabs at the political establishment. He spoke about his lifelong accomplishments that were significant in the mental health field. His initial fame was based on codifying traditional methods of discipline. His theory was based on observations of human nature that worked in creating good behavior. He related that he no longer believed in the principles that brought him fame.

Like many professional Smugger experts, he touted his innovative speculation as fact. This intellectual had a worldview where criticizing, punishing, angering, and any consequences should be replaced by encouraging, respecting, listening, and supporting to create happy people. Forgetting the basis for his own fame, he ridiculed common sense, human nature, and conventional wisdom as impeding the progressive evolution of man. His "advanced Smugger thinking" would single-handedly eliminate the problems that have historically plagued man. Eventually mental illness, poverty, and war would be things of the past. He was convinced that the adoption of his new behavior patterns would result in a better world.

His smug arrogance was astonishing. He placed himself above the thousands of years of human experience in many great civilizations. Even though the quest for power on a personal as well as on a family and national level has been a major motivation throughout history, he wanted this eliminated from his utopian world. He reluctantly acknowledged the pervasiveness of the seeking of power by men. He believed if no one used power to impose his will on another, the world would be a better place.

Obviously this would be true. It is just not part of human nature. Free choice was the answer to all social ills. However, in his theory he could not reconcile the human tendency for people to be inherently motivated by power. His positive behavior model had no explanation for why people would control the expressing of this fundamental aspect of human nature. There was no explanation for dealing with evil people in his vision. Without acknowledging the basic human power urge, his theory becomes nonsensical.

Reality has a way of crumbling Smuggers' elitist egos and utopia-driven philosophies. All patriotic Americans need to become more aware of the eternal attack on our country. To be forewarned is to be forearmed.

I have been blessed by my service to others. By doing the best I could do as a son, husband, father, laborer, professional, and citizen, I have reaped more than I could ever have imagined. I feel it is my patriotic duty to present a graphic picture of the way Smuggers are attacking our institutions and promoting evil through moral equivalency. This is necessary in order to preserve the greatness of America for our future generations and assure victory in the Culture War.

Choosing Sides in the Culture War

Almighty God, you have given us this good land for our heritage. We humbly ask you that we may always prove ourselves a people mindful of your favor and glad to do your will. Bless our land with honorable endeavor, sound learning, and pure manners. Save us from violence, discord, and confusion, from pride and arrogance, and from every evil way. Defend our liberties and fashion into one united people the multitude brought here out of many nations and tongues.

Endow with the spirit of wisdom those to whom, in your name, we entrust the authority of government, that there may be justice and peace at home, and that through obedience to your law we may show forth your praise among the nations on earth. In time of prosperity fill our hearts with thankfulness, and in the days of trouble do not allow our trust in you to fail. Amen.

—THOMAS JEFFERSON
Written and read at the opening of the Continental Congress in Philadelphia in July 1776

What the *&#*% is going on? Across the landscape of our American culture, most of us are witnessing the cherished institutions, values, and teachings of our society crumbling in front of our eyes. The modern counterculture is poisoning the spirit of the citizens of our nation—a nation that was created by men who drew great strength from and believed deeply in God. But we are too young, too busy, or too dense to notice this rapid-fire assault that is striking at the heart of our institutions. Justin Timberlake's public sexual assault on Janet Jackson during the Super Bowl XXXVIII halftime show (and in front of an audience of unsuspecting children and adults) was our wake-up call. This in-your-face invasion of our homes was the Culture War's 9/11. Like it or not, we are in the midst of an internal war for the minds and souls of our citizens.

President Reagan, through his vision and his resolve, brought an end to communism in Europe. It is time for us patriots to end the power of the Marxist-leaning Smuggers inside our borders.

There is no time for inaction in this final phase of the Culture War. People of character must stand up and act before everything is lost. In the following pages I examine the front lines of the Culture War: the institutions of parenting, marriage, school, and community. My four decades of professional experience working in the psychological and educational areas, along with my strong interest and background in political science and history, have inspired me to write this book. I am writing to say things that need to be said in order to get us back on track as a strong, moral, and optimistic society.

The destruction of our nation's values and morality will be reversed when the American people are awakened to the inherent fallacy of the "modern" agenda. It is weakening all our sacred institutions. The Smuggers must not be allowed to inject their failed Marxist-humanist utopian ideas into the social fabric of our country.

In our instant gratification, hip-hop counterculture, morals impede debauchery. In the long run, morals are inspired wisdom that if followed prevent us from making stupid decisions.

Morals do work in negotiating the dangers present in one's life.

Barry Goldwater started the process of steering our national ship towards a more moral course in his 1964 presidential campaign. As he said, "I would remind you that extremism in the defense of liberty is no vice! And let me remind you also that moderation in the pursuit of justice is no virtue!"[1]

Through this book, I tackle the destructive practices, thoughts, and behaviors spawned by both the media and the educational, psychological, and medical industries. By teaching and training children to develop a conscience we are strengthening little people to face the world and make it a better place. As the family moral bar is raised for children, it will raise everyone's moral purpose, motivating leaders on all levels of society to maintain their highest standards in order to match those of our own American family.

Misdeeds must not go unpunished in the family or in the nation.

Thomas Paine once chided Great Britain with the same thoughts in mind, writing: "Had you studied only the domestic politics of a family, you would have learned how to govern the state."[2] He realized that the very morals and discipline found in a healthy family are evident in all institutions of a peaceful society as well. The moral interface between the family and other institutions is essential for the peaceful survival of our nation.

The Marxist ideals that are the foundation of our modern child development must be exposed.

I have personally witnessed the permissive change in our culture and the negative impact this has had on children (examples of which are sprinkled throughout the book) illustrating the horrendous assault on our culture. The collateral damage inflicted on our children from teaching tolerance instead of absolute values must end.

Moral equivalency is devouring our souls. Deviance rammed down our throats is demeaning the heroic efforts of positive and stable role models. These moral role models are the people who do the right thing, often with little or no recognition. The interplay between permissive child-rearing practices, past and present, and the decline of morality is real—with serious consequences for the survival of the nation.

The permissiveness and lack of morals on the part of ancient Greek parents had a profound impact on the fall of the civilization. We are mimicking ancient Greece. "An excessive desire for liberty at the expense of everything else is what undermines democracy and leads to the demand of tyranny... it will permeate private life... it becomes the thing for father and son to change places, the father standing in awe of his son, and the son neither respecting nor fearing his parents, in order to assert his independence... The teacher fears and panders to his pupils, who in turn despise their teachers and attendants; and the young as a whole imitate their elders, argue with them and set themselves up against them, while their elders try to avoid the reputation of being disagreeable or strict by aping the young and mixing with them on terms of easy good fellowship."[3] Parents need to teach right and wrong, not focus on "easy good fellowship."

In order for a representative government to flourish, we need citizens with consciences. They may not be altruistic but they have to do what is right in a free society. A conscience is cultivated in a child by parents giving calibrated consequences followed by a conversation discussing the importance of doing right rather than wrong. Waiting too long to begin this process will have the dire results of losing the opportunity to create a conscience. Once the critical period of developing a conscience has passed there is no magic rehabilitation for a habitual criminal or an evil dictator. The responsible action in dealing with immoral and overtly evil individuals is for moral men to confront their evil behavior and forcefully remove them from power. "A republic cannot be made up of people who think they can do in secret what they would not do in public."[4] Morals and character do matter. Our founding fathers were versed in the same Roman virtues that led the philosopher Cicero to write, "Honor is virtue's reward."

Choosing the traditional camp over the selfish Smugger side is the way to win this war. Evil must be stifled. Stand up for what is right and be counted. It is the only way to keep America's greatness. Right is might. By doing the things we know to be right in our daily life, we are sowing the seeds for liberty, justice, and peace. Unconditional tolerance of all things is eliminating the essence of our civilization. Without the structure of rules and moral preferences, a nation decays. Societies need laws and justice for people to live in harmony.

We are at a crucial juncture in our history. If we choose to lose the Culture War, terrorists will conquer our weakened nation. Who wins the Culture War will decide our destiny of either living in decadence or in a vibrant society.

The American Dream is alive and well. We live in a land of opportunity with the freedom of choice to create our individual destiny. We Americans are not restrained by government or social class system in our quest to better ourselves. This is the reason immigrants are struggling—even dying—to enter our shores. Many immigrants are not even searching for a government handout, just for the opportunity to advance themselves and their families.

While walking along the beach, my wife and I saw a lady running to chase two great blue herons away from her husband's bait pail. The herons were feasting on the fisherman's asset: his bait. On the way back we observed the fisherman's wife and friends around the bait pail. Lurking about ten feet away was one of the herons waiting to get his entitlement, a free lunch. As we glanced towards the water we saw the other heron using his entrepreneurial initiative and effort to wade into the water to fish for himself. Thank God we live in a free enterprise nation that allows us the opportunity to better our lives through our work ethic. We Americans are free.

We can choose to be either self-centered takers, going down the path of hedonism to end in self-destructive chaos and eventual military defeat, or be doers, responsibly following the shared moral and valued traditions that have produced our nation's greatness.

Many older adults have been lucky enough to experience a more secure and stable world. We fortunate individuals owe our children and grandchildren our wisdom. Living a responsible, moral life is a beneficial legacy we can pass on. Through our being role models and teaching we can leave a positive blueprint of how to obtain freedom, prosperity, and a quality life.

We need to assume the role of elders and take the responsibility of passing the legacy to future generations. The shared sacrifices and disciplined lifestyles of fathers, mothers, grandparents, and other authority figures are essential in teaching our children. In the long run, the benefits of following the traditional moral path, a courageous path that relentlessly confronts the immoral deceitfulness of the Smugger agenda, is the high road. Our nation's greatness will not survive unless we assume these critical roles.

The antidote to the poisoning of our culture is for each and every American patriot to live courageously and righteously. Let us stand up and confront the moral relativist Smugger elite who systematically demean our traditions in order to erode our nation's values and morals. Shining the light on Smuggers will make them irrelevant in their divisiveness and ridicule of traditional American culture. Our victory in the Culture War will be evident when our focus is on following and improving our traditions through an open and civil discourse amongst all Americans in a patriotic manner. This book will be a reality check on our society. It is not unlike the plea of Thomas Paine's *Common Sense*. Wake up! We must once again choose the right side of a war.

Victory will be ours. By the strength of our will we can inspire each other to do our best. Let us choose the traditional commonsense methods of raising children. Let us choose moral leadership. Demand better schools, media, and entertainment. Do the right things in helping our families and neighbors. Moral ends do justify the moral means. We will be decisively triumphant in the Culture War by choosing to do what is right and good in our daily lives.

Our culture has been infiltrated. We are on the brink of losing our civilization because of arrogant know-it-alls (Smuggers) who despise the traditional values that have provided the foundations for America's greatness. When they complain about what they don't have rather than appreciate what they do have, they suck the inspirational energy from an exceptional nation. A Smugger victory will mean the loss of our identity and hard-fought freedoms. We cannot allow Smuggers to win, for then, all Americans lose.

Americans, it is time to choose sides. Total victory is necessary to preserve our nation. It is all or nothing.

Chapter 1

Defeating the Enemy: The Smuggers

"We have staked the whole of all our political institutions upon the capacity of mankind for self-government, upon the capacity of each and all of us to govern ourselves, to control ourselves, to sustain ourselves according to the Ten Commandments of God."

—James Madison, the fourth president,
known as "the father of our Constitution"

This cultural civil war is not a spontaneous breakdown. There has been a sophisticated strategy since the 1930s developed by a core of Marxist-humanists with the sole aim of destroying traditional countries around the world. Their plan was to wage a war from within. It wasn't until the 1990s that an overt frontal attack occurred in the United States. However, in America their progress during that time was real and subversive. The McCarthy hearings of the 1950s demonstrated the penetration of Marxist and humanist sympathizers into bureaucratic middle- and high-level government positions, higher education, entertainment, and the media.

One generation later, the anti-establishment hippies, who were to become the greatest champions of this subversive movement, set their sights on a wide range of our traditions and values. These misguided, affluent students were like children on a beach having fun digging random holes in the sand. There was no master plan. They were anointed by their frustrated professors to attack the "repressive social fabric of our society." The vision that these young radicals held was the failed utopian Marxist ideals of their all-knowing professors. The impressionable recruits were indoctrinated with these impractical notions, which had been historically shown, time after time, to be unworkable. Elitist teachers and students continue to construct these sandcastles of elaborate theories, only to see them continually washed away by the waves of time. Yet many naïve college students with little personal experience and limited knowledge of history became unknowing pawns in an ongoing cultural war. Some of these students' personal identities as adults were derived from this period of campus charade.

I will call these converts to the anti-establishment culture "Smuggers." "Smuggers" will be the term used to describe pseudo-intellectual, secular elite, Marxist-humanist oriented, antipatriotic, cultural and moral relativist, atheist hedonists who, for whatever reason, are wishing and working for the collapse of America. Smuggers are elitist know-it-alls who possess smug attitudes and are mugging us of our traditions, morals, and values.

Smuggers have been very effective in altering our perceptions and thus our values. No longer do we honor a person who has sustained doing the right thing in life—a person of good character. We have been programmed by the elite media to think of this person as self-righteous and dull. Instead, we are indoctrinated to view people with the latest logo on their clothes, politically correct slogans, and phony sensitivity as virtuous people, regardless of their actual daily lifestyle. Image is everything. Perception is reality. Smuggers have cultivated a morally shallow culture where selling one's soul for material wealth is not only acceptable, but is seen as smart. They have demeaned and continue to destroy our traditional culture. They are the enemy.

These Smuggers have used the vast power of the media, portraying men as oppressive macho brutes, mothers as dull browbeaten victims, divorce as liberating, and the youth of the era as saviors. These Smuggers, taking potshots from Hollywood pressrooms and the ivory towers of our most hallowed universities, cause damage to every institution in our nation. In one shameful generation, these me-first egotists began the process of eroding the very foundations of traditional America that had been built up over hundreds of years.

This describes the place where the plan to attack marriage and the family originated:

> No country better illustrates this [phenomenon] than Russia. In the first flush of its atheistic Marxist socialism, it denied the necessity of marriage, established abortion centers, ridiculed fidelity and chastity as a 'bourgeois virtue', compared lust and adultery to drinking a glass of water, after which you can forget the glass in one instance and the person in the other, introduced postcard divorces, which required only that you send a notice that you were no longer living with a certain party, and all obligations ceased.[1]

In our contemporary age, the Culture War has morphed from defending our traditions against covert maneuvers to defending against overt full-scale battle operations. For this, we have the Clintons to thank, for it was not until their presidential administration that the counterculture at last felt sufficiently strong to begin imposing the ultimate phase of their strategy. Gone were the days of negotiation, of the more insidious social change resulting in the deluded Great Society of President Johnson and the ridicule phase of the 1960s. This was to be a culture based on equality, gender sameness, atheism, and cradle-to-grave entitlement coated with a veneer of hedonistic splendor. It was, in essence, new packaging for the failed Marxist concepts.

The initial Clinton administration salvo upon their election was decreed from the bully pulpit: the acceptance of gays in the military and cradle-to-grave socialized medicine. Their behavior surprised many voters, for candidate Clinton was portrayed as a centrist and moderate.

The media have assisted both in advancing their positions and omitting their lies, relentlessly advancing the radical agenda set by the Clintons. Selective highlighting of daily news, focus groups, and unnamed sources are common subjective practices used by Smuggers in the media to bolster their Marxist principles. Where did all the Communist sympathizers go after the collapse of the Soviet Union? The answer is that they mutated into leftist supporters.

Confusion is a major tool in the Smuggers' arsenal. Smuggers intentionally create smokescreens to hide their destructive actions. They have refined the art of pretending to honor American principles by blurring moral distinctions, distorting the truth, and outright lying, while at the same time targeting American traditions without for a moment altering their own phony smirks. Whenever their blatant biases are exposed, their reflex is to attack the opposition by accusing them of their own Smugger tactics. They are accomplished hypocrites.

An illustration of the audacious tactics employed by Smuggers is the Joe Wilson saga. He testified to the Senate Intelligence Committee that he had assured U.S. officials as far back as 2002 that "there was nothing to the story." The "story" being the accusation that President Bush lied to the American people when he delivered a sixteen-word line in the State of the Union address saying that Saddam Hussein sought significant quantities of yellow cake uranium ore from Niger, Africa.

Originally, Wilson reported early in 2002 that Iraq was interested in purchasing uranium, saying that his evidence "... [confirmed] what the British and Italian intelligence services had told us from their own sources." It wasn't until after an Italian journalist uncovered fake documents indicating that Saddam was seeking uranium, that Joe Wilson changed his tune about Iraq's effort to obtain uranium. All at once he became a darling of the media, denouncing the Bush administration and saying that they were lying about Iraq's search for uranium. When asked whether he was given the assignment at the urging of his CIA wife, he vehemently stated, "Valerie had nothing to do with the matter." Contrary to Joe Wilson's statement, the Senate published testimony that his CIA wife offered up his name and printed her memo to her boss saying that "my husband has good relations with Niger officials and lots of French connections."[2]

Joe Wilson was proven wrong by Lord Butler's non-partisan panel that concluded President Bush's sixteen words were indeed true. But Smuggers never admit they lie nor show remorse.

The anti-establishment hippies of the 1960s are presently in the halls of the Congress, the boardrooms of nonprofit and Fortune 500 companies, environmental groups, the courts, and on all levels of government, including the State Department, the Pentagon, and some even in the White House. This infiltration has escalated the frequency and intensity of the Smuggers' attacks on traditional America.

The election of G. W. Bush has frustrated the Marxists who have followed a gradual reconstruction and revisionist path to altering the American tradition. Many Smuggers have responded to the disappointment of the 2000 presidential election by reverting to spontaneous hysterical outbursts. Illegal gay marriages are sprouting one after another, there are anarchist World Trade Organization protests, and pro-Saddam's Iraq and anti-Bush rallies indicate a hatred of the possibility of a resurgence of traditional America. These actions are sporadic and do not reflect the slick, well-orchestrated policy of the Clinton years. We are at a crucial junction in the Culture War.

The Culture War is raging worldwide pitting moral traditionalism against Marxist secularism. Smuggers now believe that their victory is inevitable, an optimism that comes from the knowledge of the support they will receive from their international comrades. During the Iraqi War and the 2000 presidential elections, many U.S. elites spouted the same arguments previously pronounced by their counterparts across the ocean, the European socialists. Just as the French and German political leaders were calling us a renegade nation, these statements were translated and fed to the American public by our secular elite. In another example of international secular influence, the U.S. Supreme Court judges used international law to support the alteration of United States constitutional law—an event both unprecedented and dangerous.

Smugglers are ignorant people gleefully ripping apart their own homeland like wild animals. They believe they are geniuses who have the right to condescendingly snatch away our American principles and traditions. Our own press acts as if any pro-American foreign story would indicate a bias—even when it is relevant and true. Only anti-American information ensures their objectivity. They are as dumb as any person who burns down his own home or neighborhood to correct a perceived grievance.

Smugglers are people who believe their Marxist-derived ideals give them the right to denigrate anyone who does not believe like they do. They have exemplified the tactics of "the politics of personal destruction." The indoctrination process in schools, the media, and entertainment has anointed them superior to anyone who is morally upright, hardworking, and patriotic. Whenever a patriot expresses traditional viewpoints in a room with two or more Smuggers, the Smuggers will raise their eyebrows to communicate disdain to each other that they are in the company of an inferior thinking person. The power they possess does not come from numbers or ideas; it comes from their sniper tactics.

These Smuggers are slick guerrilla goons who exploit their positions to cleverly undermine our traditions and incessantly spread their propaganda. These subversive tactics can only be repelled by recognizing the phony smiles and condescending attitudes. These warning signs should alert us to the coming attack on our values. Only through greater awareness will we be able to ward off these misguided, ignorant pawns of anti-Americanism. Smuggers must be identified and neutralized to preserve our nation.

George Soros, billionaire and major contributor to Moveon.org, has smugly flashed his money to manipulate leaders of other nations to do his bidding. "He (Soros) is portrayed as someone ... who can be offended if a leader of a country where he is involved philanthropically is insufficiently subservient, who will consort with an autocratic regime in order to see his programs carried out; and who is intent on imposing his influence generally on an ever expanding area of the world."[3] Mr. Soros prominently displayed his arrogance regarding the power he wielded in the Ukraine: "Soros makes no bones about his interventionist nature of his role in Ukraine. At one point, he remarked jocularly, 'If this isn't meddling in the affairs of a foreign nation I don't know what is ... I look at Ukraine with the same frame of mind as I look at REITS. By my intervention I make it happen."[4] This Smugger seems to think he can buy an election through the 527 Moveon.org in yet another country—America. We must identify and reduce the influence of Smuggers like him in order to preserve our nation.

Smuggers are moral and cultural relativists. They believe that God is a figment of man's imagination. They do not believe in moral absolutes and, therefore, good can be bad and bad can be good—depending on the situation. They do not believe that American civilization is highly developed or exceptional, for all societies, including the most primitive, have to be evaluated on their own merits. By blurring the lines between good and evil, moral and cultural relativists eradicate traditional standards. This establishment of a nonjudgmental world allows Smuggers to push whatever agenda they want at the moment. The lack of absolute morals encourages relativists to fabricate reality and outright lie in order to gain advantage in reaching their goals. Smuggers cry foul whenever they are held accountable for their deeds or words, yet they are ready to call any traditionalist a hypocrite if he deviates to any degree from his principles. Embracing moral relativity frees Smuggers to do whatever they think will cause them to win. In these untrue and vicious attacks, the ends of advancing their agenda justify their sleazy means.

Yet the modern Smugger agenda emphasizes the means one uses, not the ends. They would have parents believe that so long as they raise their children in a permissive and materially rich environment they are being exemplary parents—regardless of the behavior of the child. As long as we interrogate prisoners at Abu Ghraib or Guantanamo, giving them unearned civil rights that are guaranteed only to American citizens, it does not matter if we get any information from the terrorists that would save the lives of Americans. As long as New Jersey governor James McGreevey announces his politically correct homosexual/bisexual lifestyle, it doesn't matter how he has impacted his family members or ran a corrupt administration. As long as you fight a sensitive war, it doesn't matter if we win. As long as Smugger values are practiced, you are following their concept of "the means justifies the end."

The greatness of America builds upon the idea that moral means beget moral ends. We Americans use ingenuity to do whatever it takes to get the job done as long as it does not break the laws of God or man. We can get sweaty. We can mow our own lawns, paint our own homes, and raise our own children without feeling inferior to those who choose to pay for these services. We are proud of our self-reliance, our industriousness, and the outcomes of our efforts. We are the hardest working people in the Western world because we are willing to sacrifice (use the means) to gain the ends we want.

I was proud to be one of the Floridians working together to repair the damage to their communities from the extraordinary hurricane season that produced hurricanes Charley, Frances, Ivan, and Jeanne. We wanted the ends of having our communities back to normal and we were willing to put personal effort and means to achieve this purpose. This is the down-to-earth approach of the American spirit.

Smuggers are destroying our country from within. They conform to historically failed Marxist ideals and are found in every occupation and socioeconomic level of our country. Most have spent many years being indoctrinated in our best universities or on the streets of our urban centers. The beat-the-system welfare-mentality hipsters are the least dangerous Smuggers. They believe in the "world owes me a living" philosophy that predates Marx and are intuitively attracted to any redistribution of wealth rhetoric. These are the poor masses who the more educated Smuggers rile up and pander to.

The real menace to our nation is the affluent Smuggers themselves. These are people who have reached high levels in our power structures of government, corporations, media, and education. Smuggers are embedded in both the Republican and Democratic parties. These Smuggers usually are not highly motivated to gain material wealth for they are already well off. The Smuggers' quest is for power; power not to change their personal situation, but power to change the world. These powerful Smuggers are more pompous than the welfare hustlers. The hustler just wants more money for personal power and so constantly schemes to take other people's wealth. The professional Smugger's needs are more complex. He wants to relieve his sense of guilt for receiving more than he deserves according to his efforts. By fostering a utopian dream where everyone has what he has without him giving up anything, he can sleep more soundly. At the same time he gains even more power for his goodness and his establishing this new order.

It sounds familiar, doesn't it? It sounds like what has transpired in every communist country. The powerful get more power and wealth, the proletariat gets more symbolic slogans, marches, and poverty. These powerful, guilty Smuggers are leading us through their intellectual dream that ends in a nightmare of reality.

The Smuggers' hatred for their own country can only be attributed to the belief that America does not reach their unrealistic utopian ideals.

Ten to twenty percent of our population are Smuggers. These are people who would rather see traditional America lose than be successful leaders of the free world. Lynn Stewart, a radical attorney Smugger who defended Omar Abdel Rahman, the convicted bomber of the World Trade Center in 1993, stated, "I don't have any problem with Mao or Stalin or the Vietnamese leaders or certainly Fidel locking up people they see as dangerous."[5] Yet this Smugger is committed to fight anything America attempts to do to protect our citizens against homicidal terrorists. It is not possible to transform die-hard Smuggers into patriots. But we cannot allow them to sway the confused and weak to support them. Our nation is far from perfect. We have racism, corruption, and hypocrisy throughout all the layers of society. Our leaders are often self-serving. We are imperfect like all past, present, and future nations. Yet we are presently the best civilization on the face of the earth.

The downfall of our civilization will not resolve the frailties of human nature. Historically, human weaknesses have been perennial problems that have never been eliminated, just kept under control.

The Smuggers disdain everything American as primitive and unsophisticated, especially patriotism. When speaking, their smugness is displayed by a condescending smile. Their despising of the establishment somehow makes them purer and smarter than the rest of us. These so-called humanitarians are experts at ridiculing, criticizing, and degrading with practically no experience at building, developing, and governing. They are the ultimate in sidewalk superintendents and Monday-morning quarterbacks. This elite chooses to peck away at the essence of America. Our nation is not living up to their vaunted dreams and principles. These arrogant media, Hollywood, political activists, educational, and political celebrities have all the answers but possess not one iota of humility. Like most American teenagers, they think they know everything. According to their delusional belief system, the world would be a better place if only they had all the power. The proletariat masses are beneath their intellectual ability and cannot comprehend the complexities of establishing a new world order.

The main problem of the Smuggers is not America; it is their own inflated egos, their ignorance, and their unwillingness to accept the reality of human nature. Their thinking processes on the surface sound convincing, though on closer examination the infeasibility of their Marxist leaning becomes obvious. Yet they think they know better than all of us.

Smuggers have infiltrated our power structure, which has to be reversed to maintain our civilization. The cancer of these hidden Smugger invasions will destroy our society from within. Any society makes choices in developing the culture. Certain ideas, customs, food, and dress are deemed better than others. When there is a shift in one element, the culture evolves to incorporate the change throughout. There is always a priority of particular behaviors as to their value to the society.

With the advent of television in the 1950s, Smuggers were given a powerful vehicle to reengineer our culture. The force of television has created a significant group of people called TRLs. TRLs, Television Reality Lifers, are people whose most important relationships in their lives are found on the screen. They hang around the water cooler at work talking about the latest sitcom. Those who stay at home are fixated in front of the screen as they vicariously exist. The TRLs live their lives by fantasizing they are part of the show. Reality TV is not a type of show; it is everything on television for the TRLs.

Smuggers have successfully transformed a large portion of our society to be more accepting of utopian notions. Whites, heterosexuals, and the family are no longer valued while minorities, homosexuals, and gay marriages are praised. This can best be witnessed on television programming and advertising. Even the news promotes the Smuggers' agenda.

Smuggers' use of reverse discrimination is a blatant attack on our American traditions. This discrimination is the Smugger's strategy to bring America to its knees. The TRLs are being indoctrinated into a hedonistic-Marxist reality, not only in our universities as young adults but as infants and toddlers in their family rooms by television waves penetrating their brains.

The International Context:
Is America Becoming the New Europe?

The implementation of the European Union (EU) across most of Europe underscores the secular Smugger movement's worldwide influence. Many countries in Europe have been seduced to hand over their historical sovereignty in order to gain economic advantage. The EU members will gain financially from better-coordinated road building, easier access for laborers crossing borders, and a more standard currency. Yet the high cost to these countries is the loss of their national identities.

The great cultures of these European nations will vanish. The European Union's success will also mean the diluting of many cultures into a more sterile and bland modern state. This emerging entity will have a blank historical slate with a more centralized bureaucratic government that is more easily controlled by the international secular elite and is less directly responsive to the people.

Elimination of the history and culture of a people makes it easier to conquer them. America is the one major power in the world that stands in the way of international secularism. The indomitable American spirit of right over might makes us unique in the world of nations. We truly believe that the good guys win in the end. Goodness conquering evil has been a powerful force directing the course of our history. The U.S. has a history of optimism. Americans believe that fair competition brings out the best in everyone, including competition amongst nations. Consolidation to stifle others leads to stagnation and decay. Fair competition invigorates and stimulates creative juices. Maximizing freedom of opportunity with law and order leads to dynamic civilizations.

America is unique in the world of nations. President Reagan's vision of America was based on his faith in God, the creative spirit of the citizens, and our country. He knew an American military buildup would overload the USSR, eventually causing it to collapse. President Reagan was never given credit by the international Smugger secularists for this monumental accomplishment. It went directly against their international coalition concept of solving problems. It was America alone through sacrificing its resources—not the UN or international babble—that defeated the Soviet Union. President Reagan did the right thing and received no thanks.

President G. W. Bush and President Reagan both said what they mean and meant what they said. The qualities of directness and honesty do not translate well in the eloquent secular world. Both presidents reduced taxes, stimulating the economy, after they said they would. They did not believe in the redistributing wealth principle. The tax rate in the top tax bracket was as high as 76 percent when President Reagan took office.

European nations have a long history of living with repressive evil. Each nation has had periods of internal and external leaders inflicting atrocities upon their people. This suffering from loss of basic human rights left these people numb. Many of the citizens of these nations have accepted abuse and evil as inevitable. Too many no longer possess the courage to fight. Tolerating evil actions is easier than mustering the energy to defeat them.

As William Shakespeare wrote in *Julius Caesar,* "Cowards die many times before their deaths, the valiant never taste of death but once."

Our country has no tolerance for surrender to evil. Our founding fathers established a courageous course in resolving injustice. The

Revolutionary War, World War I, and World War II have demonstrated that with perseverance we can be victorious against great odds.

America is a unique freedom-loving nation. Our culture's principles of good triumphing over evil are well illustrated in our history. Each generation of our immigrants are taught about their inherent God-given "right to freedom." Accepting defeat at the hand of evil is incomprehensible to us Americans. We must not abandon our freedoms to gain acceptance in a world united in secularism. As Western civilization's main power, we may have to lead by standing alone.

Choosing the Battleground: Where to Begin the Fight

The consequences of the attack on our culture are most shockingly witnessed through our children. They are the home front, the casualties of our Culture War. The standards for raising our children sink lower every day, resulting in the most profound devastation. Under the acknowledged socialist Dr. Spock's leadership, moral relativist Smuggers have undermined our traditional child-rearing practices and replaced moral parenting with confused, inconsistent, and often contradictory principles. The subverting of our moral parenting has been the single most destructive act in the Culture War during the past fifty years.

The Smugger-influenced change in child-rearing has led to too many children acting out of control. These children are either bullies preying on the weak (including their parents), or are victims getting others to do their bidding through manipulation. We are turning our backs on doing the right thing, even with our innocent children. Instead of teaching our children not to be lazy or bullies or victims, we are being nice guys. Lazy, friendly parenting produces lazy, self-indulgent, angry, and weak children. We are ignoring, appeasing, redirecting, and reinforcing instead of disciplining. We are not teaching children to develop common sense or to be tough enough to handle everyday problems or to fight for their rights, especially when threatened by bullies. We are not communicating our traditional values, beliefs, and morals to our children. We are producing bullies and wimps. Where have all the strong parents gone?

Children raised under the modern parenting approach often are self-absorbed. Without values and morals to direct their behavior when their parents are not present, children resort to their primitive impulses of manipulation. There are the tantrums with physical outbursts to intimidate (bully) others and the "Poor me, I will cry until I get what I want," or worse, the "hurt myself until I get it" strategy (wimp). There is little empathy for the rights or concerns of others. These maladaptive children will be and have become today's dysfunctional adults.

Reclaiming Universal Values from the Smuggers

Smuggers who believe in no God and no absolute morality have infiltrated the highest levels of power in our country. These self-serving Smuggers have brought us to the depths of moral, social, and political depravity and decadence. Behind their belittling humor and smiling intellectual faces, there is disdain for everything we have accomplished as a God-fearing, hardworking people. These self-centered pleasure seekers detest the standards, sacrifice, and discipline required to reach the level we have obtained as a nation. They find conforming to a system based on historical morals and common-sense traditions repulsive, boring, and beneath their self-important illusions of grandeur. They are doing everything possible to lower our beliefs, principles, and standards to weaken us for eventual collapse.

These intellectuals demean our national successes, blame us for all the problems of the world, and want to erase the wisdom of our ancestors. Their goal supercedes their allegiance to our nation. Their goal is a world with one utopian government. "What men wish, they like to believe," said Julius Caesar.[6]

In order to achieve this goal, the Smuggers want us to believe that all morals and values are equally valid. The sinner and the saint, the criminal and the law-abiding citizen are all humans who should be accepted and treated with equal respect. By advocating this irrational notion of moral equivalency, these relativists understand that civilization will fall to be replaced by a world without any nations, a one-world government. By attempting to make right and wrong subjective and situational, society is heading down the slippery slope where people can no longer cross the line of antisocial behavior since the line no longer exists.

Senator Daniel Patrick Moynihan called it "defining deviancy down." When a forty-year-old convicted child molester is called "the accused adult lover of twelve-year-old Alex,"[7] instead of an evil sexual predator, we have moved into the twilight zone of an amoral society where evil actions are sugarcoated to protect the modern agenda. In pursuing pleasure, the self-absorbed Smuggers are creating a future world of chaos and pain. A peaceful nation is founded on absolute morals, not on individual, class, or national excuses for irresponsible behavior.

We are no longer proceeding with a clear moral road map to guide us in dealing with inevitable issues of everyday life. Terrorists are attacking our nation daily. These terrorists are the radio shock jocks and reality television programs that promote and describe immoral acts. They are the Hollywood and MTV producers who create a pseudo reality where the bad guy wins and the good guy is a boring loser. They are the corporate executives whose greed is more important than any responsibility to shareholders. They are the entertainment and sports celebrities who are anti-role models and yet heroes to our children. They are the politicians whose allegiance is to their reelection rather than the good of the people. They are the columnists, students, and environmentalists who report false information to further their agendas.

Cultural lies are marketed as fact, immorality is cool, and God is dead according to the Smuggers. A lie becomes a fact through constant repetition. A false statement is written in an article and then syndicated nationally in local papers. From *Doonesbury* to the *New York Times* to the British Broadcasting Corporation to the PETA kooks who fight to prevent us from fishing while advocating the killing of viable babies, we are under attack.

Most Americans are oblivious to the degree, frequency, and intensity of our cultural battles. The problem is most of us see our own personal portion of the decay of moral accountability without realizing the comprehensiveness of these cultural transformations. The laborer is aware of the decline in workmanship, the teacher the lack of academic excellence, the lawyer the irrelevance of truth, the doctor the noninvolvement with the patient, and the politician the unconcern for the good of the nation. Each of us experiences a glimpse without understanding the scope and progression of the decline. Unsung heroes live exemplary lives in the midst of a Smugger swamp of phony and self-serving behavior.

We Are Being Transformed

We are in trouble. Our society is not transmitting our traditional beliefs, values, and morals to our citizens—especially our youngsters. Every day we witness another attack on our cherished American ideals, principles, and traditions. We have moved from *Father Knows Best* to Homer Simpson, from the take-charge guy to the sensitive gay guy.

Each member of the family doing his own thing has shattered any concept of intimacy. Change has definitely taken place, and it is not limited to young people. Logos on clothing are more important in defining oneself than one's character. Parents act as perennial teenagers rather than as responsible adults.

Being genuine, sincere, and honorable are of little value in our mate-rially dominated culture. Artificial enhancement of the breasts, but-tocks, penis, face, and other body parts is not viewed as deception but is glorified. Natural wholesomeness is shunned as boring and naïve. Men are instructed to take Viagra and shave their chests, backs, and legs and to have piercings and tattoos to appear more fashionable in this synthetic world.

Entering a Moral Wasteland

Freaky is cool. It is chic to do anything the opposite of what once was considered decent. Manners are not cool, common sense is no longer common, and morals are demeaned. We are in a moral wasteland. The counterculture's effectiveness in attacking moral behavior is running out of targets. NAMBLA (North American Man-Boy Love Association) is openly soliciting young boys for sex on the Internet. Soft pornogra-phy is exploited on network TV and in advertising while hard porn is all over the Internet. Guilt, shame, and embarrassment are practically concepts of the past. Children are not being trained to develop a con-science and if they possess one it is attacked daily.

Our children only know a world in which divorce, abortion, out-of-wedlock births, pedophile neighbors and clergy, disrespect, violence, pornography, drugs, shacking-up, and public sexual displays are com-monplace. Their universe consists of junk food eaten while watching MTV and girls aggressively pursuing boys. Parents side with their chil-dren against other authority figures, even when the child is blatantly wrong. Children are taught they are smarter than their parents. Schools are places to party and receive free condoms, not for learning academ-ics. Teachers dress unprofessionally in these chaotic schools. Children return to single- or absentee-parent homes with little to no supervision or direction in learning right from wrong. Their role models are celebrity shock jocks whose personal lives are disasters. Children are not learning right from wrong.

The ability of Smuggers to equate good with bad behavior has had a major impact on all segments of society. Professionals, politicians, businessmen, priests, parents, teachers, and children have been morally corrupted by the worldwide saturation of their rationalizations. These man-made utopian ideals that are often contrary to human nature have permeated our country all the way to the chamber of the Supreme Court. Several Supreme Court justices have argued we have to lower our moral standards to better merge with other nations in a global culture. The Smuggers argue we need to follow the decrees of the corrupt and impotent United Nations and Western European countries. We are rapidly changing to an immoral, secular society. A Culture War is raging.

Our society has transformed from one with God-fearing people who knew right from wrong, to a hedonistic, no-rules world where people are entitled to something for nothing. An immoral nation is easy prey for conversion to unrealistic utopian ideals in a society that believes the Ten Commandments are the Ten Suggestions, so diluted regarding right and wrong that they are now meaningless to many. The authority of God has been undermined by this ignoring of His commandments. The gods of money and pleasure are now our culture's guiding forces. Living beyond one's means and seeking self-gratification are presently the litmus test of living the good life. Individuals who contribute to God, family, community, and country but fail to amass material wealth of their own are not valued in our society. Even though they have lived honorable lives, they are viewed as failures.

According to Smuggers, no one suffers rejection or loss of self-esteem when we dumb down our standards. Therefore lazy, less intelligent, or dysfunctional people have no reason to strive for a higher level, since there is no such thing as a higher level. All people are the same, period. The modern agenda promotes the lowering of standards and expectations. Sadly, the impact can be seen all around us.

These Smuggers are attacking our society on all fronts. Everything is too overwhelming so we do nothing even when we know we can do something. We retreat into ourselves. We are the "me generation" and we just go with the flow. We have been systematically brainwashed to believe anger is inappropriate regardless of the degree of provocation. We tell people what we think they want to hear rather than the truth. We don't want to get angry so we ignore evil actions of people and nations. It is easier than becoming upset and having to do the right thing. We are becoming a nation of sheep.

We will lose everything our forefathers fought and died for if we do not distinguish between right and wrong. We are a country where there are many honorable people bewildered and paralyzed in understanding what is happening to our country. We are rotting from the inside out. This cancer is destroying the essence of the nation.

Not Taking Responsibility

The media and a large segment of educational, legal, and medical professionals all tell us that we do not need to be responsible for our actions. Drinking, smoking, gambling, overeating, promiscuity, and overspending are caused by genetics, chemical imbalances, or exploitive villains. The individual is not held accountable. Researchers are even attempting to rationalize excessive partying as caused by a genetic defect.[8]

Professionals are not performing their duties with integrity and have the audacity to blame their poor results on their clients. A mother came for an application interview at my school. She related to me how her daughter was not required to do much work in her public school. Her twelve-year-old daughter agreed and added that her tests were rarely graded. The daughter noted that it did not matter to her teachers if she completed all or part of her homework since the teachers did not expect her to complete her assignment due to her learning disability. Her mother replied to a group of government schoolteachers that she thought her daughter was lazy. The teachers were aghast and replied that she should never say that about her daughter because she has a mental disorder. The mother said she felt reprimanded by the teachers for questioning her child's work ethic. But, the mother should have questioned the *teachers'* work ethic for not checking her daughter's work as well as letting her get by with doing less than she was capable of doing. The mother knew her daughter was lazy and the standards were dumbed-down. But it is easier not to fight and to believe the daughter's obvious lies, excuses, and false promises than to have the courage to change course. Naturally, to assist her daughter's education the public school recommended placing the child on medication to remain in this low-functioning program.

Our actions are no longer to be judged. Our children are systematically conditioned to accept any and all inappropriate behavior. A code of lying, cheating, stealing, and adultery are as acceptable to live by as the Ten Commandments. All pain, physical and psychological, is dealt with by pills instead of by the power of the mind.

No Outrage?

We are not protecting our children nor role modeling responsible behavior. Where is the outrage from citizens over drugging our children into submission? There is no outcry when we see professionals in casual sloppy dress or acting disinterested while delivering their services when they are receiving good money to do their jobs.

Where is the outrage when, time after time, the national media's blatant bias is exposed? Dan Rather of the CBS network attempted to justify a partisan attack on President G. W. Bush's record even after the documents were shown to be fraudulent. Tom Brokaw and Peter Jennings, national news anchors, attempted to bolster Dan Rather in spite of the fact the story was obviously untrue. Mark Halperin, the political director of ABC News, stated in a memo to his staff that they should question President Bush more vigorously than Senator Kerry, thus rejecting the concept of objective news.[9] Mark Halperin's father, Morton Halperin, was an administrator in the Department of Defense in 1994 under the Clinton administration. He advocated a greater role for the United Nations's influence over American sovereignty and was a supporter of convicted spy Philip Agee.[10] The mainstream media dismissed the Swift Boat veterans' testimonies as false without directly questioning them. Michael Moore's so-called documentary *Fahrenheit 9/11* was shown in movie theaters while the documentary *Stolen Honor* was withdrawn from being shown. After the Sinclair Broadcasting Group stock dropped 15 percent, the company decided not to show the entire documentary on its stations.[11] Anti-administration commentaries were reported as hard news appearing on the front pages and pro-administration factual reports were buried on the back pages. The political shilling of the national media was front and center during the 2004 presidential election.

Are integrity and honesty no longer guiding forces in our nation? We are numb from being attacked on all sides for expecting higher standards. We back off and accept mediocrity. We are in the midst of a civil war and we are being attacked on every front. I am fed up with the Smugger moral relativists spewing their ridicule at America's heroes and traditions and am frightened by the cultural meltdown of our major institutions. Morals, character, and integrity do matter.

Smuggers defining certain actions and thoughts as politically correct or incorrect are socially engineering our society. People want to be accepted. Mouthing insincere PC nonsense is more important than doing what is right. The appearance of being a nice or cool guy is more valued than a straight-talking, honorable person. Hollywood celebrities, crooked businessmen, and politicians prove daily that deception and crime do pay.

Political correctness pays immediate social dividends even when it is done with self-serving motives. Besides, when bad is good and good is bad, how do you know what is right? The path of least resistance is to accept everything as equal, even when you sense something is wrong. Driving in the passing lane instead of the right lane, living above one's means instead of saving, recreating instead of working, driving instead of walking, eating junk food instead of preparing a meal, divorcing instead of relating, being civilly irresponsible instead of voting—all these are indications that many of us are no longer doing the right thing. Accepting abuse to self and others is easier than standing up to defend what is right.

Easier to Be Immoral

Living an immoral life is easier than living a moral one. The immediate and concrete gratification of these belief systems is much more seductive than having to behave with personal integrity over a lifetime. The sweet life sold by celebrities offering anything from equality, wealth, free sex, perennial youth, an altered and drugged state, to power is hard to resist. The Smuggers are everywhere in our culture. At churches, schools, newspapers, unions, and television networks as innocuous as the History Channel, Smuggers are bombarding us with moral relativist preaching.

Smuggers are attempting to obliterate our traditional moral values. Instead of aspiring to traditional and moral lives, they have chosen to despise this arduous path and take the easier selfish road. Their lack of disciplined, moral resolve drives them to attack rather than to create wholesome lives. It directs them into sabotaging everything that has made our civilization remarkable in the history of the world. Their hatred of the high moral standards of traditional America has made them religious zealots of an amoral society.

These Smuggers have persuaded many that virtues are oppressive, that moral weakness not strength leads to self-liberation. Many liberal people have intellectually embraced this notion as it readily conforms to their political philosophy of generosity and tolerance although they still live a moral lifestyle. On the other hand, many holier-than-thou conservatives pay lip service to traditional beliefs while living a hypocritical, immoral existence.

Smuggers are masters at making immorality innocuous.

Many of us have been converted without knowing it and have abandoned moral traditions. The traditional moral ends are being subverted into amoral ends. Throughout history there have been phony prophets who have weakened the moral resolve of people. The false idols of biblical times such as the golden calf have evolved into "ism" doctrines: materialism, communism, hedonism, feminism, fascism, consumerism, environmentalism, humanism, and socialism. These "isms" promise heaven on earth with minimal personal effort and rapid payoff. Capitalism, conservatism, and liberalism based more on human nature than on utopian ideals are also "isms" that are doomed to failure if they discard honorable practices.

When Character No Longer Matters, Evil Flourishes

The concept of dishonor has practically vanished in the new secular culture. Our citizens have been brainwashed to view dishonor as a legitimate *means* of obtaining power. Corrupt leaders in all walks of life are emulated as role models simply for their success. The character of the person is unimportant as long as he reaches a high status, regardless of the road traveled. Historically deviant behaviors are being

erased through politically correct edicts. The acknowledgment of natural negative consequences of an immoral lifestyle is taboo in our
oppressive PC culture. We are no longer allowed to say it's the person's responsibility who eats too much and gets fat, or that people who
are sexually promiscuous and get sexually transmitted diseases, or people who drink too much and become alcoholics, or people who rely
too much on prescription drugs and become drug addicts are accountable for their actions.

Pseudoscience and hate crime legislation are intimidating us from
thinking and saying what we know is blatantly true. Citizens are programmed by PC thought patterns to stop making any judgments and
blindly accept all behaviors as equally legitimate. The lines between
right and wrong are continually blurred. Our previously cherished principles are discarded as useless baggage. We have been reeducated to
be tolerant of things we know to be wrong. Moral equivalency is a clear
and present danger to all Americans. In this brave new world everyone
and everything must be tolerated, including evil.

In a world without clearly defined traditional values and morals, evil
is emboldened. The path to self-fulfillment is to practice accepting the
socially unacceptable. By removing preferences, we become less rigid
and more adaptable to an ever-changing world. Being a bum or a hard
worker, being a criminal or a law-abiding citizen, being a freak or normal is viewed as equally valid. The heroes of our past—the Boy Scouts,
patriotism, the Pledge of Allegiance, manners, decency, and honoring
thy father and mother—are attacked relentlessly. Smuggers say that
morals and values interfere with change so they need to be abolished.
No, it's the Smuggers who need to be abolished.

The governor of New Jersey, James McGreevey, resigned his position effective November 15 on August 12, 2004. He used religious
terms to hide a series of corrupt incidents behind the guise of fur-
thering homosexual rights. With a dramatic attempt at heroics he

announced he was a gay American: "Yet at my most reflective maybe even my spiritual level, there were points in my life when I began to question what an acceptable reality really meant to me. Were there realities from which I was running? Which master was I trying to serve?" He continued, "At a point in every person's life one has to look into the soul and decide one unique truth in the world, not as we may want to see it or hope to see it but as it is." [12] Governor McGreevey was not a victim of his sexuality; he appears to be a common, unrepentant predator. God has given us freedom of choice. McGreevey has had two different wives and produced a child with each. He chose the lowest spiritual master of self-indulgence: hedonism.

The truth is that this resignation was not about his sexual preference, rather it was about his choice to run a corrupt and immoral administration. There is no "unique truth" from this moral relativist spin that should matter to the voters of New Jersey except whether or not he did illegal or immoral acts on duty as governor. The common good has no meaning for Smuggers who use their power for their own sake without concern for others. Governor McGreevey's parents and his own wife were used as props for his phony performance of contrition, a mean and exploitive act.

Edmund Burke put it best when he said: "The only thing necessary for the triumph of evil is for good men to do nothing." We should not allow Smuggers the freedom to redefine and destroy our culture. In Chapter 2, I discuss the way that the Smuggers are reshaping our nation through "Mythology as Cultural Fact." Smuggers have been effective but once they are recognized for who and what they are their power of evil will dissipate.

Chapter 2

Moving from Mythology to Wisdom

It took about fifty years for the Spock-inspired child development theories to warp the way we Americans live and raise our children. Insipid in design and disastrous in consequence, the Smugglers' movement swept across the United States with surprising ease and continues to maintain its hold on us all. Ignorant of its origins and its consequences, the general public unwittingly accepts and enables revisionism and relativism to control the way we live.

The radical changes in the way we dealt with children seeped into our perceptions of the world. The increased materialism and permissiveness with our children altered our values outside the home. Ostentatious wealth, leniency, tolerance for inappropriate behavior, and equality of roles disregarding status has corrupted our culture. This is seen with children who have been taught they are equal to their parents, workers equal to their bosses, students equal to their teachers, and media reporters and congressmen equal to the president of the United States. Disrespect of authority has become rampant.

It is helpful to first examine the origins of the altering of our traditional culture. It was during the anti-establishment years of the 1960s that university Smugglers, aided by the combined forces of television, movies, and slick magazines, first made a concerted effort to alter the institution of the family. They set their sights on the most fundamental expression of a family's strength and values—its unity—and went to work. Television sitcoms and advertisements began to relentlessly undermine traditional families. Men were portrayed as know-it-all bunglers, women as dependent victims, and children were heralded as intelligent sages with quick and outspoken wit. Marriage, family, and work were seen as obsolete. There were endless psychobabble articles selling the "scientific" basis of the modern method of raising children. All traditional methods of parenting were derided as old-fashioned and ripe for rejection. It was thought that modern child development advice was far superior to the old, repressive methods that were responsible for all society's ills.

These modern ideas of relationships, childhood, and values were so persuasively presented that they became cultural fact before surviving the test of time. Compare this to the past when those innovations that impacted our culture came from the accumulation of the choices made by the citizens. Traditional changes from the bottom up were usually incorporated slowly and with great care. Modern changes are from the top down, with little consideration for the overall impact on our society. The media, entertainment, pharmaceutical, and educational institutions are imposing their hidden agendas and propaganda on us. The astonishing success of this brainwashing was in part due to a society newly receptive to rethinking its cultural mores in anticipation of a new world order. These ideas required less effort and time on the part of everyone and were touted as more humane, more *modern,* than those of the past.

And in this they were right. Modern ways of living do have traditional methods beat on every level—*except that they do not work.* It took several generations for the Smuggers' intelligentsia and media to reluctantly document the horrendous results of these modern practices. Relentlessly the impact of modern methods could no longer be denied by the most ardent follower of the counterculture. The evidence was compiled throughout our national institutions by the secular elite.

What has emerged is a fascinating window into the rationale behind these modern cultural facts that are taught to our population each and every day. It is imperative to see these myths for what they are: a sharp departure from traditional methods that is incredibly harmful to our children and our society.

I have listed below some of the myths that form the basis for the Smuggers' modern relativist movement and that we will explore throughout this book. Following each modern myth is the traditional approach demonstrating the rationale for returning to the more effective, but at the same time more demanding, ways of living and raising children. As you read these myths, it will be apparent that the so-called cultural facts of our modern society are anything but facts. The reader will be forced to reexamine many child developmental, educational, and relational assumptions and will return to a more middle ground approach. As permissive materialism, educational, and relationship ideas persist in failing to produce positive results, one thing is clear: It is time to revisit our traditional wisdom.

◆   ◆   ◆

MODERN MYTH: Friendly Divorce Is Not Harmful.

Divorce handled amicably is not harmful to children.

Mature parents have the best interest of their children at heart and can divorce without any negative impact on their children. When the parents treat each other in a warm manner, the child can be shielded from parental disagreements. Any strong feelings should be expressed behind closed doors.

As long as each parent spends "quality time" with the child he will be reassured that he is loved by each. When parents act as if they will remain the same after the divorce, the child will have no reason to develop anxiety. Each parent's assurance of love will protect the child from the negative impact of the divorce.

TRADITIONAL WISDOM: Divorce Is Suicide to the Family.

Divorce is harmful and has inescapable negative effects.

Judith Wallerstein's twenty-year longitudinal studies demonstrate that the cultural fact of divorce being handled safely is false.[1] In her study, she finds that children of divorce suffer from intimacy and trust issues. I, too, have found that children of divorced parents never seem to walk away unscathed. In forty years of professional experience counseling children and their families, I continue to be amazed by the strong emotions children of divorce feel even many years later. A forty-seven-year-old client once said to me that, after a decade of each parent being married to a stepparent, he wants his parents to remarry. This is the fantasy statement of a wounded child, not a healthy adult, and demonstrates how far into the future divorce can reach.

Parents who act as a happy couple while divorcing can impart even more devastating consequences for the children. The children are blindsided by the phony actions of the parents. The children cannot understand why, if the parents are amicable with each other, they are breaking up the family. The confusion of the children is often released by acting out as their divorced parents continue to pretend the divorce is not the main issue. While this may seem absurd, I have seen this drama played out often in my private psychotherapeutic practice.

Another interesting common clinical observation is that often one parent is able to articulate exactly what their ex-spouse is doing wrong, while at the same time committing those very same offences. "My ex-wife said I yell at my daughter and do not provide sufficient support for her." In the very next session this man may come in and state his wife is not using his money on the needs of the child and the ex-wife is too restrictive with his daughter. Ridiculous as it seems, the ex-husband will deride his daughter's mother in front of the child. So the child is hearing the same thing from the father that the mother says about him. In this case, one parent's anger toward the other is more powerful than the health of the child. In counseling, the child can tell you *verbatim* the hateful statements one parent makes about the other. Yet when you ask either parent they say they always act decently and respectfully towards their ex-spouse in front of their child.

The old adage that parents need to stay together for the sake of the children is quite reasonable in the vast majority of cases. Excluding specific situations, such as when abuse is involved, the children will experience far less psychological confusion if the parents choose the positive step of fighting for the marriage. This is because a child experiences two acute forms of pain, first blaming himself for breaking up the marriage and then he or she feels the added pain of abandonment. Children deserve mature and committed parents, not confused and self-indulgent people who make excuses.

Divorce is not a solution for a poor marriage; it complicates the picture—especially when children are involved. Custody, visitation, redistributing finances, reentering the dating game, child-care, stepparents, and blending families are only a few of the new issues that emerge from a divorce. It may be a new beginning, but a new beginning with lots of excess baggage. Yes, marriage is difficult, but divorce is even more difficult. Committing positive energy to uniting with one's spouse pays better dividends than searching for the most perfect spouse.

Comprehending the downside of divorce and then using this knowledge to put energy into improving the marriage is the key to regaining control. Rejecting the so-called instant solution of divorce allows a parent to understand that marriage is a special opportunity for a healthier, more fulfilling existence for everyone in the family. In a committed marriage where the husband and wife grow closer in friendship everybody wins: husband, wife, and children. Parents need to view marriage and child-rearing as an opportunity for a more fulfilling personal life.

◈   ◈   ◈

MODERN MYTH: Spanking Is Always Abusive.

The well-known columnist Ann Landers once wrote a column entitled, "Hitting a Child is Never Acceptable."[2] The article ended the corporal punishment debate by establishing a new cultural fact that this type of discipline is always abusive. There are countless warnings in the media advising parents that spanking is traumatic to a child's psyche and that its emotional scars never truly heal. In turn, it was foretold, the wounded child will become overly sensitized to anger and retreat into his inner world. Moreover, any corporal punishment teaches that physical force is the way to resolve problems. Peacefully discussing the reasons the parent is upset with the child's behavior is a more appropriate and effective means of handling a child's misdeeds.

TRADITIONAL WISDOM: Moderate Spanking Is OK.

Parents can use punishing consequences, including moderate spanking of toddlers and young children.

It is because of this ridiculous myth that we see a mother having an intellectual discussion with her eighteen-month-old child concerning why it is wrong to bite the baby rather than instantly communicating "No!" with a well-placed spank on the backside. Infants and toddlers are not capable of understanding intellectual justifications, but they do readily comprehend a spank and the word "No." Spanking has been practiced throughout the ages in every country of the world. Almost everyone has been spanked at least once for doing something wrong. "A lot of people out there advocate that any spanking at all is detrimental, and that's not what we found," said Elizabeth Owens from the Institute of Human Development at the University of California at Berkeley. Owens was the co-author of a twelve-year longitudinal study analyzing corporal punishment and its effects on one hundred middle-class children. "[The study] showed no negative effects on cognitive, social, and behavioral skills of those youngsters,"[3] she wrote. "There is absolutely no worthwhile evidence in support of the notion that children who are occasionally spanked stop trusting their parents and begin fearing them instead."[4]

Ferrie Lindsay of the evangelical group Friends of the Family commented, "In a government survey in 1998, 88 percent of parents said it was sometimes necessary to smack a naughty child. Sometimes a well-timed slap is able to teach a child that what they have done is wrong if that is accompanied by words."[5] What I find when I give seminars on discipline is that my experiences correlate very well with this 1998 British survey. I ask the audience to raise their hand if they have never been spanked. Inevitably one, or at the most, two hands go up and 98–99 percent stay down. I joke that those individuals who didn't raise their hands—the ones who were spanked—look reasonably normal, but can use this previous "abuse" by their parents as another reason why they should be viewed as victims.

Yet our PC parenting experts persist in calling every form of yelling or physical punishment abusive. It is true that a parent can physically abuse a child. It is not true that anyone who spanks a child is abusive. When a parent is beating a child for no other purpose than to release rage, it is abuse. When a parent appropriately spanks a child to teach the child an important lesson, the parent is completely within the acceptable boundaries of discipline. The central issue is intimidation, not spanking. A child sufficiently disciplined at an early age will have a healthy fear and respect of adult domination. Couple this control on the part of the mother and the father, with a supportive spouse, consistent follow-through, use of the word "no," appropriate consequences, and an effective dose of properly applied guilt and reason, and any parent can produce an obedient child.

The real abuse occurs when a parent fails to use the natural fear a child has of an adult's power to keep the child in line. An undisciplined child who believes that all adults are as benevolent as his parents is naïve to the sometimes dangerous and malevolent forces that surround us.

"Yes, children whose parents treat them severely are indeed more likely to be maladjusted by the time they reach adolescence and yes, the parents themselves are dangerously close to child abuse. But does the same hold true in cases where corporal punishment means little more than swatting the misbehaving child's backside?" asks columnist Leonard Pitts. "For years the official consensus from the nation's child-rearing experts has been that it did. Maybe that is about to change. We can only hope so."[6]

The relationship between a parent and a child is a complex process passed down by traditions rooted in the very nature of man. If a slap on the hand or backside can give an exclamation point to paying attention, how can this be abusive? Parents who train their young child to listen and to respect the authority of adults place the child on the smooth, fast track to healthy socialization. A child who listens has the advantage of a direct channel to adult knowledge and values. A child who listens to the moral lessons of the parent will project a respectful attitude and keep a healthy distance from danger.

Benjamin Franklin stated that obedience is the foundation of all learning.

Today, at the beginning of the twenty-first century, we have strayed a long way from our traditional roots. Parents have been trained to be friends of and counselors to their children. Punishment and intimidation have become taboo. Parents are supposed to display only their soft sides and entertain, not discipline, their children. Today's parents are taught by experts to unconditionally love their child and to have no limit in their tolerance of obnoxious behavior. The child learns to predict his parent's permissive behavior and loses any semblance of fear or intimidation.

We must take care to heed the old proverb, "He that spareth his rod hateth his son" (Proverbs 13:24) and to reject the current interpretation, "Spare the rod and spoil the child."

◆   ◆   ◆

MODERN MYTH: Quality Time Is Enough.

Spending *quality* time with a loved one is sufficient to maintain the relationship.

Quality time is the time a husband and wife, a parent and child, and other members of significant relationships spend together doing so-called significant things. This specific quality time more than makes up for the lack of actual time traditional families spend with their loved ones. By bringing them both closer together, a "golden moment" is created, intensifying the experiences and imparting more meaning to them. As an added bonus, as modern people accrue greater resources (money), they gain the opportunity to buy these unique experiences.

TRADITIONAL WISDOM:
Quantity Time Cannot Be Replaced by Quality Time.

There is no replacement for *quantity* of time spent providing all the wisdom, guidance, and love that husbands and wives, parents and children, grandparents and grandchildren ought to experience.

This bogus quality time rationalization started during the early women's liberation movement. Its ingenious purpose was to seduce women into the workforce and away from their duties as wife and mother. This myth decreased the guilt of the mother from not being at home for her husband and children and at the same time enabled a career to replace family as the mother's top priority. The industrial revolution produced absentee fathers and now the women's liberation movement has produced absentee mothers. The outcome is that we now have absentee husbands and absentee wives, both of which are absent from each other.

Being the mother to an infant is a full-time occupation. It takes more than special events to civilize a child. A mother molds a child in every way—from touching to smiling, speaking, potty training, and laughing, her influence is unbounded. Researchers have found mental and verbal development lags for children whose mothers work full time before the child is nine months old. Developing the character of a child starts with the mother's nurturing and is enhanced by the father's discipline.[7]

During a personal interview of mine with a child and her parents, the mother focused more on the before- and after-school programs than on the academic. At one point, having realized that the only expressed concern was about convenience, she suddenly blurted out that her main concern was certainly for her children and not for her career. Her interjection, laden with guilt and defensiveness, is an example that although the imperviousness of quality time is pushed as a cultural fact, there is no escaping the guilt of not truly being there for your child and family.

This cultural fact of the effectiveness of quality time is constantly spread by the mass media via advertising. A visit to Disney World, playing with a high-priced entertainment item, going to a concert, shopping at the mall, or any other special event where the parent is with his child is considered quality time. The same goes for a husband and wife isolated from their children on a separate vacation or where the vacation plans to have special activities for the child away from the parents. In the early 1970s, playing tennis together with your spouse, board games or reading to one's child was considered quality time as long as the undivided attention was given.

In the new millennium "quality time" has to be more and more flamboyant to hold the interest of the spouse or the child. The new expectation is that the child or one of the spouses sets the agenda and the parent makes sure it takes place. Diving lessons in the Caribbean, ocean cruises to destinations chosen by the child, purchasing expensive electronic equipment, or even bringing home a brand-new car, while considered quality time by modern parents, still can be seen as mundane by the child or spouse.

It is probable that in the child's world of tomorrows an even higher standard of expectations will evolve, making daily interaction even less appreciated. In fact, this process has already begun. In the Associated Press article "Quality Time in Eye of Beholder" a telephone interview with one thousand parents and their children aged ten to fourteen found that both parents and children were dissatisfied with the quality time they spent together. The study found 52 percent of the parents admit they do not spend enough quality time with their children and 57 percent of children believe their parent's work gets in the way of meaningful time.[8] "Quality time" is a concept that was destined to cause distrust.

"Quality time" ignores the reality of time. The longer we spend time together with another person the greater the chance we have to impact the other person. In the case of the interaction between parent and child, "quantity time" allows many opportunities for teachable moments. In every instance, being there to assist the child in learning a new concept is more important than a week with Mickey Mouse.

◆   ◆   ◆

MODERN MYTH: Children Always Tell the Truth.

Children are innocent and have no motivation to lie. A child will tell spontaneous things an adult would never say. "How do you like my hat?" asks grandmother. The child's answer may be, "I think it looks ugly." Everyone would laugh at the child's remark, thinking, "I wish I had the honesty to say it." Art Linkletter made a living getting kids to say the "darndest things." Children can be totally politically incorrect without worry. The child's lack of sensitivity to others is an indication of innate honesty.

TRADITIONAL WISDOM: Children Need to Be Taught Honesty.

Parents need to be vigilant in their intolerance of lying. Insensitivity to others means a child has little training, not that he is honest. The value of telling the truth is something that must be learned, while lying often appears to be the easier way and comes naturally. In other words, parents have to train the child to exist in the world of honesty, and there is no better way to do this than to be role models. This is not an easy task in our PC world that rewards saying what you think people want to hear rather than saying what you believe. This habit is itself a subtle form of lying. As one study suggests, "the best teenage liars are often the most popular kids."[9] It appears most children seize upon our foibles rather than our virtues.

Parents who believe their child never lies must have either limited exposure to children, an only child, or a poor long-term memory. Any parent with two or more children quickly learns the dynamics of lying in their own family from the first time one child says one thing and the other child says another. One has only to think back to his own childhood, to the inevitable point when he was caught in a lie by his parents. That children lie is not a secret. "He said/she said" situations are unavoidable, as anyone supervising children will tell you. In the same vein, every day school administrators are confronted with conflicting stories from teachers, students, and parents.

It is parents who seem to have the most naïve perspective of lying. My wife and I have encountered this phenomenon time and again as parents announce without hesitation specifically what happened in a classroom between their child and another. When questioned as to how they could be so certain it happened that way, the parent answers, "my child said so." This belies their unquestionable belief that a child obviously tells the truth. Similarly, if a teacher has a different perspective than the student concerning the event in question, the parent will believe the child no matter how overwhelming the evidence. In a recent case, a junior high student failed to hand in assignments to three different teachers. Incredibly, both parents insisted the child was telling the truth. When, while at school, the student later admitted that she did not do the homework, the parents maintained that the teachers misplaced her work and withdrew her from the school. Avoiding their child's lying habit was easier and less painful than confronting and correcting her problems.

To complicate the picture of dealing with lying, young children have difficulty distinguishing between fantasy and reality. This means that parents have the responsibility of teaching them about reality, an ongoing job that takes time. However, teaching a child to discriminate between reality and fantasy will not ensure honesty. Only the daily practice of the virtue of honesty will do the trick. Children are keen observers who need honest parents in order to establish honesty in their own lives. Once a child is sufficiently trained in honesty the parent's job of supervision becomes much more manageable. Being honest with oneself and others is the foundation of an exemplary and dignified member of society, a person with character.

◆　◆　◆

MODERN MYTH: Everyone Is Equal.

Everyone is equal guaranteeing each and every person the same rights and privileges as anyone else. We are a free society to do and to obtain what we want. No one is better than another. Differences in wealth and opportunity should be eliminated to create an even playing field, raising the poor to a higher level. By redistributing the wealth of a nation every child and citizen is given the same chance to succeed. Equality for all is a civil right given to our people by the Constitution. America guarantees that each American is free to do his own thing without being burdened with the responsibilities of others.

TRADITIONAL WISDOM: Work Ethic Is the Equalizer.

Everyone is unique in developing his own destiny. Americans have the freedom to earn anything they want. They are not entitled to anything except basic human rights. We have the freedom through our own industriousness and merit to gain what we want. People have their own destinies. No one has the right to limit a person's freedom except when it infringes upon the freedom of another. Everyone should have the same rights. An individual through his own choices creates his own opportunities and results in the positive or negative accumulation of wealth. Each person has the freedom in our country to evaluate himself and decide on his best path to obtain his goals. An individual's uniqueness is often his best means to success. In our free enterprise system, Americans have the freedom to prosper but there is not any entitlement to anyone else's assets or privileges. The notion of the "me generation" is anti-American.

◈   ◈   ◈

MODERN MYTH: Protect from Reality.

People need to be shielded from reality because they are fragile and easily traumatized. (Don't say cancer, brutality, abuse, or death.)

A traumatic event can be stressful enough to cause a mental or emotional block in the healthy development of a person. A person can become fixated on the event, preventing the natural evolution of his personality.

The parent's responsibility is to screen the child from stressful events, it's the husband's to protect the wife and it's the media's to protect us all. The media inundated the airwaves with pictures of perverted American reservists in pornographic scenes with their violent enemy detainees while censoring any pictures of the enemy beheading innocent Americans. It appears the media are not protecting the sensibilities of the American society but instead protecting the enemy. Maintaining an artificially peaceful and sanitized world is better than exposing us to selective harsh realities. Adversity may develop character but at the risk of permanently traumatizing it. It is better to emotionally shield a person from unfortunate situations than to attempt to explain the inexplicable.

TRADITIONAL WISDOM: Reality Is a Great Teacher.

Dealing with reality is a great teacher of the true meaning of what is important in life. Traumatic events often bring out the best in people, making us stronger. This was evident in England during World War II when London was bombed by the Nazis, in Pearl Harbor, and on 9/11. People united behind the flag by donating blood, millions of dollars, food, clothing, and their time to volunteer where needed to aid their fellow countrymen. September 11 was the greatest surge of patriotism I ever witnessed both personally and by others. People did not hoard their material possessions; they called their loved ones. Even when a tragedy is severe, children are able to maintain a well-adjusted life. At age two, one of our students witnessed her father shoot her mother to death. Following this incident, her grandmother provided the support and discipline she needed. She is doing well in every facet of life as a successful teenager as the trauma of the murder naturally fades. There was no victimization babble to keep the wound open. The grandmother's love and discipline kept her granddaughter looking forward instead of looking back.

In a school-related incident, a parent had the audacity to complain about a lunch-exchange where children drew names and brought a lunch for each other. She demanded that an apology be given to her daughter from a seven-year-old for not buying a particular thing for her lunch. (The child seemed to enjoy the lunch that was brought for her and did not complain at school.) The mother did not ask her daughter to be appreciative of the fine lunch she received. She did not tell her daughter to deal with her complaint directly at school. Instead, she took the situation into her own hands to protect her "too precious child." Pampering parents prevent their children from developing coping skills necessary for a successful and independent life.

The idea that stressful events in childhood often have a long-term negative impact on an individual is primarily derived from the psychoanalytic medical practice of Sigmund Freud. Dr. Freud studied people with significant mental disorders during the Victorian period, a time when children were expected to act like little adults. There was limited appreciation for the child's perspective in dealing with life and children were relegated to being seen but not heard. Any tragedy the child endured during this time period was absorbed by his limited capacity and experience with practically no support from adults. The non-compassionate world of the Victorian era was the flip side of the world children today face. In that period children had to grow up very quickly, in contrast to today's children, who have a prolonged childhood and a difficult transition into adulthood. The late nineteenth century was a radically different existence than we find in the beginning of the twenty-first century. The way we view and treat children has to change according to the new reality faced by modern children.

Children are resilient and bounce back from almost anything with parental guidance. The answer is a balanced approach where a child is able to experience the joys of childhood and the parents assist the child in the transition to responsible adulthood. This means parents have to be proactive in teaching their children emotional and cognitive skills and values to face life's adversities. Children need to fly on their own into the world outside the home.

Children, like it or not, grow up to be adults. Childhood is easier than adulthood. The older we get the more of life's natural tragedies we experience. As adults we have to learn how to deal with adverse situations in order to derive spiritual strength from them. We have to let reality transform and strengthen us.

◆ ◆ ◆

MODERN MYTH: We Are Entitled to What We Want Now.

Why wait when we can have it all now? You only live once. Parents should provide for their child as much as possible as soon as possible.

A major responsibility of modern parents is to enhance their child's development by providing stimulating material and social experience for themselves and their children. The parent's function is to select a range of possibilities for themselves and their child to reach the highest level of satisfaction for both. The child gains a feeling of independence while the parents enjoy whatever experience they have chosen without feeling any sacrifice for the sake of the child. The parent is confident that selecting a well-known karate school, dance or gymnastics class, and sending the child out always in expensive brand-name clothing will ensure both their own and their child's high social status. As adults we also feel we are entitled to whatever we desire at the moment. Instant gratification is better than waiting too long and being too old to enjoy what you missed. We no longer need to save, because we can impulsively purchase what we want through over-charged credit cards or other forms of debt. This is considered acceptable because these creative forms of credit are keeping the economy humming.

TRADITIONAL WISDOM: Learn to Be Thankful.

We need to count our blessings, save for tomorrow, and learn to make a positive out of a negative. No one is entitled to anything he is not willing to work to obtain. We believe in the free enterprise system where one's personal effort and production results in what one earns. There is no free lunch for anyone except in a fantasy world such as communism. Each of us has a responsibility to do the best we can to strengthen our family, our community, and ourselves.

Thanking God daily for our blessings enables us to appreciate what we have. It is a natural antidote for the unbridled "want lust" of the modern world.

◆   ◆   ◆

MODERN MYTH: Sexual Liberation Brings Freedom, Independence, and Happiness.

Everyone has a right to his own body. Having freedom to engage in sex with whoever and whenever one wants is a sign of independence and enriches the sexual experience. Sexual independence in the modern world and the increase of contraception gives individuals opportunities for happiness without concern for unwanted pregnancies. Even if modern contraception devices fail, there is easy and safe access to abortion. Free sex is a liberating experience for everyone involved. People have a civil right to enjoy their body in any way they choose.

TRADITIONAL WISDOM: Sex Is a Sacred Act.

Sexual promiscuity causes loss of intimacy, identity confusion, and lack of fulfillment. Being a male or female whore is a destructive lifestyle. Sexual promiscuity has a long negative history. People who engage in indiscriminate sex have higher incidence of STDs, non-meaningful relationships, and unwanted pregnancies. This greater exposure to a wider range of sexual experience leads to sexual identity confusion. Bisexuality increases the probability of losing one's moral compass. Real intimacy and enthusiasm for the natural unfolding of life's journey only takes place between a man and a woman. A man completes a woman and a woman completes a man in lifetime marriage. Any substitute for sex outside of marriage between a man and a woman is destined to fail. There are biological roots for monogamy in a highly civilized society.

◈   ◈   ◈

MODERN MYTH: There Is No Need to Punish.

It is better to appease, ignore, redirect, or negotiate than punish. (Punishment is abusive and should be illegal.)

Even the most destructive criminals can and should be rehabilitated. The death penalty is barbaric and serves no purpose. Young criminals who commit heinous crimes should be forgiven and released back into society. They are too young to know the consequences of their actions. Even punishing a child leads to a negative self-concept according to modern child-care experts. Instead of confronting a spouse with legitimate grievances it is better to obtain an annulment or divorce. What is the sense of getting stressed out over something so easily dissolved? Punishment should be eliminated from our current practices. By appeasing, ignoring, redirecting, or negotiating, punishment becomes obsolete. A child demands the latest fifty-dollar Barbie doll. If you cannot afford it, give her something else to appease her instead of telling her "no." If a child does something wrong, instead of making a big deal about it, ignore it and wait until she does something right to praise. When a child becomes interested in something you do not want him to have, redirect him to something acceptable. Do not be a rigid parent by sticking to your guns; instead, negotiate as an equal with your child until both of you are satisfied. These modern flexible methods take the edge off being an old-fashioned, dogmatic parent. Your child will like you. Being a friend is better than being respected as a parent.

TRADITIONAL WISDOM: Discipline Is Love.

We need to be appropriate ourselves and demand appropriate behavior from others. Living a disciplined life is the key to being successful. When we transgress we should expect and accept appropriate consequences. These consequences can be self- or externally imposed. They can include punishment, guilt, ridicule, and incarceration.

There must to be consequences for children, too. Parents need to be parents, maintaining and demanding higher standards, values, limits, and expectations. Acting as a sensitive buddy may be a warm, fuzzy ideal but it simply does not work in practice. The child learns quickly how to manipulate this needy parent to get what he wants. The kicker to this modern farce is that the parent eventually loses his temper with the overly demanding child, while the child gets angry with his parental "friend" for not being what he needs: a *parent*.

A parent in charge is a parent who garners his child's respect and love. Whenever I punished any of my four children using the techniques of purposeful discipline, my children always ended the punishment by wanting a hug in an attempt to please me. First the child understood I was punishing him for his own good, and secondly the child understood I could and would use my power as a parent. Of course when the punishment is given, the child will be fearful or angry, but if it is administered with love the child will not hold long-term resentment. As adults most of us look back favorably on a strict teacher because of high expectations and demands. In the long run a demanding parent, like a strict teacher, is given respect. Being an in-charge parent is more difficult than attempting to be a friendly parent in the short term. In the long term, the in-charge parent realizes the dividends of a healthy, respectful child and not the anger of an under-socialized, ungrateful misfit.

◈ ◈ ◈

MODERN MYTH: Drugs Are Better than Discipline.

Psychotropic drugs are beneficial and are viable replacements for more traditional modes of punishment.

Through early medical intervention in a person's behavior, an unruly or disturbed person can be labeled and stabilized through the use of modern pharmaceuticals. Advances in science allow the mental health profession to alter the social, emotional, and cognitive abilities. In the *DSM, The Diagnostic and Statistical Manual IV Revised,* there are hundreds of diagnoses of mental disorders including over forty mental disorder diagnoses for children. There are many specific drugs to alleviate specific problematic symptoms.

The use of antiquated methods of corporal punishment and guilt to create specific behaviors is less efficient than pharmacological means with fewer residual psychological drawbacks. If a particular drug is not having satisfactory results, a slight change in dosage or another prescription will correct the problem.

TRADITIONAL WISDOM:
Good Relationships Create Healthy People.

Mentally healthy people need to have stable, significant relationships. This only happens through discipline and effort. The temporary euphoric feeling given by a drug cannot substitute for a loving relationship. There is no magic pill to create a healthy person. It takes consistency and love over time.

Parents have at their disposal methods of discipline and rules of parenting that can eliminate children's problems without the use of drugs.

Parental daily discipline and systematic training shapes the potential of the child. Through the ages the civilizing of the child has been the function of the family. These drugs cannot replace fear and guilt in producing an individual with a conscience. When a person hurts another he has to feel some physical pain and psychological guilt to learn the lesson of right and wrong. No drug will ever be able to produce such a complex mental process as a conscience. Only a parent's continuous conscientious effort will produce one.

You cannot lecture a two- or three-year-old because he does not possess the level of rational thought necessary to make it understood. Piaget has taught us this fact. A parent must be concrete in punishment and explanation. After the slap and "No!" the parent simply states, "A good girl does not bite her little sister." This ongoing message of good and bad creates the conscience that society relies on for security through the person's self-censorship of personal behavior.

Over twenty-five years ago when I moved to the community where I still live, I visited a popular general practice doctor who was known to be an advocate of giving Ritalin to children. As an experienced mental health professional, I tried to influence his view that the drugs may not be the best way to influence children's behavior. He was not convinced and continued until the day he retired to give out the drugs like candy. Hopefully the time is arriving when parents will refuse this destructive method that deflates the spirit of the child without resolving the problem. Drugging the child into submission is unacceptable in any society.

◈   ◈   ◈

MODERN MYTH: Self-Esteem Is Everything.

The greater the positive reinforcement of behavior, the higher the self-esteem.

The person with high self-esteem has no reason for self-doubt, anxiety, or depression. He knows others worship his every move. He realizes that he can do anything and the world will be delighted. The only consequences he encounters are rewarding ones that establish his positive self-worth.

TRADITIONAL WISDOM: Self-Competency Is the Issue.

People with high self-esteem are not necessarily high-functioning people. We need to teach compensation and self-competency, not false esteem.

People with inflated self-importance are annoying to everyone. A person with false esteem has been taught to believe everything he does will receive accolades. When other authority figures or peers give him less than flattering comments he will be shocked, crushed, and angry. Receiving only positive reinforcement does not prepare the person for the real world.

False esteem tends to create a slightly delusional child.

The American Psychological Society (APS) analyzed more than two hundred studies on self-esteem. The APS "found no evidence that boosting self-esteem by therapeutic interventions or school programs results in better job performance, lowered aggression, or reduced delinquency" and that "high self-esteem does not prevent children from smoking, drinking, taking drugs, or engaging in early sex."[10]

Lauren Slater's article, "The Trouble with Self-Esteem," states that renowned researchers Nicholas Ember of the London School of Economics and Roy Baumeister of Case Western Reserve University have documented the negative effects of high self-esteem. People with high self-esteem often lack social skills and score lower academically than individuals with low self-esteem. "There is absolutely no evidence that low self-esteem is particularly harmful," Ember says. "It's not at all a cause of poor academic performance, people with low self-esteem seem to do just as well in life as people with high self-esteem. In fact they may be better because they often try harder."

When the child actually conquers an obstacle like learning to walk, memorizing the multiplication tables, or performing in front of an audience, no outside positive reinforcement is needed. The child knows what he has accomplished and no one can take that away. Only through effort can you gain a sense of satisfaction. Frank Sinatra's song "I Did It My Way" is a much more gratifying theme than saying someone gave it to me.

◆ ◆ ◆

MODERN MYTH:
There Is No Good and Bad, Only Shades of Gray.

Everything is morally or culturally relative. Things are not either black or white but shades of gray. Something may appear bad to someone and appear good to someone else. Sex outside of marriage for some may be wrong but for others it may be a loving act. All morality depends on the situation and motivation of the person. All morals are personal and should be determined by the individual, not the state. Government has no business passing laws based on morals. Civil rights insure people making their own decisions about their behavior. Government should not interfere with individual freedoms by making laws based on antiquated morality. Women have a right to abortion. Government has no right to define marriage between a man and a woman.

TRADITIONAL WISDOM:
There Are Definite Moral and Immoral Behaviors.

Our Constitution was based on biblical morality and human nature. There are distinct good and evil actions. "Do unto others as you would have them do unto you" is the Golden Rule shared by religions across the world. Our Constitution is based on Judeo-Christian morals specified in the Ten Commandments and throughout the Bible. Evil does exist now and will exist in the future. The force that represses or destroys life is evil. Traditional laws are ways to enforce certain morals on citizens to maximize the common good of men. Laws against killing, stealing, lying under oath, or harming others—especially the defenseless such as children, disabled, or the old—are means of protecting the vulnerable. Biblical morality is the basis of our criminal code. Taking morals out of government would lead to the weakening and eventual collapse of society.

◆ ◆ ◆

MODERN MYTH: Don't Impose Your Values.

People will naturally make the right choices. Humans are inherently good. When you nurture them correctly they, like flowers, will blossom into healthy, moral individuals. A child is pure and innocent and does not need to be contaminated by parental inadequacies.

As the child matures physically, socially, and emotionally he will be able to discern the right choices. The level of understanding of morality develops as the child develops. Adults will only retard or even prevent the child's moral development. Children will lead us to a better world if we allow them to develop unimpeded with the nonsensical values of the past. A person will develop a higher level of spiritual value by himself.

TRADITIONAL WISDOM:
Family, Morals, and Values Are a Springboard to Spirituality.

Rousseau's Noble Savage has little to do with reality. When a lost child survives with a pack of animals the person suffers a great loss of human qualities. The human acts more like the animals that surround him than another human.

We make our citizens adhere to the norms and mores of the civilization by passing down values from one generation to another. An individual who understands the expectations of society can either build on them or reject them. Without the foundation of values provided by the family, a child is vulnerable to predatory outside influences. Cultists are easily brainwashed because their moral foundation was nonexistent or weakly developed. The strong POW does not easily switch allegiances. A morally confused and weak "Taliban Johnny" is an easy convert. We need to teach children values to have adults with strong values.

◆   ◆   ◆

MODERN MYTH: Self-Expression Is Inherently Good.

People need to be free to express themselves in any manner they choose.

People have a right to their feelings. By expressing their feelings they learn to recognize their needs and wants. A child's communication with an adult in any form encourages the child to feel more like an equal. Freedom of expression gives the child the internal signal that his life is valued. The dignity of a child is enhanced when he can speak his mind.

Even expressions of anger through tantrums should be accepted as a person's attempts to communicate with others. The tantrum will eventually run its course and the person will be better able to get his feelings under control. Allowing a person to vent his anger through tantrums will produce a more emotionally stable person in the future. An uninhibited person stands out in a group and has more self-confidence.

TRADITIONAL WISDOM: Teach Frustration Tolerance.

People need to learn to express themselves in socially appropriate ways, not venting their anger by punching a pillow. We need to end immature tantrums by channeling our emotions.

Remember when the gurus of psychology were encouraging us to punch pillows to vent our anger? This would have supposedly made us more emotionally stable. Wrong! Studies on venting anger have shown just the opposite. Anger increases when a person is encouraged to express anger.

Parents have to have zero tolerance for silly angry tantrums. A child should appropriately communicate his frustration. The younger the child, the more observant the parent needs to be to understand the child's predicament. The older the person, the more they should be required to verbalize the problem.

As behavioral patterns become evident, the person should be directed to better meet his needs. If they get easily frustrated when they do not have sufficient sleep, then ample sleep should be the rule. If a lack of food triggers anger, then provision of food at certain times should be made. Make sure the person receives plenty of exercise everyday to dissipate excess energy and allow for a natural calmness to develop.

Eating properly, sleeping properly, and getting enough exercise are necessary for everyone to be emotionally stable. Whenever a person gets out of balance in any of these areas they are more prone to outbursts.

Focusing on tantrums begets more tantrums. Eventually fixating on the tantrum gets a person labeled and drugged. The freedom of expression has limits. A person should be free to express himself only in socially acceptable ways.

◆   ◆   ◆

MODERN MYTH: Gangsterism Is Cool.

Rappers and ex-drug dealers Ludacris, 50 Cent, and Snoop Dogg are emulated by our youth. Dictators and bullies at school are cool because they know how to use power. They make their own rules and get others to follow in fear. Gangsters obey no one and are not frightened to disregard other people's rights to obtain their desires. They are courageous and creative opportunists who develop a new reality. People who are intolerant of their behavior are jealous. They would like to be like them but lack the guts to follow their desires. Bullies, gangsters, and dictators are special people who deserve everything they obtain, including our admiration.

TRADITIONAL WISDOM:
Honor Father, Mother, and Honorable People.

The Ten Commandments state: "Honor Thy Father and Mother," not gangsters, bullies, or dictators. People who disobey societal laws are criminals. No matter what they call themselves, people who act to incite others to violence or perform violence are a menace to society and should be tried and imprisoned. People who are allowed to intimidate others for their own gain will become emboldened to do ever escalating evil acts. Their influence will grow, creating a more powerful negative force. The conflict between good and evil is timeless. The moral forces in a nation cannot ignore or tolerate evil without jeopardizing the entire culture. Parents, teachers, ministers, police, and other authority figures have a responsibility to promote moral behavior and punish immoral behavior. Idolizing gangsters, bullies, and dictators is disrespecting the history of our nation.

◈   ◈   ◈

MODERN MYTH: Tolerance Makes a Person Better.

Tolerance of others and their ideas leads to spiritual growth. Everyone has a right to his actions and ideas. No one has the right to discriminate against another. By being nonjudgmental you will better understand everyone's point of view. Intolerance in any form limits the person from gaining a particular experience. All types of experiences broaden an individual and society.

TRADITIONAL WISDOM: Total Tolerance Is Decadence.

Society makes judgments of behavior in defining the culture. A nation being tolerant of all individuals and their behavior would lead to chaos and strife. All civilizations have a defined culture that rewards certain behaviors and punishes others. Discrimination based on a person's actions is necessary to develop organization and order. A virtuous or an immoral person cannot exist in a totally tolerant society. Depending on its definition, virtuous people have to consistently perform certain behaviors. An immoral person can only be immoral when disobeying certain sanctioned behaviors. Tolerance for deviance does not lead to spirituality; it leads to confusion and immorality. Only by ignoring history can a nation embrace deviance that ends in weakness and decadence. He who doesn't acknowledge evil is spiritually lost. Citizens need to be able to discriminate between good and evil to create a strong nation.

◆ ◆ ◆

MODERN MYTH: Obedience Is Destructive.

Obedience is destructive to a child's IQ and critical thinking.

A bright child thinks for himself. He has his own mind. He needs to explore his environment to learn things for himself. A parent who artificially programs the child by telling him what he can and cannot do is impeding a natural learning process. An obedient child is like a robot: The more the child listens, the more he loses the opportunity to think for himself. Obedience sucks the enthusiasm and spirit out of a child. The child becomes totally dependent on the parent for the next action. A child should be given free rein in making his own choices, for the child will need to do this throughout life.

TRADITIONAL WISDOM:
Obedience Is the Foundation of All Learning.

Benjamin Franklin once wrote: "Let thy child's first lesson be obedience and the second will be what thou wilt." In America too few people have taken this cultural myth to heart. We are raising disobedient children in epidemic proportions. We have ingeniously labeled them with Attention Deficit/Hyperactivity Disorder (ADHD) or Oppositional Defiant Disorder or Conduct Disorder or one of many other labels. The fact is we have a blight of children who do not follow the instructions of adults.

Ask any teacher. A child who listens is like gold. An obedient child for the most part is an A student. Following instructions is not a horrible act that will lead down a path to becoming a non-thinking fascist. Attentive children learn more effectively about the world around them. As a foundation of knowledge is firmly established, a person has the basis to think outside the box. To critically think you need lots of knowledge. Minimum knowledge leads to faulty thinking, while a large breadth of knowledge allows a person to make educated choices, resulting in what we call critical thinking.

This is America, where there are many competing ideas. We have freedom of speech. A child will have plenty of time to explore different value systems as he grows into an adult. But first children must learn their culture by learning to read, write, do math, and study science and social studies before they can teach the class.

◆   ◆   ◆

MODERN MYTH:
The More Schooling, the Smarter the Person.

Learning in a school environment enriches a person's life. The knowledge gained from various professors discussing their expertise expands the student's mind. Educated people are more well-rounded than people who do not attend institutions of higher education. The experience of being a student creates a superior individual.

TRADITIONAL WISDOM: Living Is Learning.

Education since the 1960s has become indoctrination into the counterculture. Too many students and professors are frozen in perennial adolescence. Their counterculture focuses on sex, drugs, partying, and eternal youth: hedonism. Too many professors and professional students choose to be shielded from reality in their ivory towers and miss out on the most normal and basic life cycle challenges to gain wisdom. Their elevated status in a university community inflates their egos, often making them insufferable snobs. I was a university professor for a decade. I taught many older students with only a high school diploma and plenty of life experience and found them to be far superior to students who went straight through school. These older students had the maturity and ability to evaluate and integrate material that only comes from life experience. Anyone who is alive is learning every day from facing reality. Wisdom comes from conquering the natural challenges of life.

◈   ◈   ◈

MODERN MYTH: Fathers Should Be Friends.

Fathers should be friends or counselors not to be feared by their children.

Children can relate better with friendly fathers. Fathers should not be feared but liked by their children. When father comes home a child should want to greet him, not be frightened of being punished for something the child did during the day. Children should want to share their lives with their fathers as much as with their mothers. Fathers should enjoy their relationships with their children, not be placed in the position of disciplinarian. Children are to be enjoyed, not punished. Children are only young once and the father should create a friendship that can grow into adulthood.

TRADITIONAL WISDOM: Fathers Need to Be Fathers.

The fact that fathers are natural disciplinarians should be used to your advantage in raising respectful children. "Wait until your father gets home" always got my attention as a child. I would laugh when my mother slapped me with a wooden spoon but snapped to attention when my father entered the door. I had a healthy respect (fear) of my father's power.

Like most children, I knew the limits of my protective, loving mother but I was unable to predict my father's reaction. In a word, I respected my father's power, especially if I had done something wrong. My father's stare (evil eye) was enough to stop me in my tracks. I knew as sure as the sun rises that my father meant business. In my respect for my father there was an undeniable, healthy dose of fear.

I followed in my father's footsteps with my own four children and they knew I was to be respected. If they did not treat their mother right I was there. Being the ultimate top of the disciplinary chart has been the historic role of fathers. I learned, my children learned, and hopefully my grandchildren will learn that doing the right thing keeps "Papa" from being upset.

Eliminating discipline from the role of the father probably has been the single most destructive attack on the family. The impact on the family due to the absence of fathers has been well documented. There is a high correlation between fatherless families and children involved in crime, drug addiction, dropouts, and teenage pregnancy. Fathers do play a greater role in the family than just providers of material goods. The deeper voice, bigger body, and more physical reactions have been underestimated in keeping children in line. The natural fear of fathers used to be utilized to help children develop good habits in learning to control themselves and we need to return to it. It is difficult for a mother or father to be friends with a child they do not even like. It is easy to love a good child.

◈　◈　◈

MODERN MYTH: The Family Is Obsolete.

Government schools and social programs can replace the family.

The family has become obsolete in modern society. In an advanced society like ours all family members need to do their own thing to become self-actualized. The choices today are unlimited and every member of society should be encouraged to take advantage of them.

Government can better handle many of the mundane functions of the family. Social programs already exist to take care of education, health, social, and emotional needs of our youth. Food programs, mental health programs, prenatal programs, and senior citizen programs have decreased the need for families. Professional personnel such as teachers, counselors, daycare workers, and doctors can do a better job than a generalized parent. The modern world belongs to specialists, not the out-of-date family.

TRADITIONAL WISDOM: Family Is the Best Social Unit.

The loving relationship of a family cannot be replicated by government. Socialism cannot replace the traditional family in producing healthy citizens. All viable civilizations have had strong families that are the building blocks of society. Parents need to realize creating a healthy family is the most important thing they will do in life.

Being a parent is not a part-time job; it is a commitment for life. The dividend for this incredible effort is in turn an incredible payoff. Children, grandchildren, and great-grandchildren allow parents to experience the meaning of the unfolding of life. The good work of raising a child is felt for several generations. What legacy is of greater value than raising children to be good, solid citizens?

◆　◆　◆

MODERN MYTH: Cynicism Is Politically Correct.

Being cynical of our government is a sign of political awareness. All governments, even our own, are out to deceive the citizenry. Citizens should not believe anything expressed by its government to keep the government honest. Any feelings of patriotism should be repressed, for it indicates naïveté. It is more intelligent to listen to our enemies and negative press reports than to accept our government's perspective.

TRADITIONAL WISDOM: Patriotism Is Wholesome.

People flying in first class who voluntarily give up their seats to soldiers flying in economy class make all true American feel proud. We have a responsibility to show appreciation to fellow Americans defending our nation. Defending what is good in our country is the right thing to do. Our government represents all the people of our nation and it certainly is not inherently evil.

During war we all have a vested interest in being united. Patriotic backing of our government officials and military demonstrates internal strength to our enemies, minimizing the need for further combat. Patriotic support of our nation is necessary, especially in time of war.

◈ ◈ ◈

MODERN MYTH: Experts Are Better Than Parents.

Why should you rely on your own devices when you can go directly to an expert?

Experts are better than personal observation and common sense in raising children. Specialists have studied children throughout their professional lives and have written countless books on the subject. In any bookstore in the nation parents and grandparents of all ages heavily frequent the child development and parenting section. There are new approaches and techniques articulated on an almost daily basis.

Television talk show hosts profile child development experts with a different slant on producing a healthy child. The expert's clinical observation and research have enlightened the American public in how to employ more subtle approaches in their role as parents. The payoff for parents is intellectually, emotionally, and socially superior children.

TRADITIONAL WISDOM: Observe Your Child, Trust Your Intuition.

Parents need to observe their children, trust their intuition, and return to traditional child-rearing methods. The result of the modern child-development expert's advice has been a disaster. The advice is often situational, confusing parents instead of giving them any direction. There are no cookie cutters we can use to mass-produce the ideal child.

Each family is unique and each child is unique so we have to fashion the exact recipe for each child to fulfill his God-given talents. No expert can do better than a parent because the parent has the intimacy of observation. Parents who grow wiser as their child matures will have greater insight into the child's behavior. There are general principles that have to be adjusted for each child.

In my book *Essential Parenting,* I discuss the POISE process that encourages the parent to trust his own instincts in child rearing. There are no magical technological innovations or approaches that can replace good old parent-to-child training. The modern permissive-materialistic approach to child rearing has been tried in the past, as described by Plato in ancient Greece. It did not work then and it will not work today for the same reasons. In fact, most of the permissive-materialistic approaches defy logic and common sense.

◆ ◆ ◆

MODERN MYTH: People Are Smarter Today.

Each successive generation is becoming smarter as they have more exposure to modern technology. Children are more aware of things around them than children of a half-century ago. Computers, television, entertainment advances, and more educated parents have given children advantages that they did not experience in the past.

Children today are more verbal and can discuss almost anything with their parents. Their awareness of sex, finances, or marital problems is sometimes shocking. Children are precocious in these areas because we no longer treat them as children. Children are treated as equals. No longer are children seen and not heard. Today children are both *seen* and *heard,* knowing no limit to their status.

TRADITIONAL WISDOM: Cuteness Is Often Detrimental.

An eight-year-old boy was in a special education program for mentally deficient children for three years before coming to see me. His mother thought he was cute and was still feeding, bathing, and dressing him. He stared into space whenever anyone spoke to him. By teaching the parents to demand that he become more independent and more attentive to them when they spoke, he was able to develop normally.

People are smart today in some ways and totally lack awareness in others. It depends on how you define the word "smart." Granted, people today are more verbally uninhibited about almost everything but often lack common sense. There is something to be said for listening to one's elders to learn about the world. Modern children may appear precocious or cute, arguing and negotiating with adults over matters that were taboo a few generations ago. Being "cute" can be seen as obnoxious and can get in the way of gaining knowledge.

Obnoxious, know-it-all children become obnoxious, know-it-all adults. Bright but reasonably courteous people are much more likely to be successful in every facet of life. In the American culture we have moved from parents focusing on children acting appropriately to children demonstrating how smart they can be. When the mother in front of me in line asks her three-year-old the color of everything in the child's sight, I realize I am in the middle of a performance. Of course the mother gave a smile to the onlookers to solicit approval. The child wanders around darting in front of others, for the most part oblivious to the mother's questions. Occasionally she may answer when she is about to test another limit. This mother has been led to believe that teaching her child a cognitive skill while ignoring her child's inability to listen and follow directions is sufficient to make her child successful and to make her an exemplary mother.

Children who do listen become adults who listen and better learn how to function in the world. Only by teaching children to listen will we be able to reverse the epidemic of mental illness sweeping America for children as well as adults.

◈   ◈   ◈

MODERN MYTH: He Who Dies with the Most Toys Wins.

Money is everything.

The accumulation of money demonstrates a person's importance and success. Money is power. The obtaining of wealth is more important than the manner of getting it. People should be judged on their personal assets. Anyone who attempts to justify his life on any criteria besides wealth is only rationalizing. Money talks. It makes the world go round. Living a moral life unnecessarily restricts a person from reaching his potential. Cumulative wealth is the most basic and accurate sign of a person's value on earth. Only religious fanatics will deny this obvious truth. The ultimate success of a person's life is directly measured by the amount of money amassed in his life.

TRADITIONAL WISDOM: Living Right Is Most Important.

The spirituality of one's life is its essence. How morally one lives every day determines his spiritual blessings. Being pious on the Sabbath while acting hypocritically the rest of the week may be a method of becoming materially rich but spiritually destitute. Selling your soul to the altar of money will bring you wealth and maybe fame, with its negative accompanying cost of self-importance, pompousness, and lack of meaningful spiritual and personal relationships. The old adage "money cannot buy happiness" is true. "What a person gives out comes back" is another truism. The good works we do come back as a fulfilling and satisfying life. The person who develops the habit of doing what is right gains positive power and strength. We will be ultimately judged on doing the right thing in our lives, not on our bank accounts. Upon dying we cannot take money with us but we will leave behind the moral quality of life's choices. Living the Golden Rule, "Do unto others as you would have them do unto you," is the essence of living an honorable existence. Our spiritual legacy is the most meaningful in our life and afterlife.

MODERN MYTH: Humans are Inherently Good.

People who have their basic needs met have no motivation for committing negative acts. Even unsupervised individuals will behave appropriately—it is part of human nature. It is only when people are socially deprived that they exhibit harmful behavior to self or others. These actions may be inappropriate, but the individual is only misguided. Evil is a false concept that was produced by primitive and ignorant people of the past.

TRADITIONAL WISDOM:
People Have a Choice to Be Good or Evil.

God has given humans freedom to make their own decisions. People make extraordinary personal sacrifices for the good of others. Other individuals are so self-serving that they will force others to do destructive things to themselves and others. When a person continually does evil actions, eventually he cannot turn back from evil. He *is* evil.

While working in a prison, I gave psychological evaluations to inmates who were not only troubled and misguided, but were downright evil. Evil and sainthood are not antique concepts. They existed in history and both exist in the modern world. We have to prepare ourselves and our children to deal with these forces of good and evil in our lives. Honorable people should be promoted and evil ones incarcerated to prevent them from hurting innocent others.

The Impact of the Myths

The Smugger myths have to be recognized for increasing personal vulnerability in a complex world and be immediately eliminated as excuses for our self-destructive tendencies. We have been bamboozled into believing the time-tested traditional methods of living are passé—in the phraseology of our modern, forward-thinking psychological experts, "old-fashioned." These "old-fashioned" methods seemed to be too strict in a new dawning of the "Age of Aquarius" permissive world. The truth is most traditional practices are moderate when considering the entire spectrum of choices. The current Smugger experts are skewed, being far to the left in their permissive advice. By returning to the traditional middle of the continuum, we can bring relationships, families, and values into a more highly functioning state. Eliminating guilt, fear, punishment, and evil from our society is the extreme position. Calibrating guilt, fear, and punishment to gain desired results is necessary and wise. Handcuffing authority figures—especially parents in a PC world—is destructive to our culture. Encouraging fathers, mothers, and community leaders, as well as all citizens, to perform their roles more effectively is a more moderate, healthy response. Living a morally disciplined existence, not a self-serving "me generation" existence, is the way to insure a strong and peaceful nation.

Unwarned is unarmed. After reading this chapter you are armed and enlisted as an American patriot. The following chapters will examine in greater depth the destructiveness of these myths and the wisdom of our great traditions.

Chapter 3

Dismantling to Building Community

A middle-aged black male is pumping gas in a gas station directly off I-95. He hears a muffled sound and feels a burning sensation in his back. The man takes two steps forward and falls flat on his face. The next day a thirteen-year-old student is shot in the back as he is walking into school. Two days later a wife and husband are loading purchases into their car in a Home Depot parking lot. She is shot dead. These indiscriminate attacks seem to be endless. Civil, business, and school events are postponed out of fear. People in the area under attack remain hidden in their homes rather than risk personal safety by going out. As the physical risk to the people of the area escalates, the cohesiveness of the community dissolves into everyone fending for himself. We are confronted by uncertainty and fear. Every day the media bombards us with negative news about our local communities. We are losing the courage to fight for the safety of our neighborhoods. We are retreating into our barricaded homes.

Americans are losing their connection with their neighbors. People go from their lonely cubicles to their high-priced vehicles. They pay their tolls, the bar codes on their car window opens the security gate, they press their garage door opener, and quickly disappear from sight. These people are self-isolated cave dwellers. Their advanced technological features and upscale furnishings make for an upscale cave, but a cave nonetheless.

There is little ground separating them from the next cave, but walls and blinds give them the sense of isolation. When the cave dwellers leave their caves, their headphones and straight-ahead gazes minimize any possibility of social contact. After their brief excursion into daylight, they again disappear into their caves. It is much safer; it takes much less time and energy than maintaining relationships with people in the next dwelling. With the breakdown of our moral standards, we have difficulty trusting our neighbors.

Individuals are healthier when they have a sense of belonging. A close community where people share the same values, morals, and beliefs provides a needed predictability. This safe environment allows people to relax and to enjoy others. It takes moral community leaders to create this type of environment.

Authority figures need to demonstrate moral behavior. When we must iterate that authority figures need to conform to community standards, it demonstrates how loose our standards have become. Authority figures—teachers, policemen, clergy, coaches, scout leaders, and politicians—are by their positions role models. When role models are not conforming to the standards of the community, they are sending a message that the community standards need not be respected. Teachers talking about their alternate lifestyles and coming to work in jeans or provocative clothing defame their position. Policemen having visible tattoos or earrings and attempting to impress by telling others of their drinking and partying exploits are doing the community a disservice. Any member of the clergy, politician, or scout leader who uses his power to sexually abuse others should be removed from his position and prosecuted to the full extent of the law.

Dumbing Down Standards

When a Smugger argues that addiction, gambling, and pornography are victimless crimes, we begin to realize how dishonest and corrupt many of our leaders have become. The millions of aborted babies, the ever-increasing violent acts caused by lack of judgment or the need to obtain another fix, the broken families from parents' or children's addictions, and the sexual abuse of children are not without victims. The big lie of victimless crime is at the heart of the cancer devouring our communities and producing modern cave dwellers.

Our standards for role models have been "dumbed down" to make a mockery of the positions of our community leaders. Only by communities holding their leaders to a high moral standard can the community expect to be a highly functioning one. Does any clear-thinking person believe it is in the best interest of our children to allow an active alcoholic, drug addict, felon, womanizer, or homosexual to have access to influence our children's thoughts and beliefs? Whenever authority figures indicate by their actions that the breaking of the moral code of society is acceptable, these role models need to be removed.

The recent images of dishonorable corporate CEOs being carted away in handcuffs are somewhat reassuring. We Americans believe bad guys eventually get their just reward. Personal profit and greed at the expense of shareholders is a prosecutable criminal act. However, there are other acts that do not reach the level of violating the laws, though they still are morally reprehensible.

Immoral corporate acts are devastating to our faith in our enterprise system. Employees' lack of confidence in the leadership of their companies decreases satisfaction and productivity. It undermines the employees' allegiance to the corporation as well as everyone's trust in the economic system.

Not Protecting the Innocent, Not Punishing the Guilty

Too many employees are being disrespected and emotionally abused. Recently two clients came to see me on an employment assistance program for mental health problems. Their appointments were scheduled one right after the other. They each worked for different departments in the same credit card corporation. Even though these clients did not know each other, they reported almost identical scenarios. The company was outsourcing their jobs to India, the Philippines, and Costa Rica. Each related that they received high recommendations from their superiors until recently. One of them noted that many people were being "boxed." She explained a person was instructed to wait in the lobby while their belongings in their office were cleared out and placed in a box. The box was unceremoniously given to that dejected worker in the lobby who was then instructed to leave the building.

In separate sessions each client said she was systematically demeaned to prod her to quit her position. Each described a form of psychological torture. Even though each had exemplary evaluations in the past, recent monitoring of her telephone conversations had become an ordeal. The more she saw her fellow workers forced to depart, the more dispirited she became, and the more the supervisor stressed her lack of enthusiasm in her conversations with customers. This vicious cycle of receiving negative feedback brought them to a destructive state which generated more negativity. As one client stated, it felt like one enduring drop after another, a Chinese water torture of unbearable stress.

Outsourcing is a profitable and economical means of staffing a business. There is not an inherent immorality in the practice of using cheap labor. A problem only arises when corporate leaders maliciously manipulate their employees to gain a short-term advantage by creating artificial and falsely negative environments for employees. It is at best irresponsible and at worst an evil practice. Immoral corporate leadership is a destructive force that affects the employee, the company, and society overall.

We can no longer take the side of the perpetrator over the victim without destroying our social fabric, the social mores of society. The constant assault of the bleeding-heart Smuggers is attempting to excuse every evil act as a result of a social injustice that caused the horrific behavior. The January 2003 indiscriminate clemency granted by Governor George Ryan of Illinois to over 160 inmates legally sentenced to death was a hideous act of injustice. This scandal-ridden governor slapped the victims, their families, friends, and all law-abiding citizens in the face. He was elected as a representative of the people to follow the rule of law. Governor Ryan's despicable disregard for justice was cowardly decreed as he left office. Community leaders must ban together to overturn acts that countermand the just punishment of evil.[1]

The transgressions against an innocent victim do not end with the initial act. The victim that has been hurt by an evil act sadly often displaces this anger on another, often actually duplicating the act done to him on another victim. I shockingly witnessed this phenomenon when working with adolescent sex abusers in community mental health. Each one of them shared that he was abused at an early age. They related that their abuse of another was to see how it felt to be the person who had the power. There are no victimless crimes. Citizens have a right to be protected from criminals.

Elevating Community Virtues

The exemplary families of the community have a responsibility to ensure that the standards of the community are the highest they can be to prevent crimes. For community leaders to accept anything else is a disservice to the citizens. Community authority figures need to be on the same moral page as parents in the community to send a clear and strong message to children that following the highest standard leads to a socially approved and successful life.

Our nation was firmly established by moral men. Benjamin Franklin spoke about thirteen virtues in his autobiography.[2] George Washington was influenced by the powerful Roman morality in his late teens and quoted Roman phrases throughout his life.[3]

America has been a great nation because all institutions have worked together to instill traditional morals and values. It is based on common sense, knowledge, and wisdom that work. We were raised in a culture where the good guys won and the bad guys were locked up. Our heroes were moral people who overcame the odds through their perseverance. We rooted for the moral underdog who was inevitably victorious. Our culture teaches us to move forward by solving the current problem, not to wallow in the past. We have been an optimistic people. Our traditional culture is based on universal morals taught in all institutions and practiced throughout the community.

Dimming the American Dream

The epidemic of bullies among our youth, the criminal behavior in all social strata, and the domestic and foreign terrorists all demonstrate the eroding of America's moral, cultural message. We are not training our children in our historical values and morals. We are not insisting that our children have courage to fight for what is right. Instead, the counterculture is perversely teaching our youth that the dark side of life is preferable to goodness. We need to get back on a moral track or suffer the pain of a nation in decline. We have to turn toward the traditional culture that built our great nation.

The pompous European notion that America does not have a definable culture is international Smugger elitism. Our traditional values and morals unite all the nationalities and religions that comprise our melting pot. No matter what part of the world our ancestors came from, we learned the American dream was real and obtainable. This dream had to be earned and was not just given to anyone as a birthright. Traditional Americans will never accept the idea of entitlement.

This American dream is alive and strong outside our borders, too. This is seen every day by foreigners putting their lives in danger to enter our nation. Yet in education, the media, business, and political institutions we hear only about the broken American promises. We as a people are fed a steady diet of negativity. First-generation immigrants are thriving on our freedoms, while the children of families living for generations in America are languishing in the same nation. Instead of augmenting the Horatio Alger stories, our institutions are diminishing and eroding the importance of a moral lifestyle.

Americans of several generations in our nation have lost their traditional roots, as they have lost its anchor: the traditional family. Our local communities have faltered as the counterculture has redefined and eliminated many of the duties to the family. Withdrawing from responsibility as a member of a traditional family and community has created a weaker local community that is negatively impacting the mental, social, and emotional health of the entire nation.

Unbridled Materialism Has Uprooted Communities

The movement from an agrarian to an industrial to a post-industrial society has moved people away from the family, home, and community. Social mobility that means moving for career advancement has become part of modern America. This mobility has uprooted many of us from the communities of our families. Increasing our material wealth has weakened our traditional communities.

Americans are no longer "keeping up with the Joneses." We have become the Joneses. In pursuit of the god of money we have sacrificed the time we spend with our family in our community. It takes time and energy to develop and maintain relationships. Our dedication to the material god to the exclusion of family has adversely impacted our communities. Many decent people are no longer dedicating their time to volunteer in their neighborhoods or towns. The weakening of our community has made life unhealthy for our children.

Prioritizing Our Lives in a Glut of Choices

We Americans live in a great country where we have a multitude of choices. Many parents are out of balance choosing more and more material wealth or "want lust" over having time to spend with their children and establishing ties in the community. To these parents, time is money; but more than ever, we need to spend more time with our children. And time is more valuable than money: It is our life.

We will never adopt Mexican time where time stands still, but we can choose not to take a second or even a third job, not to take a salary increase that will require more hours in order to purchase more useless things just to fill up a mini storage unit. Consumerism in its most vulgar form, compulsive buying, has made it nearly impossible to cut back on work without risking bankruptcy. Parents need to see the importance of spending time with their children and developing community connections instead of spending their lives and money at the mall.

Too Little Quantity Time, Too Much Fantasy Time

Modern children are not sufficiently connected to family or community. Fewer and fewer children are having intimate involvement with their career-oriented parents. Many children are part of a close-knit group outside the home that has an investment in their well-being in a functioning community. Our materialistic permissive lifestyles have camouflaged our need for a viable community. With material wealth has come a multitude of objects: televisions, videos, CDs, DVDs, Game Boys, and computers that encourage one-to-one involvement with a self-absorbed machine instead of old-fashioned human interaction. Who needs human friends when a child can play with his Game

Boy or go online meeting "friends" in a chat room? Too many children are not learning the important lesson that social skills and common sense are necessary tools for lifelong success.

With little parental supervision, children are creating their own fantasy worlds. Teenagers may have a difficult time retaining essential historical information, but they surely know the personal lives of meaningless celebrities. I asked high school students who was a teenage idol and Eminem was immediately mentioned. The student spoke about him as if he was his best friend, even mentioning his daughter's name was Haley. I did a small survey and amazingly each and every student from high school through elementary school student knew Eminem's daughter's name. Yet these students do not know the name of our current vice president nor do they want to know about the history of the founding fathers of their nation. These music celebrities are an integral part of their fantasy lives, which play a large part in their conversations with their peers.

Children are not learning about reality and gaining what was called common sense. Their lives are involved with electronic fantasy instead of wise, caring adults or even concerned peers. Today children know less and less about reality, living mostly in some form of fantasy. Modern parents find it easier to play along with their child's "cute" dreams rather than deal with everyday reality training. Britney Spears, Eminem, SpongeBob SquarePants, Powerpuff Girls, or phony reality show winners consume the child's life, in essence becoming the child's imaginary playmates. There are no substitutes for the real thing: friends and adults to look up to, to learn from, and be protected by.

Amoral "Cave" Communities

Materialism has lead to selfish isolation, creating amoral communities. Too many geographic areas are not communities that share a consensus of morals and values. Instead there are many locations that are comprised of people living lonely lives in isolated houses. Often family members live in their own self-serving worlds with little motivation to develop a common view of life, even amongst family members. Needless to say there is little time devoted to being part of a community. People do not even attempt to follow common rules of decency because they are not anchored in the community. Too many people litter our beaches and roads, drive in the passing lane slowing traffic for others, and never turn on their turn signal when making a turn. Other drivers are ready to kill for the slightest reason in what is now commonly labeled "road rage." Businesses sell contaminated food to their local customers and fire loyal employees rather than grant them their pensions. Modern isolated people pay $30 for the privilege of touching strangers in "cuddle parties."[4] Even criminals have stooped to the newest low of "home invasions" that unnecessarily place innocent people at a life-and-death risk. The lack of personal knowledge of and contact with the people in the neighborhood makes it easy for people to stop being neighborly.

Most people do not have time to spend being around their home, much less their community. With the majority of both parents working and only limited extended family members nearby, there are no longer grandparents, aunts, uncles, or even mothers to keep their eyes open to protect the neighborhood children. There are even fewer children in the neighborhood who need to be watched over. Many children spend their time inside the confines of their own house or perhaps the home of one friend. Much of what was once considered the characteristics of a community has evaporated. We are left with venues where parents continually take their children for some type of instruction. Modern parents realizing the sadness and isolation of their children have taken to transporting them to more interesting environments. Geographic neighborhoods and communities are becoming extinct.

Modern Security Does Not
Stop the Media's Home Invasion

Parents should do more than use their material assets in attempting to protect their children. Living in a gated community seems to be a reasonable response for the safety and well-being of children in the twenty-first century. The security guards, the upscale homes, and high gate do nothing to protect the child from the media home invasion that is corrupting the morals and traditional values of our children. The threat is not so much from thieves, robbers, or rapists physically entering our homes as it is from electronic waves of the media penetrating our homes and the minds of our children.

In our present permissive and materialistic society, we are overly preoccupied with the physical well-being of our children while ignoring their mental health. We make sure our children wear crash helmets when they ride bicycles yet we allow them free access to over one hundred television channels totally unsupervised. We rush them to the emergency room or doctor's office when they have a virus but have no idea what they are doing on the Internet. We attempt to superficially know at least the families of our child's closest friends though we have no clue about their electronic friends, heroes, and activities. Besides being inundated by pornographic sites, children have the opportunity for online gambling. "The Delaware survey found 9 percent of eighth graders had gambled on Web sites offering electronic forms of slot machines and card games."[5]

Bullying is on the Internet. "[It is] no longer confined to school grounds or daytime hours. 'Cyberbullies' are pressuring their quarries into their bedrooms. Tools such as email messages and logs enable the harassment to be less obvious to adults and more publicly humiliating as gossip put downs and embarrassing pictures are circulated amongst a wide audience of peers with a few clicks."[6] The Internet can be dangerous to the health of our children.

The most intricate electronic device cannot substitute for an actively involved parent developing moral character to protect a child against the trash on the airwaves. The importance of daily interaction between child and parent will never have a substitute.

Parents need to better balance their priorities to be good parents. A TV-censoring filter (V-chip) or computer programs that allow only certain material to get through gives parents a false sense of security. A determined child can override either of these. The only foolproof method of protecting a child is to instill a strong value system in the child, a traditional moral value system that clearly defines good and evil. A value system should be based on honest communication of reality rather than the indiscriminate confusing and blurring PC toleration of all thoughts and behavior.

False Safety in Artificial Relationships

Modern parents have attempted to develop safe havens for their children. Without time to spend at home with their children or the support of the extended family, child protection becomes a priority. These parents spend their brief free time with their children as chauffeurs. They take their children to activities to form an artificial community based on the parents' perceived needs of their children. These synthetic associations have more, not fewer, problems than the traditional community.

These modern parents place their faith in strangers. Coaches, ministers, karate or music instructors, and other authority figures train and provide safety for their children. Not only do the parents pay for these services and lose valuable opportunities to impact their own children, but they also place their children at risk. Often authority figures in our modern, transient communities have not established their reputations from their good works over time in a close-knit neighborhood. Instead many charlatans use marketing techniques to disguise past failures, often immoral intentions, and sometimes even their criminal histories. It is the fear of possible deviance and lack of personal supervision that puts guilt in the back of the mind of the parent. This guilt propels the parent's knee-jerk response to initially support their child when a sincere authority figure makes a legitimate complaint about their child. This empowers most children to believe their parents can overrule any authority figure's decisions. There are many liabilities for modern parents who farm out their own responsibilities to acquaintances.

Children Being Robbed of Childhood

Children are losing their childhoods. Constant supervision in organized activities does not allow children to learn from each other. Unorganized games teach children important lessons of life, how to lose and how to win. A group of properly socialized children does a better job of teaching other children the rules of a game and enforcing the rules than do adults. All games have rules that have to be followed or you are penalized or disqualified. A child learns that other children acting like the referee, judge, or umpire are not always correct but the call needs to be accepted and made up for by better play. It becomes evident to participants that working together increases the probability of winning the game. Playing sports has many valuable lessons to teach. As a child moves up in organized sports he may even become inspired by a dedicated coach.

Children Are Losing Their Freedom

Children no longer have an opportunity to develop their own social skills in relating to each other. Children have limited opportunities to make personal decisions amongst themselves and learn the skills necessary to stand up for themselves against bullies. This lack of opportunity to have freedom of interaction with other children in a stable community is handicapping their development into responsible, independent, and self-reliant adults.

Parents do not hold their children to high standards of behavior. Regardless of their child's academic performance parents are pressured to present their child with a car as soon as they can legally drive. The parent's lack of faith in their child doing the right thing has motivated many of them to purchase cell phones with GPS tracking to monitor the child's location and speed. Instead of teaching their adolescents to be trustworthy, parents are once again relying on electronic equipment to monitor them. Any adolescent can thwart their parent's tracking of their driving behavior by turning off this device. Parents are not willing or able to understand the importance of their child's internalizing mature and responsible behavior before granting them adult privileges.

Instead, too many adults attempt to live through their children. We see them coaching their own children and showing them favoritism. They are in the stands booing at the other team of little children who are doing the best they can. These same parents yell at their children's teachers and coaches before they determine the facts of a situation. These parents are not teaching their children sportsmanship and are not following any moral path. These parents' personal need for their child to win at any cost is a sign of moral depravity.

Parents' Egos Are Out of Control

Parents are abusing adults and other people's children for the needs of their own egos. A homicidal Boston hockey father who killed his child's coach because he disagreed with the way the coach handled his child is an indicator of the extent of the disintegration of our sense of community.[7] How far off course is our moral compass? The winning-at-all-costs mentality, evident in blatant cheating to win, parents verbally and physically abusing their children in competition, and brawls amongst parents over the outcome of their children's games is disgraceful and immoral. The valuable lessons of winning and losing are being lost in the perverted ego needs of parents living vicariously through their children.

Parents who prematurely encourage their children into social events is another illustration of living through their children. Preteens spending the night at sleepovers, going to pop rock music concerts, and precocious dating seem to be more exciting events to parents than to their children. It appears as a way parents can attempt to give their children what they desired as a child and never were able to satisfy. The problem with parents' unfilled sexual fantasies being imposed on their children in today's "anything goes" community is that there are no longer built-in moral and relationship safeguards.

Modern Enclaves Attract Evil

There is no longer a moral consensus that sex between children or even sex between children and adults is immoral! The moral relativist Smuggers have subverted our morality. Let kids be kids and have fun and pleasure as a sentiment is much easier than attempting to hold a high and restrictive moral standard. Being morally old-fashioned is out of vogue in our modern, sexually free culture. Being "open-minded" about boys and girls having sleepovers together, "touchy feely" drug infested rock concerts and clubs, and blatant displays of sexuality means to ignore all the potential long-term possible sexual and moral negative consequences to one's child. This is a modern form of parental neglect and abuse. Sexual permissiveness is harmful to the particular child with a negative ripple effect throughout the entire local and national community.

There are child sex proponents who say adults have a right to have sex with children. The belief that a child has a right to consent to experience sexual pleasure at any age is a convoluted way to justify an adult having sex with an innocent child. There is documentation in past hedonist civilizations of the evils of sexual abuse. Sigmund Freud, the founder of modern psychology, was confronted by the psychic destruction of his clients through sexual abuse during the Victorian period. The negative impact of sexual abuse is undeniable throughout history. Currently, past sexual abuse incidents are major determinants of the course of therapy. The manner in which the victim interpreted the abuse often has an influence on the life path of the individual. A victim who was showered with attention and gifts in exchange for sex with a molester often has confused feelings. On one level the child feels special and on the other, knows it is wrong. Some victims go into a shell, avoiding any display of their sexuality. Other victims become sexually flirtatious and sexually promiscuous. Frequently these victims of sexual abuse raise families where children continue to act out the unresolved conflicts of the abused parent. In one case I saw the children of a family after the father was removed from the home for having an incestuous relationship with one of the daughters. Eighteen years later I saw the same girl, now a mother, bringing her thirteen-year-old daughter for counseling for defiance, sexually provocative behavior, and nearly being raped by an older teenager. The mother's ineffectual method of coping with her sexual abuse was passed directly down to her flirtatious daughter.

Other times childhood sexual abuse will cause withdrawal. A forty-two-year-old mother came for counseling because she was unable to show affection toward her two pubescent sons and had little sexual interest in her husband. As therapy continued she shared that as a young child her father would drink and slip into her bed as she acted as if she were asleep. She attempted to tell her mother, who rejected the thought. She had buried the incident but her distrust for men surfaced in her distaste for sex and her inability to love her sons. By learning that she was a victim and discussing her anger toward her father, her behavior changed toward her family.

Ask the children whom priests molested if they were thankful. A thirty-nine-year-old client who was molested as an altar boy at age thirteen came for marriage counseling with his wife. After several sessions it was obvious that he had been dishonest about his feelings—especially sexual feelings—for the entire twenty-year marriage. He had several long-term affairs to drown out the fear that he was a latent homosexual. As it turned out, he was a classic victim who was running away from a horribly destructive experience.

Any adult who has sex with a child is committing a criminal act. A twenty-six-year-old married woman had been sexually abused by her history teacher from the age of fifteen until graduation from high school. She came to see me for her inability to feel the passion for her wonderful husband that she had felt for her teacher. She described the excitement of meeting with a grown man who was married with two children. She had found out that he was continuing his ways with other students but she was not fazed by his continued abuse, she just knew how she felt being with him. The problem was she was unable to connect that her sexual dissatisfaction with her husband was connected with her abuse that began at fifteen years old. The adventure of experiencing an illicit, perverted relationship obliterated her ability to appreciate normal relationships. Her sexuality became distorted. Like most abuse victims, her perspective became warped. That the cycle of sexual abuse is in no way helpful to children is an understatement. It destroys their innocence and robs them of a morally healthy perspective on sex.

Yet there is an association dedicated to the sexual abuse of children that is gaining legitimacy in intellectual circles. The North American Man-Boy Love Association is receiving legal support from the ACLU to continue to market their organization. NAMBLA, in its literature and Web site, advocates sex between a grown man and teenage boy as beneficial to the child. The ACLU defends the group's right to seduce and corrupt children under the guise of free speech.

Advocating sexual abuse under the rationalization that it is good for the child to be around cultured adults is not anything new. The ancient Greeks called sex between a man and a boy "pederasty." In decadent Greece children were tossed aside by the noble pedophiles as soon as the child reached puberty. Of course, according to the Greek aristocrats, there was no damage to the child, who was treated like a sex object. At the twilight of his life Plato concluded pederasty was abusive to children even after partaking in the practice throughout most of his life.[8]

Abusers today are just as gifted as ancient Greek pedophiles in justifying their evil acts. I heard many different excuses while dealing with sex offenders in prison and mental health centers. "I was attempting to teach my daughter how to have good sex." "He enjoyed it, he came back again." "I was quite gentle and gave many gifts." The abuser thinks only about his own needs, not the child's. It is for this exact reason that children need to be protected by moral adults since young children are easy prey for immoral adults. We need to protect our children's innocence, trust, and feelings of social security.

The rationale advocating pedophilia has a new champion in Judith Levine. In her book, *Harmful to Minors: The Perils of Protecting Children from Sex,* she weaves numerous pseudoscientific studies, mostly women's studies and dubious self-reporting of national and international sexual survey statistics, in a skillful and sophisticated manner.[9] Ms. Levine is a professional journalist who has honed her craft well. Her writing skills are used to push her personal agenda with shocking disregard for the truth.

In June 2002, I appeared with Ms. Levine on *The Cathy Fountain Show* on FOX television in Tampa, Florida, to discuss her controversial book. She repeated many of the absurd premises found in her book. She assumes that a child has the maturity to become sexually involved with an adult and believes if a child feels pleasure in molestation and does not perceive the act in a negative manner, the act can be good for the child. Ms. Levine implied to the host, Cathy Fountain, that it is the interpretation of the sexual incident by the significant adults in the child's life that is more important than the act itself. Ms. Levine related that you have to separate the morality of the act from the psychological pleasure of the act. In other words, if the molester acts caring and touches the child gently to give him or her pleasure, then this would be a positive sexual experience—especially if no adult puts a negative connotation on the immoral act. The molester might satisfy his power and hedonistic needs but this is immaterial to the child, according to Ms. Levine. The main issue is that the child has a right to his body's pleasure and the maturity to know what is in his best interest. The immorality of the act will have no negative consequences on the child as long as everyone remains nonjudgmental.

Her rationale for sexually abusive acts on children is either naïve at best or at worst, criminal. Her fallacious thinking does not take into account the context of our culture. The social and emotional maturity of children is not equal to that of adults. Children do not have the necessary life experiences to develop the judgment and emotional maturity to make decisions in their long-term self-interest. A molestation that may initially be perceived by a child as a pleasurable experience will eventually turn sour. Whether a child is gently seduced or raped, there is eventually a high level of psychological damage. A child is usually devastated by the ending of a relationship and may go into a shell or act out promiscuously in search of the illicit pleasure. Once a pedophile, a seductive molester, or a power rapist robs the premature innocence of a child, the child becomes more susceptible to being harmed by others and has a distorted view of sex for the remainder of his or her life. It does not matter how long a child keeps "the secret" or rationalizes the actions of the pedophile. The immorality of the act is

destructive to the child no matter how initially pleasurable the experience. This thinking is naïve and fallacious because it is devoid of any
context of cultural reality.

Children in the United States are generally ill-equipped to make
even simple choices. When children are given greater freedom of
choice over their intake of food, the results are chilling. "One-fourth of
school-aged children are overweight and one-eighth are obese, twice
the proportions found two decades ago."[10] Teenage drivers are noted for
their recklessness resulting in a high rate of auto accidents. Developing the ability to make good judgments takes an accumulation of real
experiences over time. Most children today live in a media fantasy
world and have minimal exposure to real and intimate relationships.
These limited in-depth relationships with significant others make them
more vulnerable to the attentions of older people.

Both NAMBLA and Ms. Levine's book are highly dangerous to children. They would allow adults to have sex with children as young as
twelve without any possibility of criminal prosecution. Yet both have
proponents in this cultural civil war. Judith Levine's above-mentioned
book, *Harmful to Children,* in April 2003 received a *Los Angeles Times*
Festival of Books Award.[11] This means there is a cultural current that
would place children in peril by legalizing pedophilia in our communities. The decriminalizing of this deviant behavior can only be contemplated in a troubled society. The reality is pedophiles protected by laws
will proliferate, becoming more insatiable in their hedonistic gratification without legal restriction to their evil acts. Decriminalizing
pedophiles can only be contemplated in weak communities. The Smuggers need to be exposed for justifying evil. We are in a cultural civil war.

The Impact of Gay Issues on Our Communities

Homosexuality and bisexuality have always existed and will continue
to exist. We are a free country that allows us to live the lifestyle we

want in the sanctity of our homes. God has given us freedom of choice. The issue all societies have to face is whether to promote it or not. I believe not.

The far-reaching negative impact of gay marriage has recently been confirmed by statistics emanating from Scandinavian countries. Stanley Kurtz of the Hoover Institute stated, "The majority of children in Sweden and Norway are born out of wedlock. Sixty percent of first-born children in Denmark have unmarried parents. Not coincidentally these countries have had something close to full gay marriage for a decade or more. Same-sex marriage has locked in and reinforced an existing Scandinavian trend toward the separation of marriage and parenthood. The Nordic family pattern—including gay marriage—is spreading across Europe. And by looking closely at it we can answer the key empirical question underlying the gay marriage debate. Will same-sex marriage undermine the institution of marriage? It already has."[12]

A thirty-nine-year-old woman came to see me about her lesbian relationship. She informed me that she had been in an abusive relationship for sixteen years with her husband, from which she had produced a sixteen-year-old daughter and thirteen-year-old son. Both of her children had significant mental health issues. Her female partner stated that she was unwilling to accept her son living in their home. Her partner was several years older and had recently gained custody of her own two children, a girl age nine and a boy age four from in vitro births with her previous female partner. As the more dominant female, she told my client that her son had to leave their home.

Shortly after the two young children arrived, the thirteen-year-old son was shipped off to boarding school. This presented major problems for everyone. The children had to explain to themselves and others that their mother had changed sexual orientation. Her sixteen-year-old daughter was being released from a residential mental health facility but could not move in with her mother. Both of these children were outside their mother's new life. My client was placed in a nanny role with her partner's two young children. Her partner had a thriving business and was the main wage earner. However, the children's main bonding was with their birth mother. But she chose to have an affair with a young woman and wanted freedom from the responsibility of raising the children. She shipped them to her old lover, who had been the motivating factor for the two conceptions.

These two younger children's issues were unfairly complex. They cared for my client though they knew she had minimal power. The four-year-old boy realized there were no males in his world, saying, "even the dog was female." His sister was placed in an embarrassing situation when she was in a horse show. She had the misfortune to have the four women in her life come to the show at the same time. Her birth mother and her girlfriend, my client and her partner—all were there. This nine-year-old had to introduce all four women as her mothers to her friends. Imagine the embarrassment and stress on the child. Both of these youngsters were shipped back to their biological mother and her young lover after a nine-month period. Homosexual relationships are difficult for everyone, especially children.

These clinical observations have made me homophobic. My motivation is not from personal fears; I am long past the possibility of sexual confusion. My fear is for young children. Many, if not most, preadolescents and adolescents in today's America are sexually confused. They are exposed to vivid pictures of homosexual and bisexual images in the media and bombarded by a "nonjudgmental" media that equates all forms of sexuality. There are homosexual and bisexual clubs in many government schools that persuade students to experiment sexually and to interpret their confusion as a sign of their homosexual orientation. One of the adolescent students in my school just had a painful breakup with a boyfriend and told her teacher she might turn to girls. This was probably a ploy for attention but it does show the impact of the homosexual agenda on children. Lucky for her, the teacher explained it was normal for her to be upset with her ex-boyfriend but in a short time her interest in boys would return. It miraculously returned as soon as a new male student entered the classroom a few days later.

Political correctness in our institutions has a negative impact on our children. My youngest son was attending a highly regarded state college in Florida. He was assigned a homosexual roommate. Even after informing the institution that his roommate was engaging in homosexual acts in his room, my son was told he had to "tolerate" this behavior. He was ridiculed and ostracized by active homosexual groups on campus for being homophobic. He did not want to witness these indecent and immoral acts. He stood firm in his objections and eventually the student performing homosexual acts moved out to find another roommate. My son knew that heterosexual acting out behavior performed in his room would have more easily resulted in the student being transferred or disciplined by the administration.

Things have radically changed. Until 1973 the American Psychiatric Association diagnosed homosexuality as a mental illness.[13] Clinicians noted many self and interpersonal destructive acts were associated with this deviant lifestyle. Throughout history those who are aware of the homosexual subculture know the difficulties of the lifestyle. Even if the majority of Americans choose to be homosexual, the emotional difficulties of their lives would not be resolved. The problem is not the homosexual's ability to fit into the heterosexual world. The real issue is the deviance of homosexuality.

The bottom line is that same-gender sex is contrary to human nature. Only a man and a woman can naturally procreate. No homosexual psychobabble agenda can change this obvious difference. No religious tolerance proclamation can change this fact. No pseudoscientific genetic nonsense about homosexuality being pre-determined by a particular gene can change this fact. It is an abomination to equate a homosexual with a heterosexual act to attempt to change the natural order of life. No amount of homosexuals mocking the traditional family can legitimize their actions. When a man and woman choose to join hands in sacred matrimony, two people can learn from their inherent differences to fulfill themselves and unite as one.

Virtual Reality: No Substitute for Caring Relationships

Many modern people choose to live in fantasy world. In the absence of live flesh and blood relationships, people go inside themselves into the recesses of their imaginations. An individual without a significant relationship is at high risk of becoming mentally ill. People in the past often read literature to search out more ideal relationships. Today individuals have more powerfully seductive substitutions for human relationships.

Virtual communities have invaded our homes. The media have created them. It started with sitting around the console radio listening to weekly programs. Next pictures were added and the television became the focus of our living rooms. The television in its infancy was a big deal. Everyone in the family circled the one TV to eagerly watch the one or two stations then available. Affluence has allowed for multiple television sets in the home, thus leaving children to their own devices in making program choices from hundreds of possibilities and then interpreting what they see on their own. Many housewives watch morning talk shows and soap operas and become disillusioned with their lives as wives and mothers. Weird combinations of degenerate people are relentlessly promoted as chic to promote alternate lifestyles. It has corrupted our culture.

Television has insinuated itself into the heads of Americans. Slick advertising creates wants and transforms them into needs. It provides intellectuals a forum to change our values and perceptions through agenda-laden programming. Television was the engine ushering in the consumer economy and the permissive and materialistic philosophy of our current society.

For Too Many Children TV Creates Their Basis for Community

The ghetto has become glorified in music and on television and is the current model for most American youth. The baggy pants worn below the hips exposing the underwear, the streetwalker attire for the girls, the hat worn at an angle, and the gaudy shoes complete the outfit of today's ghetto wannabe. The ghetto rap music and its pimp imagery is constantly bombarding our children through radio, television, commercials, and MTV-type video programming. Our children have developed their own community and it is in their minds. It is the "war zone ghetto."

By adding picture stories to sound the media industry has produced the powerful music video to spread their glorification of hedonism. Sex, drugs, violence, and grotesque videos added to the current music took on a virtual reality. Deviant actions and looks inundate the minds of our children. Evil, abusive acts are desensitized by rapid and numerous exposures to the dark side of life. The word "bad" began to mean "good," and the word "good" disappeared from the vocabulary. Our children were taught to tolerate all deviant behavior and to view all traditional values as corny, old-fashioned, worthless behavior.

Computer Danger

The newest home invader, but probably not the last, is the computer. Its potential for good and bad is unlimited. This is virtual reality in a highly sophisticated form. I learned about the practical positive implications of the Internet from my wife and my four children and the real dangers from my counseling clients. When traveling outside the USA, the Internet allows people to keep in close communication with friends and loved ones. It brings everyone together. In the business world it has been a bonanza to many industries and the ability to access knowledge has been greatly improved. The many positive influences have just begun to be realized.

However, the computer opens our homes to unknown individuals. The computer can be a horribly destructive machine for lonely, isolated people. My first negative Internet experience with a client happened when chat rooms first gained popularity. This man, who worked as a fireman and was married with two children, was having problems in his marriage and found a receptive woman through his chat room connections. One thing led to another and he fell romantically "in love" typing his ideal image to a lady who typed back her ideal image. He went a great distance to visit her only to find out she had a child she had not mentioned and was not who she wrote she was. In the meantime his wife found out about his escapades, which further complicated their fragile relationship.

I was stunned to see a steady drip turn into a flood of clients turning to virtual-reality relationships rather than working on their long-term invested relationships. People find it easier to create a fantasy relationship than use their energies to correct their ongoing meaningful relationships.

It is ironic that parents of young children are delighted to inform my wife and me that their three- to six-year-olds know more about the computer than they do. This means the child is not learning to use the computer from the parents but is left unsupervised for extended periods of time "playing" on the computer. This time spent progresses from simple educational games to more elaborate action games and then to Internet access and chat rooms. Many students are "instant messaging" late at night or early in the morning, depriving themselves of needed sleep. How can these children be sufficiently alert to learn in school? If parents do not take the time to learn about the computer their child is using for hours each day, how can they protect their child? Parents need to know what their child is doing, give guidance, and utilize censorship. Parents must realize and appreciate the power of the computer.

With younger people, the stakes are higher of being corrupted by cyberspace. Adults have the power to reevaluate and change course. Young children have more vulnerability to the effects of pornography and the effects of the stalking pedophiles. The damage of a rendezvous with an evil person can permanently alter the course of a child's life or even end the child's life. There are practically no internal experiences for children to draw upon to protect themselves except the values given them by their parents and other loved ones.

Belonging Gives Us a Sense of Security

People need a community. The area where the twin towers stood was a business section with intermittent residences throughout. This was not a close-knit community by any definition. Most people living in this pricey section of Manhattan are originally from somewhere else. Yet everyone in the area immediately reached out to each other forming an instant community when the 9/11 disaster struck. People came from all over to assist each other in whatever way possible. Watching on television, Americans from all over the country became New Yorkers.

It is during a crisis that people turn to loved ones for comfort and support. The survivors of the twin tower disasters and even those who did not survive were immediately on their cell phones connecting with their loved ones and in many cases saying good-bye. They were returning if only by telephone to their intimate community. Survivors did not concern themselves with their status or material possessions; they needed to hear the voices of their loved ones. It is human nature to value significant relationships over inanimate objects. Our relationships with our loved ones give meaning to our lives. The knowledge that there are people who we love and love us in return gives us a sense of security. The sense of security provided by strong leadership is more powerful than physical safety. The Nazi bombing of London during World War II did not demoralize the citizens. In fact, the city became an inspiration to all the free world. Under the leadership of Winston Churchill everyone in London became united as fighters for freedom.

Natural dangers can also bring a community together. The citizens of New Orleans are generally ecstatic about their community. The city of New Orleans is seven to ten feet below sea level, making it a death trap in the event of a flood. The real physical danger of flooding is unimportant as compared to the enthusiasm and cohesiveness of its people. It is as if by defying the odds against nature everyone in New Orleans is a vested member of the community. The contagious, happy, spirited atmosphere of its people may be derived from year after year conquering together the fear of being annihilated by nature. Being a part of a community, no matter how precarious the setting, enables people to experience a sense of security. When people belong to a well-defined and intimate group they are more secure.

Responsible People Make a Peaceful Community

Traditional communities were formed inside a geographic area. Growing up in Bensonhurst (Brooklyn, New York), my neighborhood started out on 79th Street between 17th and 18th Avenues. When I entered elementary school, the neighborhood reached to 76th Street and 19th Avenue. It expanded to my church and then my junior high school. Eventually the concept of my neighborhood grew as my relationships moved outward. Yet almost everyone shared a well-defined moral belief system that provided a guide to become an honorable and distinguished citizen.

Besides the family home, other institutions like school and church bind a community together. While I was visiting a friend in beautiful Madison, Mississippi, he made an interesting observation. We were in a restaurant on a Sunday sitting near what I assumed to be an extended family. His assessment of the apparent group of family members was that the group was in fact several families who had come from church. In the Bible Belt the churches are numerous and serve as the nucleus of the community. The present community stability of Madison reminded me of the more structured period of the 1950s.

Everyday human relationship problems exist in any community worldwide. Husband and wife, parent and child, boss and worker; these all can conflict, but there used to be agreed upon rules and expectations based on a traditional moral code. This consensus of moral code worked to help keep people on the straight and narrow. This conforming mentality restricted self-absorbed individual freedom but produced community peace. Looting, home invasions, and indiscriminate killings were practically non-existent. Authority figures were respected. There has to be a balance between freedom of the individual and responsibility to others to have a functioning community.

It is easier to raise children in a cohesive and friendly environment. People in a healthy community keep their eyes open to protect each other and provide a sense of security to community members. Developing a healthy community takes individual leadership and the effort of its citizens. Viable communities were the rule throughout the USA when I was growing up in the 1950s. These communities were broken down into neighborhoods. This was true in a big city or small town. Each neighborhood was further broken down into blocks where children played with children on the street from adjacent apartment houses or in the backyards of private houses. The parents were in charge setting the limits for their children outside the home. Children were told a time to be back in the house for dinner and the children responded to their directions. Mothers who appeared from everywhere quickly noted any deviation in the daily routine. Mothers at home were the single most important element in creating healthy communities. Fathers who provided for the family enabled mothers the privilege to remain at home. The absence of a mother in the home and a father's enforcement of discipline to monitor the child's friends and use of time has made the community less safe for children.

Traditional Parents Know How to Say No

In a traditional community children had to ask permission to do anything and most requests were denied. Any stranger was closely observed by the grandparents or retired neighbors who looked out for the children. The elders watching out gave us a sense of security and thus freedom to travel.

Children looked out for each other, too. A physical disagreement between boys was allowed as long as both fought fairly. There were no weapons or ganging up allowed by the other children. Boys would form a circle to insure a fair fight. As soon as the disagreement ended, the game continued with the worst case being one or two boys feeling sore. Children taught and learned games and supervised each other. The spontaneous interaction between neighborhood kids was a treasure chest of learning experiences that helped the children to better understand the fickleness of humanity. As the children branched out to larger geographic areas, they were wiser through the common-sense experience that was learned in the neighborhoods. Being part of a defined area with shared values gave its members a sense of freedom as well as security.

Children today have fewer limits and less knowledge of potential dangers that exist outside the home. Unlike children in viable neighborhoods, today children have little firsthand experience of standing up for themselves. Learning social and assertive skills are limited to the adult-supervised sport activities or to the virtual world of electronic waves. We need morally responsible adults to revitalize our communities to allow children to return to being children.

Restoring the Sense of Community Begins With Parents

As our affluence has increased, so has our children's isolation from a neighborhood community and face-to-face friendships. It is through the daily trials and tribulations of friendship that children have an opportunity to learn about the ups and downs of relationships. Getting into a disagreement with one peer and getting advice from another of how to handle the situation, learning from another friend's mistakes, and ultimately having a safety net of interested parents and other family members appears to be essential in raising a healthy, peaceful child.

Young parents have the most to gain from having a viable neighborhood. Once their children reach school age, the children will naturally want to explore the world outside their front door. Parents have to balance their material pursuits with the responsibilities of providing a safe environment for the children. Creating a safe haven for their children means parents have to devote time and effort to become known and helpful in the community. To become a member of the community means parents have to be there.

Parents have a responsibility to establish relationships with neighbors. Associations between people insure the safety of everyone in the community. Neighbors who keep an eye on elderly persons bind those individuals into an element of community. The monitoring of children by people outside the family provides more cohesiveness to bring separate people into identifying with each other as members of a community.

Parents have to spend time in their home and community. By being there in the home and the community, parents will teach their positive values that protect their children from perverts preying on their innocence. Teaching a child a traditional moral value system is giving the child self-censorship that is an antidote for the amoral environment. By having both parents as role models the child will learn what is normal and what is abnormal.

Parents have the responsibility of being knowledgeable about the dangers in their community. Just like I was taught by my mother and father to avoid certain people or sections of my neighborhood, children today deserve the same level of involvement by their parents. My mother told me not to accept any candy from an adult. At the moment I got that advice it did not mean much. A short time later, a man in a raincoat did offer me candy while waiting for a subway train. I refused the candy. He then opened his raincoat and exposed himself. My mother did her job well to protect her son. Setting limits of where children can go and what they can do in and outside the home is a loving act. By demanding honesty from their children and observing their behavior with their peers, parents can monitor the character development of their child.

Intimate community knowledge by parents protects their offspring. Setting aside time to go to the store, the library, the parks, and school functions establishes a network of relationships. These neighborhood contacts act as auxiliary eyes and ears for the parents while their children interact alone in the community. This network of interrelated community relationships multiplies rapidly as the children make their own contacts.

Having a parent at home when the children arrive back from their adventures outside the home is invaluable in the sharing of their ever-expanding knowledge of their environment. Most children will openly convey what happened in their daily activities. Some children may have to be prompted with questions, while others will not shut up. There is a window of opportunity to know the details of their lives before all is forgotten. Parents have to be there in the home and the community for the optimal development of their children.

We are squandering the precious times that foster intimacy like when the child arrives home from school. Mothers who work outside the home are being robbed of opportunities to greet the child and hear about their day, to teach their children about potential dangers, and give timely moral lessons. Children are being robbed of the secure feeling of knowing there is going to be someone there when they arrive home. The mothers are being robbed of the opportunity to be mothers. The security of knowing your mother will be waiting for you with a snack and a smile after school cannot be measured.

Family and friends are the child's security blanket. When grandparents, uncles, aunts, cousins, and friends spend time in the home, the child's sense of belonging in a larger community grows. Children in contact with others are healthy children. Knowing that Mrs. Harrison, their teacher, is a friend of their parents goes a long way in validating his parents' power in the community. It makes the child aware good and bad behavior will be reported back to his parents. It keeps the child on the straight and narrow path. As the web of family contacts spirals outward so does the umbrella of protection for the children. It is the parents who are instrumental in the process of developing a community.

There is no substitute for investing time and energy in the community. No amount of money or dedication to business can substitute for spending time in the home and community. Parents have to realize the investment of time and effort in the home and community pays great dividends in emotional, mental, and spiritual health of their children. When children or adults are lonely and isolated they are susceptible to drug and alcohol addictions, criminal behavior, or mental illness. Relationships are essential for keeping all of us on a healthy track. Not developing a solid community base means there are fewer possibilities for meaningful relationships. Fewer meaningful relationships mean more isolation and loneliness. This leads to a greater vulnerability to negative and evil predators. This old proverb says it well, "Idleness is the devil's workshop."

Voluntary Association Creates a Peaceful Community

Parents are not the only ones to have a vested interest in a community. Everyone is affected by the quality of interaction that shapes the ambiance of the neighborhood. When rudeness, intimidation, and lawlessness prevail, everyone suffers. The opposite happens when decency, empathy, and lawfulness are the rule. When people give of themselves to their neighbors, everyone profits, especially the givers. When citizens volunteer in schools, hospitals, churches, athletic programs, civil and professional organizations, and share themselves with others, the person adds meaning to his life and develops a positive identity. The caring act creates a force for good. Each of these acts of voluntary association insures a strong sense of community. People feel safe and secure in a giving environment and feel more in control of their destiny.

Benjamin Franklin understood the power of voluntary association. He inspired the public library system, hospitals, fire departments, and professional associations where young men were mentored by more knowledgeable elder men. Through his leadership he assisted the vibrant development of Philadelphia from a small town to a major community in the early history of America.[14]

The same dynamic exists today. Voluntary associations are a more powerful means of uplifting the community than channeling resources through government workers. Volunteers do their work out of personal purpose and choice—not for a paycheck or by the direction of a supervisor. When the nest is empty, parents have more time without direct responsibilities to their children to share their wisdom with others.

When people gain a sense of community, private sector and even government workers perform their duties at a higher level of effectiveness and decency. Performing a quality service, even when paid, contributes to the betterment of others. Teachers, ministers, police officers, postal workers, plumbers, or retailers who are pleasant, conscientious, and moral in all their interactions make for a wonderful community. In such a community evil cannot take root and grow. It would be a community that has heightened levels of trust, spirit, and pride: a stable community that promotes all citizens to flourish physically, mentally, and spiritually. Each of us, regardless of our background, has something to give to others. It is about time we begin to rebuild our communities for the good of all.

It takes effort on every level to cultivate a peacefully functioning community. It starts with solid families with fathers, mothers, and children working together. Fathers do their job as providers, disciplinarians, and leaders. Mothers are everywhere securing the home, nurturing the family members, and developing the friendly associations that act as a protective network. As the children grow and expand their horizons in the neighborhood, the family overlaps more of the community.

Everyone, young or old, businessman or employee, rich or poor, relative or non-relative has a lot to gain from a peaceful neighborhood and a lot to lose from a community in chaos.

Neighbors need to realize that they are interdependent with each other. "Do unto others as you would have them to do unto you" is a universal strategy to produce a peaceful world. Adults need to automatically stop any bullying behavior by any individual, old or young. The demanding of a high level of decency produces a quality place to live. It makes everyone's life better.

Leaders are the catalysts for making everyone perform at their optimal level. There are no substitutes for people setting standards and holding themselves and others to those high standards. Authority figures that do their moral duties reinforce the family's religious and cultural teachings. Leaders throughout the community give the same moral message. Everyone is expected to do the best he can do and must strive to reach this goal. This is the profile of a highly functioning, peaceful community. This is a community where healthy families can release their children feeling comfortable for their safety, security, and future. This is the local world Americans want.

Peace and freedom come with a hefty price tag. It takes disciplined, courageous, and moral decisions on the part of responsible people day in and day out. There should be no tolerance for the immoral concept of victimless crime. There should be no tolerance for deviant exploitive parasites that suck the vitality and goodness from those of us who are desirous of living virtuous lives for our families and ourselves. A few self-centered immoral people should not be allowed to jeopardize peace for the moral, hardworking majority. Evil should no longer be allowed to hide behind the veil of non-judgmental tolerance for all behavior. Communities have a responsibility to set and demand moral standards from citizens to protect us from evil.

We can no longer accept the Smuggers' nonjudgmental ways; as deviants, they consciously undermine our traditional values and morals. The whittling away at our traditional moral lifestyle has enabled deviants to gain greater acceptance while weakening our resolve to live an honorable existence. The cultural civil war is real. Either we fight vulgar, immoral behavior with righteous, moral behavior or lose our families, communities, and nation to chaotic self-indulgence. The tolerance of evil in our communities will bring destruction and harm. The adherence to goodness brings peace to our community. It takes effort to develop healthy and safe neighborhoods. The choice is clear and is ours.

Chapter 4

Indoctrinating to Educating Students

Basic academic skills, moral values, and an appreciation of the greatness of our nation are disappearing across America. We are no longer teaching in-depth American and world history that demonstrates the exceptionalism of our great nation. Americans are systematically losing the knowledge of our culture, making it easier to indoctrinate our children into a new world order founded on Marxist doctrine. The result of this diluting of our basic culture is seen strikingly in our government schools.

Every day American junior high and senior high students take part in a chaotic scene as they rush through their school hallways from one class to another. The running and shouting, displays of inappropriate affection, yelling put-downs, threatening, and bullying have become the rule rather than the exception in school. Administrators, teachers, and even parents have become numb and blind to the institutionalization of abuse at school. Administrators and teachers have diminished in status while the status of student bullies has skyrocketed. Bullies have become popular role models for other students to emulate. The unpopular social outcasts find each other, plot, brag to other students beforehand, and then execute bizarre violent acts destined to end in death and infamy. Instead of morally responsible students who respect their fellow classmates, many social isolates are joining the ranks of the popular by disregarding the rights of others.

Our public schools resemble immoral war zones. It is not unusual to see police officers stationed in our schools as security guards, a last-ditch attempt to keep the peace. Police resource personnel, as they are often called, have spread from inner city schools to schools throughout the nation. Parents' concerns that may in the past have focused on abusive teachers have shifted to protection from other students. Teachers are also fearful in today's schools. Physical and sexual attacks, even killings of teachers by students as well as sexual encounters between teachers and students have become commonplace. "More than 4.5 million endure sexual misconduct by employees of their schools from inappropriate jokes to forced sex, according to a report to Congress."[1]

When sex and violence are temporarily in the background, social issues are placed in the foreground: lifestyle issues, revised history, the rights and entitlements of everyone, the environment, recreation, and extracurricular topics—not academic skills training. Too much sex, violence, and socialistic propaganda are taking place during the hours our children should be learning academics.

Smuggers Have Transformed Our Public Schools

Children in many government schools are being indoctrinated into an immoral and hedonist culture alien to traditionalist America. The counterculture of the past has become their daily reality. Immersed in this unhealthy environment, kids quickly learn either to adapt or receive the full brunt of their peers' attacks. An environment of sexual permissiveness, rampant drugs, vulgarity, nasty attitudes, and physically abusive behavior has become the cultural standard. In this world, it is survival, not studies, that matters to the students.

The bottom line is that our students' young minds are languishing in the public schools. The tenets of the counterculture have ravaged both the academic and the social atmosphere of government schools. In the name of "equality," the emphasis is placed on identical output; productiveness of students could never vary from student to student or there would be claims of discrimination. While the triumphing of the importance of self-esteem has ensured that many children are more than confident that they are doing well, the simple fact is that they are grossly unable to perform fundamental skills. How can students take algebra without mastering the multiplication tables? Students are able to fumble their way through writing short essays only by employing "creative" spelling and little, if any, punctuation. Inflated grades and acceptance into accelerated classes or "writers' workshops" leads many below-par students to believe that they have the skills to become journalists.

"Today's college freshmen get more A's than ever in high school while studying a record low number of hours within their senior year."[2] Teachers' dishonest evaluations on report cards and a sophisticated marketing campaign by the school superintendent's office ultimately hurt the students themselves, who, when they finally enter the real world, must face the harsh reality of a job market unable to massage their egos with the same unrealistic expectations.

The parents are also being conned. They are unaware of the full impact of their children's lack of basic knowledge. The only thing the parents know is their child has received high grades, is usually on the honor roll, and goes to school daily in an impressive building. The parents know their child is in a magnet school or specialized curriculum such as drama, forensic science, music, television production, technology, oceanography, photography, and so on. Certainly the parents want to believe these sophisticated courses of study are far superior to the education they received. How wrong they are.

There is a fraud being perpetrated in America.

Government schools are robbing students of their futures. It is a criminal act to tax all our citizens without providing the stipulated service. The National Education Association's propaganda that the lack of student achievement is due to the lack of tax dollars is utterly false. A July 2004 Cato Institute report stated that there is no relationship between the amount of money spend on education and achievement.[3] The contract is not being honored. Too many children are being promoted without advancing academically. Year after year the student moves to the next grade but his knowledge and skill level remain stagnant.

It makes me angry to witness students who are satisfied with their education when they are functioning years behind the most meager standards. I am frustrated with the child for being lazy, the parents for lying to themselves, and my colleagues for not stopping this charade.

State standard tests are an attempt at some form of accountability to reverse this criminal practice. Interestingly, the parents usually do not get irritated at the child's laziness or the school's deceitfulness. No, they become irate at the state test. They do not seem to want to know the truth.

When I ask parents why they waited so long to take corrective action for their child's academic shortcomings, they squirm. Usually they mutter some excuse about not knowing. The real answer is not caring enough about the child to want to know.

Parents who have not kept a watchful eye on their child's academic ignorance are living in a dream world. But eventually the extreme harm that this negligence has allowed them to ignore hits both the parents and their child right between their eyes. It is a fact that students who are stifled in a dull learning environment often regress. The unchallenging and uninspired activities lull the child into an educational and developmental coma. Poor academic habits dull the brightest of students. The students receive high grades for academic work that is more appropriate for two or three years below their grade level. Yet these artificial grades placate parents who only want to hear good news.

Children are being labeled with mental disabilities, drugged, and socially promoted at an epidemic rate. With both the child (through drugs) and the parents (through laziness or self-delusion) in a semi-conscious state, they are shattered when forced to confront their children's appalling ineptitude as judged by the more reality-based standards of higher education or the job market. The jig is up and both parents and child are shocked when the child is unable to pass a qualifying test to be promoted in public school, pass his freshman year of college, or pass a simple qualifying test for a job or the armed forces. The student and his parents eventually face the fact the child has been cheated out of developing intelligence through a good education.

Close to half a century of Smugger engineering has left our government educational institutions in shambles. We have students attempting to make career choices in elementary and middle school in the new "school-to-work" initiative while the basic academic skills have dropped from the radar screen. The "school-to-work" concept is disgustingly reminiscent of the central government of the old Soviet Union. Young students are by no means sufficiently mature to make adequate life-long decisions. Even if the student had the maturity to make reasonable choices without basic math, language, and thinking skills, the student would not have the ability to perform the job. The utopian approach to education has been a lose-lose experiment. The students have increasing academic gaps and society has more and more dysfunctional people adding to the rolls of the disabled.

Our K–12 schools need to return to teaching our children the universal academic skills and traditional character values that will be as useful twenty years from now as they are today. The purpose of education is to prepare children to be successful in tomorrow's world, not to manipulate our youths into accepting a socialistic agenda. Removing history as a requirement necessary for graduation from high school and revising historical facts in textbooks are calculated attempts to undermine the American way. Career choices, lifestyle issues, gender issues, and other attempts to change human nature should be left to the mature person's choice. We have gone so far as dispensing condoms to students without their parents' permission. Socialistic propaganda should not be the basis of education in the USA.

Schools have become so impersonal that within their walls bullies are given free rein while wimps learn the art of victimization. It is an immoral world where right and wrong are almost impossible to differentiate. We desperately need to return to more manageable, small schools where students know all the teachers and the teachers know all the students. It is only in this atmosphere that parents can maintain high expectations for their children's schooling, standards can be upheld, the best traits of students can be celebrated instead of the crudest, and where strength of character underlies it all. It is necessary to return to this world where a child will have a structured, peaceful school environment and where he can strive to reach his maximum potential, unlocking the key to success throughout his life.

The Role of Teachers in a Manageable School

Teaching is a dedicated lifestyle. As in the past, teaching today requires multi-tasking, a fine character, and the perseverance to never give up on a student. Teaching is an all-encompassing way of living.

A real teacher is more than degrees, specializations, the ability to put on a dog and pony show in front of parents, or eloquence. It is an ability to help each and every student be the best he or she can be that defines a teacher. A good teacher is analogous to a good mother. It is not what they say; it is what they do when no one else is watching.

***It is all the little but important tasks that need
to be accomplished to do the job well:***

- ▶ Completing everything that needs to be done without complaining.

- ▶ Correcting all the assigned work of the students to ensure quality.

- ▶ Following through on keeping his word no matter what the circumstances.

- ▶ Motivating and inspiring students instead of becoming frustrated.

- ▶ Juggling various tasks to meet the needs of many.

- ▶ Being everywhere.

- ▶ Doing what is best, not what is easiest—regardless of the difficulty for students.

- ▶ Believing involvement makes a difference when there are no positive signs of change.

- ▶ Talking precisely.

- ▶ Avoiding talking about personal issues that are unrelated to learning.

- ▶ Observing and knowing everything possible about the students.

- ▶ Keeping records to demonstrate change and document progress.

- ▶ Communicating honestly about social, character, and academic development to students, parents, and administrators.

- ▶ Working alongside students to accomplish a class or school goal.

*Teachers need to relate with students
in a positive manner by:*

▸ Preparing the room and lessons before class begins.

▸ Establishing structure, order, and rituals to promote classroom stability.

▸ Persuading students to do more and to do it better.

▸ Making no excuses, just doing what is right and necessary.

▸ Keeping perspective of long-term student goals.

▸ Remaining professional instead of becoming personally angry or punitive at student failures.

▸ Giving respect and demanding respect.

▸ Refusing to choose favorites.

▸ Adhering to school policies and being a team player.

▸ Recognizing, celebrating, and appreciating small changes in students.

A good teacher must be a consummate professional. He should possess good character and a strong desire to expand the academic skills and character of the students. Learning and teaching are both lifelong processes, and the more effectively you learn, the better you can teach and live. As an example to students, an effective teacher's role modeling is more powerful than words. Just as students learn from and imitate their teacher as a natural part of the teaching process, the teacher, too, draws energy, enthusiasm, and strength from his students.

▸ Motivating, encouraging and helping students be the best person possible, not money or awards, are the driving force of teachers.

▸ The day-to-day role model is a powerful instrument of change.

▸ Teachers who obtain a level of excellence in their profession enter with these qualities or gain them during the teaching process.

▸ Moral clarity of what is right and wrong for the individual student.

▸ Enjoy the growth of the students.

▸ Reach a level of maturity to be patient and calm yet firm, loving, and strong in disciplining.

▸ Admit mistakes to students.

▸ Possess personal integrity, self-respect, honesty, and courage.

▸ Understand the human nature of students to push the envelope to take the path of least resistance that results in laziness and cheating.

▸ Fight the battles to detect, correct, and defeat negative traits in students.

▸ The ability to keep learning with enthusiasm while maintaining courteousness and humility.

▸ View every minute as a learning experience.

▸ Allegiance to the school community.

An effective teacher has to develop his spiritual side. His purpose is to be an important part of the cycle of life in lifting students to a higher level of awareness. To obtain this commendable goal, teachers have to rein in their own ego needs to create a productive learning environment for others. The spiritual growth of a teacher can most effectively be accomplished in a school where the focus is on student development instead of following a bureaucratic whim that changes with new administrative fancies. The guiding force of teachers, parents, and administrators should be the individual action that would help each student uniquely grow to reach their optimal potential, academically and personally. A real teacher receives more than he gives in being the best person possible for his students. Teaching is a spiritual journey.

Teachers, like students, need an emotionally secure world for them to perceive the subtle influences that encourage meaningful changes. No teacher can be productive with the knowledge that a bureaucrat is looking over her shoulder second-guessing her every instantaneous decision to protect one student from another. Teachers need to be free from government regulations that hamper them from doing the right thing for the development of their students. Increased teacher gratification blossoms best in a structured yet loving and happy environment where teachers know all the students and students know all the teachers. This school community where everyone knows everyone else is by definition a manageable school.

Specialization Has Weakened Our Social Fabric

In an underdeveloped society, the means of functioning is passed down from parents to children. In a primitive society, the knowledge and information is limited to what can be transferred in normal daily interaction. As society becomes more sophisticated, the information becomes more vast and specialized. No longer do parents possess the expertise to fully educate their children. More formal learning skills and knowledge are better taught in school. After the completion of schooling, a young person has the ability to successfully enter the job market. As their work experience increases, their knowledge expands. They have joined the world of adulthood.

Our students are being held captive by our institutions of higher education. The education process has been distorted, alienating the lives of students and professors. Anything taken to an extreme can become unbalanced, including education. Today's higher education students are required by universities to put their lives on hold for as long as a decade before receiving a graduate degree. A degree is like a union card that allows them to enter their chosen profession. This increased interval may act to limit competition in particular professions but it is creating a narrow and superficial academic world. This academic world is negatively affecting our society. Professional students and professors are not in tune with the best interests of our nation. This higher-level learning process has become progressively more abstract, making it more tedious and less integrated into everyday life.

Being a college professor or a student demands time and energy. The students as well as the teachers are isolated from daily reality, leaving them susceptible to impractical ideas. The effort to obtain specialized knowledge leaves little energy or time to develop a well-rounded personality. The student's life is left in suspended animation. Many important decisions are postponed until after graduation. This hiatus from the traditional world of producing, earning, and marrying impedes the maturation of the individual. The effort to obtain specialized knowledge limits the motivation to become a fully functioning member of society.

Our higher education process rewards students who are willing to postpone or even abandon the natural progression of the life cycle. Putting a person's life on hold creates personal imbalance. The people who deviate most from a traditional lifestyle are at an advantage in an abstract world of higher education. Through graduate teaching assistantships many of these students evolve into teachers in their area of specialization. These inexperienced graduate teacher assistants are ordained to pass on their newly acquired and untested knowledge to even younger students. This higher education process is thwarting the natural development of its members and indoctrinating our younger generation with unworkable Smugger ideas.

The time between learning and reaping the rewards of education is so delayed that the natural frustration of learning turns into excruciating personal pain. Frequently teachers and students join hands in revolting against the basic principles of the nation, not because of the inherent incorrectness of the tenets or a better-thought-out strategy, but because of self-centered immaturity.

The suspension of reaching natural milestones skews the perception of these perennial students. Student and professor are not grounded by ever expanding life-cycle responsibilities, leaving them vulnerable to unrealistic and utopian ideals. Many intellectuals have little knowledge and appreciation for the effort it takes to translate an idea into a reality. When many of their plans are rejected as impractical, often their response is to become indignant. They experience these people as less intelligent with antiquated traditional morals and values impeding them from obtaining their vision. They are convinced their ideals would make life richer with minimal effort for everyone.

Their top-down thinking is often infeasible in the real world. These intellectuals used to be separated from the rest of the world by their ivory towers. It wasn't until after World War II that these people had significant exposure to large segments of the population, providing them an opportunity to adversely impact our society. These Smugger professors taught us as fact that physical effort would be unnecessary in an automated world. In their minds, work was for the dull bourgeoisie while the pursuit of pleasure was for the enlightened. Their hedonist sermons inspired many youths to turn away from a disciplined lifestyle toward a decadent one. It is a lifestyle based on Marxist nonsense that argues against personal initiative and effort. These notions have eroded standards on many fronts, leading us to a society based on the most common denominator, not on quality standards.

The institution of higher education has been the vehicle to transform local public education into facilities of socialist propaganda. Every student is equal regardless of his effort. No student should suffer the pain or frustration of setting high goals. The dumbing down of curriculums throughout our local schools made life easier for both teacher and student in the short run. In the long run, it has diminished quality. As quality has waned, students with years of indoctrination and even with completed credentials as high as doctorates have joined the ranks of the unemployed.

Many of these professional students have become a burden rather than an asset to our nation. The lack of effort in one's pursuits translates into a decrease of quality affecting the entire nation. The Smugger attack on our traditional institution of education has weakened the entire fabric of our society.

Consolidation of Schools a Colossal Mistake

Simultaneously with the Marxist indoctrination of higher education students, the Smugger engineering of our public schools was beginning to take shape. Our local schools were combined into huge consolidated school districts. These districts required more specialized personnel who marched off to higher education. These teachers became extensions of college professors assisting in the changing of traditional education. No longer were schools accountable to parents through easily accessible and direct contact with them. No longer were schools teaching basic skills. Instead, administrators, teachers, professors, and many politicians formed an alliance to bring young students into a changing world: a society based on socialistic ideas where public schools become the primary institution for social change.

Government schools are a protected industry for the politically connected. A superintendent of schools has become a political rather than an educational position. The head of a large school system has to appease many special interests. Children, parents, and teachers are usually on the lowest rung of that ladder. Business, media, political leaders, and accreditation bureaucrats have to be appeased and cajoled to maintain power. Too many school administrators have no connection to the classroom. Their function is to enhance the image of the school system and themselves.

A bureaucrat's purpose is either to advance up the organizational chart or, barring that, simply to survive. The politics of school committees are their world. They are sales representatives. They sell to teachers and other administrators an agenda generated and approved by accreditation agencies. The political agenda ranges from prohibiting any mention of God in the classroom to explicit sex education, homosexual sensitivity training, arbitrary teacher certification, and school facility requirements that help to eliminate alternatives to government schools.

The agenda is imposed from the top down rather than the bottom up. These bureaucrats are the middlemen in government schools. They receive free dinners and hotel stays as rewards and are happy to be out of their chaotic schools. The social programs and ideals fashioned in isolated committees are introduced into the classroom without any field-testing. Their job is to be on the accreditation circuit happily socializing with others also removed from direct responsibility with children. The long-range interests of students, parents, and even teachers seem to have been moved to the bottom of the government school agenda.

In my county and many others, the budget of the local school district is larger than the entire county government budget. Schools have become a profitable big business that community leaders rely on for asserting influence. The school industry's expenditures and movement of local financial assets profit the community leaders.

Students, parents, and teachers are having a difficult time getting their concerns addressed by a non-educationally responsive school system. I recently spoke with a parent who was new to the area and wanted to make an appointment to visit with the principal of the school in the district his child was to attend. He was told he would first have to appear before the school board to receive such an appointment.

The influence of instructors is limited in a bureaucratic environment. Teachers have to disband programs and strategies that have achieved results as new administrators attempt to demonstrate expertise with their "new" ideas. There is little continuity in the big business of schools. Who are government school officials accountable to, special interests or students and parents? The answer is the larger the school and school district, the smaller the influence of parents, students, and teachers.

Schools did not become as large as factories because of an educational rationale. The reason for larger and larger schools was "the economy, stupid." Neighborhood schools became too expensive for the local county government to maintain compared to the economy of scale gained by consolidating a school district. Herding children into large complexes made it cheaper to build the facilities and to buy supplies. In the 1950s the bottom line directed education, not reason. The high schools of today are indistinguishable in size from the factories of the fifties but the attitudes and values of students today are radically different from the population of the 1950s.

In the beginning of the twenty-first century, teachers are more accountable to bureaucrats than to students or parents. Teachers have little ownership in government schools. They are directed to follow bureaucratic policies. Teacher initiatives are stifled. They quickly learn how to get around the system by doing just what is asked, no more, no less. Teachers also have to please an army of bureaucratic specialists who are accountable to the superintendent. Teachers learn to play bureaucratic games.

The lack of creative freedom for educators to educate has demoralized many of the best school personnel. Teachers who develop and implement effective programs are reprimanded for not following existing procedures. Teachers have to disband successful programs and strategies as new administrators attempt to demonstrate their expertise with their "new" old ideas.

Innovation is frowned upon not only by bureaucrats but also by fellow teachers. A teacher going above and beyond what is expected is often demeaned instead of celebrated. A friend and government schoolteacher told me war stories of working in public education. He ran fund-raisers on his own time to finance educational field trips. The students and parents were ecstatic about the educational opportunities offered by these experiences. However, the negative reaction from colleagues and administrators was unexpected. His peers wanted the additional funds without doing the extra work and the administrators were distressed that the favorable reaction by parents and students would force them to implement the program throughout the district. My friend was pressured to abandon his initiative. Innovation from the classroom teacher up to the administrator is stymied in centralized public education.

Modern government schools have isolated teachers as well as students. Teachers have to spend more than ninety minutes with their young students to obtain a social and emotional knowledge of them. More often than not teachers and students become alienated from each other in these impersonal schools. Being just a number and an anonymous person has forced many students to do unusual things to be noticed and accepted in this anonymous environment.

Popularity Replaces Merit in Large Schools

As schools have lost control of education, students' evaluations of fellow students' attractiveness is more important than the teacher's scholastic evaluation. Most students today dress, talk, and behave in school to impress other students rather than parents, teachers, or administrators. In a micro society led by immature youth, many inappropriate and antisocial habits are encouraged. Focus on piercings, tattoos, sexy clothing, and designer jeans takes precedence over becoming a productive adult. The practice of the Golden Rule is shunned in favor of "popularity makes right." Bullies, addicts, freaks, and other sociopathic individuals become school celebrities while the weak become victims and the traditionally raised child becomes estranged and left to battle his way through the insanity.

In a large impersonal school the "popular at any price" child, not the honorable child, is at a distinct advantage. Superficial relationships generated in large schools are breeding grounds for developing phony identities. There are the so-called goths, skaters, preppies, druggies, headbangers, and so on. A student might talk the talk, trash talk, as a member of a group without having to walk the walk, be able to back up his words. The bully-liar, like any conman, can move from one peer group to another, decreasing his chance of being exposed. Large facilities give impunity to the cowardly bully. As the number of students decreases, the percentage of unsavory characters noticed by both students and teachers increases.

Large and Impersonal Fosters Parental Distrust

These immense, impersonal schools have changed the parents' allegiance from the teachers to the children. Most parents no longer wholeheartedly trust or support their children's teachers. In the past, the teacher was always right, today the child is always right. The shift has a lot to do with not personally knowing the teacher or other parents in a consolidated school. Parents today are apprehensive concerning their children's safety. When the child hears his parent question the teacher he believes no matter what he does the parent will believe him. This emboldens the child and deflates the teacher. The parent becomes an ally of the child while the teacher becomes an adversary.

In order to compensate for his lack of status with the parents, the teacher has become more of an expert in an area and less of a friendly neighbor. It is more important today what credentials a teacher has than her personal character or how well she can teach. The lack of traditional moral convictions has lead to dubious role models. One of the reasons for dumbing down school standards is to appease parents who have little involvement with their children's teachers. Teachers who do not know the families of their students have had to relax their standards.

The communication between the teacher and the parent has shifted from direct contact to more impersonal report cards. The decrease in personal contact with the parent has nudged teachers to err on the side of being more permissive. The decrease in personal interaction between parent and teacher has allowed the teacher to be less directly accountable to parents for the daily instructions of the child.

Homework and tests have been diluted or even eliminated in many grades. This has led to dumbing down standards with little outcry from taxpayers. Most daily problems are left unresolved and underreported. The cumulative impact of this impersonal process is for teachers to have less power and validity in the eyes of the parent in evaluating their child. In order to minimize hassles with parents, teachers and administrators have become ultra liberal in their praising, grading, and promoting of the student. Teachers have attempted to replace student mastery with artificial praise to motivate the student. The cultivation of high esteem (false esteem) has led to questionable practices of paying prize money to take state exams, eliminating traditional grading formats, and pushing children through school without reaching grade level milestones. My small county school system in Florida has motivated students to do well on the state-required FCAT exam for the past three years by giving more than $300,000 in prize money. In many school districts elementary honor rolls comprise 50–80 percent of the entire student body. So much for the intrinsic value of learning being the natural motivator of the student!

Parents Micromanaging

Modern parents have lost faith in their children's ability to become strong individuals. In the past fifty years, parents have been urged by experts to move away from the conventional wisdom where parents are in charge in the home and children are responsible for their own behavior outside the home. The "modern approach" where children are in charge in the home and parents are responsible to protect and personally supervise children outside the home has been a fundamental change.

Parents are not making their children accountable for their behavior in school. Instead they are attempting to control the teacher's reaction to the child's irresponsibility and disruptiveness. Modern parents are insisting on parental involvement in their child's classrooms. To too many parents, being involved means direct input in the daily functioning of the class, which is actually interference. The motivation for this interference is an attempt to ensure special treatment for the success of their child.

The responsibility of controlling all facets of their child's life is a characteristic of modern parents. Any adversity has to be softened by the parents to prevent traumatizing the child. On some level the modern parent realizes that a lack of direct training leaves their child vulnerable in facing a harsh world. The parent's unwillingness or inability to be an in-charge parent motivates many parents to compensate by becoming involved outside the home. These parents become the child's chauffeur, driving her from one activity to another; her bodyguard, speaking up for her in disagreements with other children; and her social director, finding entertainment activities that meet her approval. Most importantly modern parents feel obliged to micromanage the child and her teachers.

The concern of many parents is to protect their child against the possible abuse of school personnel. There is little support of teachers as legitimate authority figures to help properly socialize children.

Parental disrespect often is seen in their disregarding the most basic school rules. I see this scenario happen more and more frequently. Even though there are specific policies established by the school, parents often attempt to bypass them if they believe it is in the interest of their child. A father of a three-year-old had his son's ear pierced during Christmas vacation, knowing it was against the school's uniform policy. He argued that the policy was sexist. He wanted his son to be able to do what he wanted.

It appears parents have a self-righteous mandate to protect their child at all costs from any negative consequences. The parents first announce to the child they will come to school to meet with the teacher and correct the unfairness done to the child. Before speaking to the teacher or other students involved, the parent will know exactly what happened. As an administrator I am amazed by the lack of logic and ask, "How can you know what happened when you weren't here?" The answer is always the same: "My child told me. My child doesn't lie." I do an investigation and I bring in the teacher and children to demonstrate in every case there is another side to the story. The parent becomes subdued when the child alters his once adamant account.

As ridiculous as it seems, parents attempt to directly bully their children's friends. Another change from the past is today's parents actually get involved in their children's petty disagreements with their friends by directly confronting the other children. Instead of saying to their child, "you need to iron out your own problems" or "you need to fight your own battles," today's parents charge in on their white horse saying, "My daughter said you were not speaking to her," directed to another child without that child's parent present.

This is bullying of a child by a parent. Shocking as it sounds, many modern parents do not view this as inappropriate. After several incidents of this, our parent handbook now clearly states that a parent has no right to directly confront a student and must arrange a conference with a teacher or administrator if there is a problem between their child and another student. Their child knows no boundaries nor does the parent in protecting their child.

Students Working Hard at Not Working

There is an epidemic of bright children who have learned the art of playing dumb. These students have found a way around the system to meet their immediate needs. By working hard at not working, they are frustrating both their parents and their teachers. It is not until they are confronted by a strong and strict teacher or parent that they realize it is to their advantage to do the right thing the *first* time. Too many students are not fortunate enough to meet authority figures who care enough to put a stop to a child's cycle of counterproductive behaviors.

Only the truth can stop this counterproductive cycle of lies and laziness. When teachers ignore the excuses of both the student and his accompanying parents, while demanding reasonable production from him, they eventually arrive at a win-win situation. It takes monitoring by the teacher and consequences for the student for them to stop lying. It also takes conferences with the parents to deflect the arguments over why their child cannot do it. It also takes time to uncover the creative deceptive practices of the student. Gradually the child learns that "getting by" takes more effort than just doing the work. A high-functioning school can teach a child the value of the work ethic with little or no support from the parents.

A rehabilitated lying, lazy child is on the road to becoming a functioning individual. The student learns through effort that he can accomplish whatever he wants. He develops positive work and study habits. This frees the child and parents from playing the laziness game.

Unbelievably there are parents who, even after being shown that their child can succeed through his own efforts, derail this beginning process of becoming a quality student.

A thirty-something Dominican engineer and his wife brought their ten-year-old only child to our school. He was labeled ADHD in public school for his inability to concentrate and was two years behind academically. I immediately noticed in the initial interview that the child never made direct eye contact and constantly had a silly smirk on his face. After two months, the child made significant academic progress and, after receiving negative consequences such as missing recess, field trips, and socializing with his classmates, he began to understand that he had to *earn* his privileges. He gained motivation and increased his ability to concentrate on tasks and to produce quality work. The father and mother saw the positive results not only academically but also the positive change in his attitude that resulted in a more genuine smile, pleasantness, and an increased inclination to do chores at home without prompting. His parents acknowledged this positive change. His father sat silently while his mother insisted the workload and consequences were too harsh for her child and demanded her child should receive school privileges without earning them. This school administrator informed the parents that the child was making good progress and the school policies could not be altered without jeopardizing the gains of their son. Four days later the mother withdrew her son. No school can make a lasting impact on a child with overprotective parents sabotaging the work of the school.

Miserably Parented Children Labeled for Federal Dollars

The habit of putting conscientious effort into whatever is being taught is out of favor in the modern world of parenting. It appears, in fact, there is a conspiracy between children, parents, and schools to promote the "big L"—laziness.

A child can only be lazy if she has lazy parents who do not keep their word with the child. They don't do what they say, often right after they say it. These parents might be dynamos on their jobs but expend little energy in enforcing family rules. This is the reason why parents who have a lazy child react violently if their child is called the "L" word. Parents will attempt to frantically ward off the "L" word by using creative excuses. "My child was ill." "He has not slept." "She had too many other things to do." "My child has a learning disability." "He has difficulty listening due to his auditory processing problem." I have had parents attempt to show me psychological evaluations that give a bogus label rather than accept the more accurate observation that the child is lazy. On some level parents understand laziness is a reflection of their parenting.

Our public schools discovered a gold mine in our modern dysfunctional parenting of children: federal dollars. By persuading the parents to sign the necessary documents for special education, the school district becomes entitled to additional money from the federal government. I had a personal experience with this process. When my third oldest child was a first grader, the guidance counselor requested a conference. At the meeting I was informed my son had a superior IQ, granting him acceptance into the public school gifted program. I was also informed that he was having difficulty with reading, making him a candidate for the learning disabled program. I was asked to decide into which program I would like him to be enrolled. As a former school psychologist I knew it was not the LD class. I chose the gifted program. It was one of the worst educational mistakes I ever made for any of my four children. This particular gifted program inflated my son's self-esteem to the point where he thought his native intelligence made it unnecessary for him to study. His work ethic was trampled. It took him until the third year of college to realize there is no substitute for devotion to studies.

Federal programs appear—on the surface—to be a winning solution for everyone. The parents obtain a more sophisticated program for their child and are removed from any direct responsibility for the child's poor habits, skills, and character development. The school can receive more funds and has, for perpetuity, the parent's signature verifying that the child has inherent problems making education difficult to almost impossible for him. The child appears to win when he becomes less responsible to produce like more normal children. His diagnosis with his IEP (Individual Education Plan) lowers everyone's expectations, especially his own. Everyone thinks he is beating the system.

The fact is government schools are cheating everyone. The parent, the school, and the child are losers in this fraudulent process. The parents have a child who will receive an inferior education and remain dependent on the family for many years. The school moves from the primary mission of educating children to warehousing them. Lack of direction forces the schools to appease and entertain rather than lead students into functional adulthood. The schools have lost their moral imperative. The students fall further behind without much chance of turning their lives around. All the while the budget of public schools continue to spiral upward, out of control.

Even though government schools are often dysfunctional there are many people who want to do the right thing for children. It's a dysfunctional system that, instead of supporting these people, forces them to battle every step of the way. There are incredible teachers who do inspire children to escape from the web of low standards and expectations. They encourage, persuade, and shove the student forward, fighting the bureaucrats all the way. These teachers who impacted many of us in the past, including myself, are being crushed today by the disincentives structured into our modern schools.

In my private school I have had an opportunity to interview many special education students and their families. The state of Florida has recently established the McKay Scholarship that allows children with an IEP, meaning they are labeled as a special education student, to attend alternative private schools. It is somewhat incomprehensible to see students who believe they are doing well academically when they are actually functioning two to three years behind their academic grade level. These students receive report cards with an A in subjects followed by an E (meaning exceptional student). They are second-class students without knowing it.

They are promoted to the next grade. Everyone around them—parents, teachers, administrators, and themselves—promotes the big lie that they are doing well. No one has the kindness and courage to tell them the truth. The fact is they are sinking in the quicksand of public education. Only by facing their deficits can they decide to change their ways. This institutionalized farce of government education is sapping the strength of our local communities and is producing spiritless, defeated, and nonfunctioning adults.

Historically, labeling started with the slow-learner remedial student. Over fifty years ago, when I was a child in New York City, you were mentally retarded or you were not. Each grade in school was segregated from the best students to the worst. For example, the top sixth grade class would be 6-1 and 6-6 would be the bottom class. In my seventh grade I was placed in 7-16, obviously the lowest of all sixteen seventh grade classes. We were all label-free but had academic or emotional difficulties. The motivation for some of us to get out of these slow classes was simple. We did not want to be in this rough environment where teachers carried baseball bats to keep order. Without formal stereotyping labels and sacred documents that imprison, a simple change in behavior or attitude meant a corresponding climb out of a world of self-destructive and limiting education.

Our sophisticated educational labyrinth today is much more difficult to escape. The labeling has become progressively more creative with such names as minimal brain dysfunction, hyperactivity, Asperger syndrome, or Tourette's syndrome. Today we have over forty mental disorders for children. In my forty years of professional experience working with children, I was there before and during the rise, and now in the current frenzy of labeling.

The latest fad label is Asperger syndrome. John Ortiz, PhD, related in his October 15, 2004, seminar in Tampa, Florida, that parents prefer the prestigious label of Asperger syndrome to autism or pervasive developmental disorder for their children. Children with Asperger syndrome have average or above average intelligence and sophisticated knowledge in specific intellectual areas. He noted that in his clinical practice many adults are now diagnosing themselves with this syndrome before they even enter his office. Of course it is a wonderful excuse for impairment in social interaction, narrow interests, and idiosyncratic behavior. Besides, who would not want to be in the company of Einstein, Thomas Jefferson, Marie Curie, Carl Sagan, and Bill Gates, who, according to the scientific expert's sales pitch, had or have this Asperger syndrome. It is interesting to note that many of these same names were used to sell ADHD.

The more pseudoscientific education people have, the harder it is for people to recognize the phony snake-oil salesman. Since everyone is unique, will we eventually have a label for each of us? This labeling process is as out of control as our children.

The twin culprits, federal dollars for special education and the pharmaceutical companies, have contributed greatly to labeling our students. However, the main cause has to be attributed to the nation moving away from traditional child-rearing practices. At the same time, it is the responsibility of teachers, administrators, and parents to help students resolve behavioral and academic difficulties in school rather than just document, label, and drug children to obtain federal special education dollars. The inappropriateness of children may begin at home, but large and impersonal schools are doing little to address the problem and much to aggravate it by shirking the responsibility of educating the child.

The Pharmacological, Psychiatric, and Educational Industry's Scam

Documenting, labeling, and drugging poorly parented and poorly educated children has become a very profitable business. Parents and their idiosyncratic children are coerced by certain teachers and administrators to be evaluated by mental health professionals after being inundated by reams of checklists and forms demonstrating that their child is not functioning like an average child of the same age. The parents are seduced into the special education trap offering more academic service with a lower student-teacher ratio. The parent is told to go to particular doctors who will prescribe the right medication and label, sealing the fate of the child. The psychiatric, professional, and educational industries have another dependent child in their grasp insuring a future federally subsidized income with no expectations or demands for improvement. This is scandalous!

No-nonsense education is the antidote for fraudulent special education labels and their associated drugs. This designation has become too common in American schools ever since we began the process of lowering our standards. Estimates show that every classroom in the country has at least one ADHD child, the label for kids who are chronically impulsive, fidgety, or unable to focus. It is the second most common disorder in children behind only asthma.[4] "There has been a 90 percent increase in ADHD between 1989 and 1996."[5] "Dr. Julie Magno Zito and her associates at the University of Maryland found a 200 to 300 percent increase in behavior-altering drugs between 1987 and 1996." The largest part of this increase occurred when federal funds were made available after 1991.[6] Most people who have contact with a child having difficulty focusing in school realize that the ability to concentrate may be selective. These children labeled ADD and ADHD often have no problem being engrossed for hours in television programs, videos, games, or sports. Obviously it is a selective form of paying attention. Even adults can receive a tentative diagnosis on the Internet. There are various Web sites that allow you to take a click-on test for adult ADD or ADHD. It is difficult when answering honestly not to score as a moderate risk for ADHD. Our common sense tells us this ADHD label is not a precise and accurate scientific disorder.

The fact is there is no scientific test for ADHD.[7] Yet our schools recommend or require that students be psychologically evaluated or take drugs for this disorder.

Other modern societies like Japan and Western Europe do not have anything close to the rates of ADD and ADHD that we do. "American youngsters consume 90 percent of the world's Ritalin."[8] Obviously it is not a true mental disorder that is genetically linked to American children, whose ancestors came from all over the world. Our common sense says there is something wrong. As we have moved away from traditional methods of dealing with children the incidence of all mental disorders has escalated.

The labeling of children with ADD and ADHD has become an epidemic in America. Arthur Caplan, chairman of the Department of Ethics at the University of Pennsylvania Medical School, says while ADHD is a serious condition, he wonders if drug companies may be pushing self-generated diseases to people who don't have problems but who can be led to believe they might by savvy marketing campaigns.[9] The pharmaceutical corporations do indeed appear to use marketing campaigns to create prescription-drug-dependent children. The drug companies' initial steps in promoting one of their existing drugs for children is to finance a study to demonstrate the effectiveness of the drug on children. The hired researchers highlight any positive and disregard any possible negative interpretation of the results of the study. The study is published in a scientific journal to create a sense of legitimacy and finally heralded in the media as a viable treatment for a particular problem.

A typical example of this process is Pfizer's commissioning of a study on their Zoloft product used on depressed children and adolescents. Leaving aside the issue of whether or not children can be diagnosed as depressed, a study was conducted to demonstrate the effectiveness of Zoloft. The author of the study, Karen Wagner, concluded, "the study is both statistically and clinically significant." The report by Wagner was published in the *Journal of the American Medical Association*. The headline in the *New York Times* article, "Zoloft Does Well in Study—Drug Used To Treat Childhood Depression," by Erica Good, is the payoff for Pfizer's marketing investment.[10]

Under closer examination this process appears less than scientific and borders on fraudulent. According to their own report, 69 percent of the subjects improved significantly on Zoloft. However, 59 percent of the children taking a placebo also improved significantly. This means only 10 percent in the study might have been positively impacted by the drug. This study does not factor in the negative side effects that would force one to conclude that the headline is at best misleading and at worst false advertising. This practice is much too common.

We now know that Glaxo Smith Kline's version, Paxil, a drug frequently prescribed for moody children, has serious side effects. On June 19, 2003, the Federal Food and Drug Administration recommended doctors refrain from treating children with Paxil while they reviewed current research concerning this drug. There is research evidence linking Paxil to suicide thoughts in children and adolescents. Furthermore, "the FDA also pointed to a lack of evidence Paxil was effective in treating depression in children and adolescents."[11] Elliot

Spitzer, New York state attorney, accused Glaxo Smith Kline of consumer fraud for misrepresenting data on Paxil for children.[12]

Pseudoscience and professional marketing are powerful methods of subverting our traditional schools and culture. A new study shows teenagers have no choice in being lazy. Now laziness is said to be caused by age-related brain development, not personal decision.[13] There is a manufactured biological explanation in our counterculture for obesity, inattentiveness, depression, alcoholism, drug, sex, and gambling addiction, and now laziness. Tomorrow there will be a gene found and a specific preventative drug developed for throwing garbage out of the car window. Of course, being a slob is not a choice.

Pharmaceutical companies are involved in immoral practices that place our children at risk of becoming dependent prescription drug consumers for life. Dubious statements commissioned by the producers of a product like a cleaner may be common practices in media advertising. This is wrong. Yet the impact of selling questionable drugs to children is a far greater crime that needs to be severely punished. Drug-dependent children become drug-dependent adults. This is unconscionable in a free market society.

Through the process of emphasizing certain information, no matter how dubious, the Smugglers are changing our society. Our government schools latch on to this pseudoscientific nonsense to justify their lack of academic success. It is a gradual eroding of the character of our citizens. Irresponsible people without a strong sense of values and morals are easily manipulated. This strategy of lowering the common denominator of acceptable behavior does change the perceptions of almost everyone, including the strongest elements of society. Condoning people's negative choices is deteriorating the social fabric of our nation. Raising our standards and expectations of schools, teachers, parents, and students is the way to expose and reverse the Smugglers' ability to implement their agenda.

Traditional Education Is the Answer

Traditional education of our students will minimize the possibility of scams. Schools are a powerful institution in an advanced technological society. Without developing literacy in verbal and math areas, a person cannot productively function in a civilized world. There are very few functioning adults who were not positively impacted by a representative of the school they attended. It may have been a teacher, an administrator, a coach, or other staff member. A child has an opportunity in school to view the world in a broader perspective than the child would have solely with his family. Conscientious educators can help a child become better balanced. In school a lazy child can be trained to become industrious, an overly aggressive bully type child can learn the social skills that may not be taught at home. The wimpy, passive-aggressive, manipulative child can find a more productive means of getting his needs met at school. The healthy, strong, peaceful child may receive the message from concerned authority figures that she is on the right track. As the breakdown of traditional families continues, the institutions of education are more important today than ever in influencing the lives of children.

School is the coming-out party for children separating from their mother and home. With the advent of almost universal preschool this separation takes place at an earlier and earlier age. Most parents with young children have some concern about their child leaving their protection and direct supervision to enter school. It is the first time the child comes out of his home and enters a new world controlled by a different adult. Unfortunately, for too many it might be a few days or weeks after birth in a home daycare, or at age two or three in a preschool. Certainly by age five, the child will enter a kindergarten program. With the exception of the growing home school movement, a child will be thrust into a world where he will no longer be the center of the universe or receive what he wants from doting parents. Other children will be competing for materials, activities, space, and the teacher's attention. A child learns to become cooperative, patient, and obedient or faces difficulty with the adjustment of being away from the home and parents. Even the best quality schools inadvertently teach a fundamental lesson: Life is not always fair.

Delaying gratification is one of the characteristics of a civilized world. A child has to learn to raise her hand and wait her turn. In a well-supervised program, one that is administered by a knowledgeable, caring adult, a disciplined child will flourish. If the child is placed in an under-supervised daycare or kindergarten, the cruelest child will often be king and the kindest will often be seen as weak. The decision for a conscientious parent of whether to raise a child with traditional values or allow a child to remain his egotistic self should be a no-brainer. A child without values may be popular and successful for a time but will eventually end as a failure. It has happened throughout history and will continue to happen. What goes around comes around. A child needs to become responsible for his own learning and behaving or suffer the consequence of being a failure in a complex society. It is the joint responsibility of parents and educators to work together to mold a child from a self-centered bully into a strong, competent, and peaceful adult.

In our PC world, teachers have to be directed not to allow children to bully their parents. Today the child is empowered by the presence of his parents. The student will attempt behavior such as whining, talking back, or responding with inappropriate language in front of the parents that he would never normally do in the classroom. My staff has been trained to help the parent by taking charge when the child is taking advantage of the parent in school. "You know you need to be respectful to your parents." This conforms to school expectations and the parent is relieved.

It is easier for today's parents to be stricter with other people's children than with their own. Whenever students from our school go on a field trip, any parent who volunteers to go along is assigned a group of students excluding her own child. It appears parents can be more forceful in getting other children to follow the rules than they can their own child. The traditional behavior of parents holding their own children to a higher standard than other children has flip-flopped to parental advocacy of their child. In recreational activities like coaching, in social situations, and at school parents appear to want to give their child an immediate edge over other children at the cost of developing their child's character. The high self-esteem and protection from the pain of reality seems to override the concern over the child developing positive traits and virtues.

Intimate Schools Correct False Notions

As a board member of the National Independent Private School Association, I have the opportunity to participate in the accreditation process of private schools. These schools have a median population of two hundred students. The common element of these schools is the family atmosphere. Students, teachers, administrators, and parents know each other very well. Everyone exchanges greetings, calling one another by name.

The personal communication in small school communities lessens the negative impact of modern parenting. Dedicated teachers sharing precise feedback about the child's habits can re-ignite the modern parent's understanding of the importance of training the child. Honest and thoughtful appraisal of the child's performance can help the parents change their ineffectual orientation.

Self-competence, not falsely high self-esteem, should be the goal. In our Smugger world teachers have to assist the parents to understand that certain current notions of raising children are detrimental to children. Teachers know from being in the daily trenches with groups of children that stressing high self-esteem through positive reinforcement is a destructive practice, not the panacea for raising them. Too many children believe they are better than they really are. These children are suffering from self-delusion. Many have no anxiety about their gaps in ability or knowledge to motivate them to improve. Eventually their false-esteem ends in being labeled.

The hands-on process of teaching and training the child in specific skills pays much greater dividends than the nonsensical practice of being a cheerleader spewing positive reinforcement to create an artificially high self-esteem. Self-competency allows a child to function in any setting, while the high-esteem approach leaves the power to continue the reinforcement in the hands of someone else, usually authority figures. Whenever authority figures do not respond with high doses of positive reinforcement, the person becomes confused and then alienated.

One of my clients wanted me to raise the self-esteem of her thirty-four-year-old daughter. She informed me her daughter has a long criminal history of robbery, drug, and sexual addiction issues. Through questioning this sixty-one-year-old mother, I learned her daughter was raised with a total immersion in the high self-esteem philosophy. This mother gave her daughter everything but was robbed by her daughter and never gave a thought to the possibility that she gave her daughter too much.

The current practice of high self-esteem reinforcement at the expense of honest evaluation is setting our children up for failure. When the young person realizes she is not going to be a famous actress or sports celebrity or some other improbable occupation the child becomes disillusioned about her entire future. Often the parent's inability or unwillingness to cushion the child's inevitable disappointments through reality training can propel the child into depression or even chronic mental illness.

Parents and teachers should work together to instill basic skills, values, and morals into the minds of these young people. Training in competency, honesty, right from wrong, the work ethic, empathy, and tenacity can give the child the tools needed for success. These valuable morals and skills are a solid foundation, not a phony world of false esteem that leads to a dependence on others. Our national strength requires productive adults, not perennial self-centered takers.

Of course a child who is confident and independent will naturally receive acknowledgement for her behavior. "Your daughter is so grown up." "She helps you prepare dinner," or "she does her homework without any prompting," or "she eats everything we serve without complaint." The compliments come because of the child's proper behavior. The proper behavior does not occur because of artificial compliments. It occurs when certain behaviors become habits through repetition. The training by the parents and teachers will impact all aspects of the child's life. These positive habits enable the child to become organized. Confusion fades, leaving a clear picture of how to gain control of one's life by delaying immediate gratification. The young student armed with the skills and knowledge of the adult world realizes her destiny is in her own hands to create if she is willing to work and be patient as it unfolds.

Legalizing Self-Defense

Too many children in the modern child development era are not being taught right from wrong. Bullying is now a full-scale epidemic in the U.S. The National Institution of Child Health and Human Development recently found that 29 percent of students in grades six through twelve are affected by bullying—either as a victim, a bully, or in many cases both. According to the article "Bullies are Everyone's Problem," "60

percent of bullies in grades six through nine will have at least one criminal conviction by age twenty-four."[14] As reported in *Psychology Today,* "A
new national survey found that 80 percent of U.S. children are bullied
at school. The effects can be devastating, impairing concentration and
self-esteem and even deadly, as seen in the Columbine shootings."[15]

To limit evil we need once again to make self-defense against bullying legal and honorable. The modern parent believes that teaching one's
child to become independent by fighting back in self-defense is barbaric. In a seminar I gave in Atlanta a member of the audience asked
what she should have done when another child her daughter's age and
size attacked her daughter in an unsupervised schoolyard. I responded
that her daughter should have physically retaliated. She was aghast. She
meant she wanted to know what I thought about bringing a legal suit
against this child's parents. I responded that she has to give her child
encouragement to fend for herself because she will not always be there.
She became visibly upset and raised her voice stating her daughter
deserves to be protected by authority figures. I agreed that authority figures should protect children but unfortunately authority figures are not
always there or often ignore student-to-student incidents.

In another case, a sixteen-year-old client coming to me for psychological counseling noted her mother was a wimp and could not stand up
to her school department head. Her mother confirmed she let people
walk all over her. In her next breath the daughter admitted being teased
by a group of fellow students wanting to know about the test her mother
(a teacher in her school) was giving. I said to her to firmly tell these students if they had any questions, to ask her mother and leave her alone.
She said that would be rude. Her mother remained silent even though
she had just told me that her daughter was so depressed about being
bullied that she had threatened suicide. Her mother did not support my
assertion that she had a right to stand up for herself. The mother continued to exemplify and communicate that putting someone in their

place when they verbally abuse you is inappropriate. The mother and daughter did not return for a second visit. In both cases the parents believed no one has a right to defend oneself against bullying or thought their child could not learn to independently defend herself.

At a presentation to an educator's conference in San Diego, a teacher asked me if she should intervene with a six-year-old child picking on a three-year-old child. I went through a series of questions that pointed out a three-year-old cannot physically defend against a child twice his physical maturity. She reluctantly realized that she had to intervene to protect the younger child and punish the bully to teach him a moral lesson. Inevitably the question arose, "How is intimidating a bully any different from the behavior of the bully?" I explained that the bully was hurting the younger child to control him for his own selfish reasons while the teacher was attempting to extinguish an evil action.

Another person asked what to do to a child who physically retaliated to defend himself against a bully. It took awhile to convince the teacher that the retaliation was a natural consequence of the aggressor's actions. Of course her knowledge of the students and monitoring of the incident made her judgment more valid. As teachers, we have the responsibility to take advantage of the teachable moment by either taking a proactive stance or directly intervening or by allowing a child to defend himself.

When a teacher observes a child bullying another she is responsible to intervene and immediately put a halt to it. In this PC time in the USA, many people view self-defense as a violent act, not a heroic one. The ridiculous reasoning is both acts are violent thus equally bad. When teachers realize that the natural response of self-defense is a deterrent to bullying, reluctance changes to cautious acceptance. Self-defense is heroic because often the unprovoked aggression of a bully is a surprise that has to be immediately countered by decisive action to prevent the bully from continuing this hurtful behavior.

An unreformed bully will proceed to develop more habitual negative behavior that will be defined as evil. Regardless of the widely held belief that evil people do not exist, only evil acts done by good people, the fact remains that evil must be stopped. I learned as a clinical psychologist in prison that there are some people who cannot be rehabilitated.

Growing up in Brooklyn, I learned as a young child that evil exists. When I worked in the Florida prison this was confirmed by the inmates. The inmates' definition of an evil person was anyone who attempted to control another for his own personal gain with total disregard for the self-interest of the other person. A bully fits this definition. A bully verbally or physically abuses someone else for his personal pleasure. "It has always been a mystery to me how men can feel themselves honored by the humiliation of fellow beings," said Gandhi.[16] A bully is a coward who will always run from a fair fight. He will prey on the weak and avoid the strong. When unable to feel capable of bullying, he will revert to a "wimp" strategy. The bully or wimp has an almost nonexistent conscience. The bully's motto is "do unto others before they do unto you" and the wimp's is "cry for mercy instead of defending your rights and beliefs."

Their journey down the path of evil has been so long that they need a miracle to turn back. It is the duty of parents, teachers, and other authority figures to confront bullies, to stop them from going down a road of habitual immoral acts. In large government schools the anonymity of students allows all sorts of problem children to fall between the cracks.

Good Things Come in Small Packages

Small schools are inherently superior to large schools in the academic, social, and emotional areas because they can immediately confront problems. There is no justification for anyone falling between the cracks. The manageable number of students in the school allows everyone to know each other and the teacher to know each student. There is year-to-year continuity of the faculty knowing the progress of a particular student. The faculty's previous knowledge of the student's traits and academic gaps eliminates the time-consuming need for formal evaluation. The school community takes on the characteristics of an extended family. The students' familiarity with each other leads more to brother-sister relationships rather than boyfriend-girlfriend fantasy relationships often found in large schools. Students will tend to be more supportive and cooperative with each other to avoid unnecessary open confrontation. Bullying does not have much of a chance to flourish in a tightly supervised environment if teachers do their job of reprimanding this type of behavior.

The shorter time needed to go from point A to point B in a small school limits unstructured time, an ingredient for chaos. Training time is maximized, leading to greater obedience to the rules of the classroom and school. Students become more comfortable in the system, joining rather than attempting to "get over," to be "cool." The concept of "coolness" is hard to maintain in an intimate world, while genuineness is hard to develop in an anonymous world.

The teachers not only know the academic, emotional, and social makeup of individual students because of the continued year after year exposure to the students, but become well acquainted with their parents as well. Through teacher-parent contact, students can be held to higher standards and expectations without wiggle room. When students demonstrate a particular level of competency, they are hard pressed to explain a regression in their production. The school is held accountable to the parents with their frequent person-to-person contact.

A small community population encourages the student-teacher-parent communication and puts checks and balances on the educational process. Teachers naturally give guidance. There is little space for favoritism and popular groups to exist. Friendship occurs between students and staff members but any excess is quickly recognized and modified. The school community keeps any deviation from the norm in balance. The comprehensive knowledge of the teacher enables her to make precise decisions in enhancing the overall attitude of the child.

It is a myth that a small number of students in a classroom enhances pupil performance. There is no correlation between the pupil-teacher ratio and academic achievement.[17] Catholic nuns have had more than a 50 to 1 ratio and have produced excellent students. I have seen students who have had a 6 to 1 ratio in affluent schools who describe their classroom as a chaotic, non-learning environment. A school without a mission is doomed to failure regardless of the student-teacher ratio.

When children enter my school from a large anonymous school, an obvious transformation takes place. Even though we have uniforms, the entering student dresses several years older with flashy jewelry. Their focus is on impressing students with their "coolness" rather than their academic knowledge. The face has a callous "I don't care" attitude. As they get into our program the child returns to a more traditional child-like behavior. The frown or defiance melts away to display the happiness and openness of a normal child. Their attention becomes more focused on school-related issues and less on peer-related matters. The child joins the school community and learns to appreciate his role as a student.

The teacher in a small school is a generalist, not a specialist. The economic reality of small schools requires everyone to be versatile to make things run smoothly. Teachers in a small school have more power with students and are prone to use it correctly. When the student realizes the teacher has the lever of power to make his life better he conforms more to the teacher's prodding. The close and ongoing contact between student and teacher gives the educator more opportunity to teach the "whole child." The cognitive emotional and social aspects of the student are unavoidable to the teachers in the intimate world of a small, manageable school. The teachers shape the child's character.

The opposite is true in large government schools. The system does not allow many dedicated teachers to do their job effectively. Teachers do not have the personal time with students or the mandate to easily impact the child. Large schools hire subject specialists and use their knowledge with many students. The methodology courses that specializing teachers receive in universities are rarely practical. They are taught by professors who have limited classroom experience with the type and age students that these teachers will have in their classrooms. Their specialized knowledge, not their practical skills, becomes their career meal ticket. As long as these specialists can update their credentials, their status is secure.

On the other hand, a regular classroom teacher has to do a little of everything. Her worth hinges on her ability to interact effectively with an intimate number of students over a long period. Most often the teacher is a generalist who knows how to teach in many areas. Her value lies in her ability to motivate and influence a child to become a learner. The generalist does not have a specialty to impress the administration or parents, instead she must be accountable for progress and personal knowledge of the students in her class. As did the teacher in a one-room schoolhouse, a teacher in a small school must wear many hats and be more directly responsible to students and parents.

Maintaining a High-Functioning, Just, and Peaceful Classroom

A child in a structured, organized, interesting, and emotionally secure learning environment will naturally gravitate toward the peaceful pursuit of knowledge. A child concentrating on an activity has little time for mischief. A quality teacher understands her preparation of the classroom and her lessons set the tone for the actions of the students. The class-room develops a positive learning culture.

Everyone, especially children, acts more appropriately when they know the rules and understand that the authorities enforce the rules. There is little room to slip between the cracks in a small school. The good, the bad, and the ugly are brought to immediate recall when the student crosses the visual field of the teacher. Other students and teachers will act as reminders when needed, insuring the proper action is taken.

Classroom meetings led by the teacher for 15–20 minutes starting and ending the school day are instrumental in setting the tone, laying out individual expectations, and handling any unfinished business. Student input gives the teacher a gauge of how well particular strategies are working for each individual child. A directed discussion of a famous quote, reading of a fable, or current events gives students the opportunity to deal on a critical thinking level and sharpen their understanding of character and moral issues. Celebrating student success in front of the entire school encourages all students. These shared classroom experiences allow the teacher to build a sophisticated classroom culture. As the class develops an esprit de corps, obnoxious behavior decreases and academic involvement increases.

The integration of learning formal and informal lessons increases when children are trained in class meetings to discuss serious issues. Cultural studies of past and present civilizations give students an appreciation of the dividends of being physically, emotionally, and morally strong to maintain a peaceful state. Cosmic studies show the interconnectedness of the universe and develop an appreciation for the spiritual aspects of life.

Purposeful discipline provides the foundation of character. Children are a work in progress. The process of education is supposed to guide the student on his journey in life. The administering of rewards and punishing consequences shapes the child's behavior. Eventually, through repetition, good habits are developed, creating a person of positive character.

In an effective school, students become aware of the impact of their smallest action. In conflict resolution, the first step is between students and is handled by the students. If unresolved, the teacher acts as a clarifier and then, as a last resort, as a judge. When a child refuses to understand the implications of his behavior, the administrators become involved usually with a parent and student meeting. There is immediate feedback from other students and teachers. Any success is celebrated, inappropriate behavior is discussed and effective consequences are given. Formal and informal lessons with concerned teachers and engaged students provide ongoing learning opportunities, laying the foundation for a strong, positive character. The daily guidance of a teacher who appreciates being a teacher is a powerful spiritual pulpit that positively impacts the course of a child's life.

Teachers persuade students to join the world of reading and thinking: the rational world of adults. This conversion to becoming a member of the adult community motivates the student to learn the required skills and knowledge. As a child becomes more competent in successfully completing tasks, he becomes more self-assured and confident as well. This is clearly seen every day in a well-managed classroom as the children learn mastery over their lessons. The child responds in a more upbeat, confident manner without any need for outside praise. This upbeat manner will be reflected in the home.

When the goal of education is defined in global utopian terms, little will be accomplished. There is no direction. There is no way to measure progress. Students will "just get by" in school when school is not stressed for any higher purpose. Administrative bureaucrats run the school for administrative bureaucrats, not for students, parents, and teachers.

When the objective of education is to "help the student become the best person he can become," the mandate is clear and precise. Not only do the teacher and student know that academics in all areas are to be mastered but also the entire child's development in social, emotional, and moral issues has to be addressed. Through the procedures discussed this chapter, purposeful discipline is administered to impact the whole child in a real and concrete process. When developing a school and classroom culture centers around the student becoming the best he can be, miraculous positive changes in the character of a child will take place.

Making Children Normal

After the parents, the second line of defense in society for producing normal children is our schools. Large impersonal schools are increasingly unable to efficiently devote their resources to attacking and altering basic behavior and values. Government schools are motivated by increased federal dollars to label children rather than to change them. Only in the more manageable schools of up to four or five hundred students do the administrators, teachers, parents, and students have enough personal contact with each other to develop a community that will educate them. John Alspaugh, PhD, urges the elimination of middle school and junior high by extending kindergarten through eighth grade. He reasons that emotional bonds between fellow students and teachers help to stabilize the academic functioning of the student.[18]

Teaching a student to develop the habits of observing, doing his best, and completing what he starts takes a dedicated and demanding teacher. This is a teacher sufficiently patient to convince the student that he can become responsible for his learning. This process takes time not only to alter the thinking and behavior of the student, but to get his parents to jump on the bandwagon, too. Fundamental changes in a child's behavior are accelerated with parental support. A parent's faith in their school and child's teacher is essential in rehabilitating problem children.

Not only do teachers have a responsibility to prevent students from bullying them, now the teacher must stop parents from telling them how to run their classrooms. It is a current reality that schools need to impose limits on parental interference. Parents often enter schools as advocates for their child, attempting to bully the teacher into accepting their child's version of an incident.

Pampering parents must unite with the school to bring about the normalizing process. "My child is open and honest with me. He tells me he did this negative act." These parents' statements are a means of explaining away the child's horrendous behavior. These parents have to be convinced that a teacher giving consequences is a sign of conscientiousness, not a sign of discrimination against their child. Parents and teachers must communicate and unite for the benefit of the child. In the past, discipline by the teacher was supported by parents. Parents would say, "You must have done something wrong, take responsibility for your behavior." The onus was placed on the child to figure out how to adjust to the world of the teacher. Parents would punish their child for doing something inappropriate in school or at home. I remember as a child being reluctant to bring notes home from my teachers. I knew I would have to face the music. Often the teachers' notes were mysteriously lost before my mother greeted me at the door. The knowledge of the alliance between teacher and parent kept many students from pushing the boundaries of acceptable behavior at school. I can testify to this myself.

My school and other highly functioning schools have remediated many children with the ADD/ADHD label. Through the use of traditional teaching methods, a problem child can learn to compensate and become an excellent student. This is not shocking since over one hundred years ago Maria Montessori devised methods that took "defective children" out of the slums of Rome and "normalized" them. This happened through working with attractive, concrete materials in a small, dedicated environment. It does take administrative, teacher, and parental effort, but it pays the greatest of dividends: producing a drug-free, label-free, healthy child. The process of turning a student around often takes more than one school year. Smaller institutions of learning can better track students with the gratification of firsthand observation of the student's development. The growth of a student over time is often lost in a large school.

A Syracuse University professor's son was in a large affluent high school in the suburbs of Syracuse. His father took a position as head of a department at Southern Mississippi University in Hattiesburg. The Syracuse high school teachers told the professor and his wife that it would be abusive to their son if he were forced to attend an undoubtedly inferior school in Mississippi.

The assumption of incompetence of the Mississippi school by the Syracuse high school teachers proved to be absolutely wrong. The fourteen-year-old flourished in the new school. Besides enjoying his high school experience, he did well on the SAT, and continued to excel on the university level.

Small schools' lack of sophisticated facilities, specialists, and credentials is more than compensated for by the emotional security of their family atmosphere and teachers who know the students well enough to motivate them.

Traditional Education: The Key to Our Civilization

The institutions of education in an advanced nation like ours have to give our youth the skills, body of knowledge, values, and morals that define the culture and make the civilization work. Any attempt to undermine one or more of these pillars of the culture will weaken the society. Like it or not, teachers, like parents, are responsible for assisting the child in internalizing the necessary elements of the culture to be a functioning member of the civilization. This conveying of the elements of the culture to the students is the main function of education.

Learning from the successes and failures of our ancestors has propelled advancement in all civilizations. When knowledge is lost, the society suffers and as knowledge is gained, the nation advances. Education is the wise guiding the less knowledgeable on a more efficient path. Passing on knowledge from teacher (wise person) to student (less knowledgeable person) is instrumental for survival. Wise individuals are essential for the progress of a civilization.

The Marxist-humanist intellectual Smuggers have hijacked the government educational institution. Their primary agenda is to precipitate social change through eroding each element of our traditional culture. There are no more studies of the greatness of our founding fathers. There is no more discussion of the roots of our Judeo-Christian morals and values. There is no more prayer or display of the Ten Commandments. "Merry Christmas" has been replaced by "Happy holidays." No longer are bullies bad or is self-defense good. There is no clear-cut right and wrong. Our government schools teach cultural and moral relativism and have a blanket acceptance of cultural diversity with total disrespect given to our cultural accomplishments.

The Smuggers' cultural and moral relativist agenda has led to a self-centered, hedonistic culture that is in direct conflict with our traditional American culture. The selfish counterrevolution has brought out the worst rather than the best of our nation. The counter-revolution has weakened America in every way.

Aristotle noted, "The roots of education are bitter, the fruits are sweet." This proverb is true for the individual as well as the civilization. A people or civilization that does not advance or maintain its value of knowledge will regress into mediocrity. A viable institution of education is imperative to an advanced nation.

The U.S. must return to its core values, morals, and knowledge to maintain its preeminent position in the world. Our nation cannot afford to allow our schools to entrench themselves further into mediocrity. The resurgence in education will only take place when people realize the importance of education to their children and the entire culture.

In order to revitalize education, parents and teachers need to unite to motivate the students to develop traditional values and morals and a broad range of basic skills and knowledge. Teachers need to be experts, not in a particular subject, but in knowing each and every individual student in all areas. In other words, to be effective, a teacher needs to be a generalist not a specialist.

A small school provides the best elements for effective and peaceful education in this country. The small school allows students, teachers, parents, and administrators to know everyone on a first-name basis. Safety and communication are enhanced by personal contact throughout the school community. Administrators can inspire and support teachers, students, and parents in focusing on the importance of education that begins in the classroom and spreads out impacting every facet of a student's life. Appreciated teachers can inspire each other and students to join the classroom culture of being the best students they can be. Successful students can help other students do a better job. Through joining hands, everyone in a small school works closely together to create an effective environment, producing healthy and peaceful students.

Parents who have firsthand knowledge of the beneficial changes in the child tend to encourage their child rather than discourage him. Appreciative parents become active members of the school team. Most importantly, students blossom academically, socially, and emotionally in a peaceful environment where harmony exists between parents and the school.

Our institutions of education must communicate to our citizens what de Tocqueville called the "exceptionality of traditional American culture." These principles and values of our forefathers guided our nation to internal strength and peace. Schools need to extol the virtues of traditional American culture, not indoctrinate the students with immoral, degrading cultural values and behavior. Schools should meet the needs of students instead of the desires of bureaucrats and social engineers. Manageable schools are vital for the transference of the best and most important features of our culture from one generation to another.

Chapter 5

Battling to Uniting the Sexes

The first bond of society is marriage; the next, the children; then the whole family.

   —CICERO, *De Officiis*, 78 BC

The family is the seminary on which the commonwealth, for its manners and as well for its numbers, must ultimately depend, as its establishment is the source, so its happiness is the end, of every institution of government which is wise and good.

   —JAMES WILSON, *Lectures on Law*, 1790–91

A healthy marriage is essential for a healthy family. Our founding fathers understood that functioning families are the foundation of a viable, free nation. Yet throughout history leaders were aware that the marriage of a husband and wife is a difficult relationship.

Smugger myths are excavating the topsoil, preventing many marriages from taking root. It is a conscious strategy. Smuggers are exploiting the natural battle of the sexes.

A man reminisced that Kasturbai "could not go out without permission."[1] "Kasturbai was a beautiful young woman and he felt more jealous of her than ever. Once they quarreled so fiercely he packed her off from Rajkot to her parents in Porbandar."[2] "He grabbed her by the hand, dragged her to the gate, opened it and was about to push her out." This jealous, controlling husband was not a madman; he was, in many people's opinion, a saint. Mahatma Gandhi's relationship with his wife might have been a more difficult accomplishment than leading the Indian nation to independence from Great Britain, yet Kasturbai Gandhi died in her husband's loving arms.[3] The journey of marriage is indeed difficult for all who walk down its path.

This inherent difficulty of marriage has historically been exploited to topple the social order of a nation. Revolutionaries understand pitting one group against another creates animosity. Smugglers have done a masterful job of undermining the institution of marriage in the United States. There seems to be an endless supply of mother-in-law, wife, children, and husband jokes. There are jokes about older men tossing out their stable marriages for younger "trophy" wives. Couples are still divorcing even though it is common knowledge that many divorces end up in bankruptcy court.

Marriage is probably the hardest endeavor undertaken by a person in a lifetime. Many married couples are in a perpetually fighting state. The battle of the sexes of a young couple is not evolving into a mature united team. Instead it is ending before it has taken root, leading to skyrocketing divorce rates. Yet the same recent divorcees are likely to cohabitate or to tie the knot again with a person similar to their previous mate. The institution of marriage has been severely wounded.

Divorce is suicide for the family unit.

It must be remembered that the casualties of divorce are the children. The cycle of intimacy is often like a revolving door with individuals entering or leaving the house. Commitment, loyalty, and fairness are at a historical low. Although the emotional, financial, and known health benefits of marriage keep a steady supply of people seeking a meaningful relationship, the institution of marriage and the family have been weakened. The positive aspects of human relationships make it almost impossible to extinguish marriage and family since they appear to be hardwired into our DNA.

Marriage, with its hopeful and blessed production of children, has been the backbone of all great civilizations. The state of the family is a barometer of a society. There is no other institution that can be as effective as the family in inculcating the culture and morals of a nation.

Husbands and wives have a vested interest in civilizing their children as it makes for harmony in the community and leads to family success. Traditional parents are emphatic in demanding that their children conform to cultural norms of decency. There is no democratic vote by family members as to the acceptability of behavior. Lying, cursing, biting, hurting, destroying property of others is wrong, period. The parents punish the child in a dictatorial manner because the parents have the most to lose from raising uncivilized, sociopathic children. Either the parents are directing their children into being functioning human beings or the state attempts to fill the void. Fascists, communists, and others have tried to replace the traditional family with disastrous results for the children and the entire society.

Husbands and wives are necessary for strong families. No alternative lifestyle configuration can substitute for a man and a woman in the process of growing in love. The incredible differences that attract each to the other are also the same differences that force both partners to look at life through new eyes. No same-sex relationship gives the opportunity for intimate knowledge of the opposite sex. It is a world that initially frustrates both spouses after the infatuation fades, though it eventually enriches both beyond their wildest dreams. Marriage between a man and a woman has no rival throughout history. Merging a man and woman in love is a miraculously blessed journey.

It is a long and difficult journey. Too many people are turning back in divorce before the journey has ended. They and their children are the losers.

Marriage is a spiritual journey. Two very different individuals learn from each other the differences of the male and female world. They show their children the differences just by their being. As they move forward, their differences fade as their similarities grow. Acceptance, approval, and appreciation anchor more of their interaction. It takes time for love to be recognized. The support of other family members and friends encourage them to remain on the path long enough for them to unite. To move from being against each other to uniting is the essence of marriage.

This chapter will discuss the guidelines for developing a functional marriage.

The Assault on Marriage Has Been Intentional

Like any social unit, marriage and the family unit are imperfect. During the past half century the family in America has been under attack by Smugger intellectuals who have infiltrated the media, education, religion, and the entertainment industry. These Smuggers have introduced many hedonistic concepts that ridicule institutions and traditional values like marriage, family, God, the Golden Rule, individual responsibility, duty, and sacrificing for others.

These American values have been made out to be "corny" in our "hip-hop" world.

By successfully attacking the family, the traditional definition of marriage, and moral code, a society can be brought to its knees. This has been a historical strategy for totalitarian revolution. In a free society dissent serves a useful function of keeping a balanced course.

The anti-establishment, hippie movement of the 1960s was not spontaneous dissent but a strategically planned and implemented counterrevolution to eliminate our free enterprise system and replace it with Marxist ideals. The assault continues today in a subtle and insidious manner by relentless attacks on our common sense, replacing it with hedonistic notions.

These hedonistic notions temporarily delight the individual but wreak havoc on the institutions of our country. The "free sex" revolution was a thinly disguised method of weakening and destroying the institution of marriage. The strategy has been effective in steadily undermining marriage for the past fifty years. If sex is free and acceptable in many perverted forms, then marriage becomes less attractive. In a hedonistic world the raising of children becomes a burden instead of a privilege.

As marriage loses its main purpose of procreation and the definition of marriage dissolves into any type of consensual relationship, the institution of marriage weakens. The Smuggers are elitists who make spurious arguments that highlight specific examples of a father's or mother's abuse to undermine traditional values and morality. These so-called objective, scientific experts, Smuggers, use the power of their position to further their agenda by producing biased studies that undermine traditional morals and values. Alfred C. Kinsey's research was distorted to further his agenda.[4] A society without limits is heading toward anarchy. A society where children remain untrained and confused about their responsibilities as members of a functioning family in a community leads them to become narcissistic and self-absorbed parasites.

Undermining Marriage Has Crippled Our Children

The supreme test of any civilization is whether or not it can teach their men to become good fathers.

— Margaret Mead

There are twenty-four million children in the United States who do not live with their biological fathers. These children are two or three times more prone than children who live with their fathers to be poor, to use drugs, experience sexual abuse, and have emotional, health, criminal, and educational problems.[5] The mocking of the value of fatherhood has led many to assume that the child-father relationship is insignificant for the health of the family.

The absence of fathers has become so common we no longer consider the consequences of raising a child outside of marriage. Usually the mother has custody of the child in non-traditional families. A boyfriend or stepfather or even a biological father without primary custody quickly learns that disciplining the child will be self-defeating. The mother's natural instinct will put her on the side of the child. The boyfriend or stepfather backs off from disciplining the child, treating him with kid gloves so that he doesn't lose intimacy with his girlfriend or spouse. The biological father is fearful of being reported to the courts or a child protection agency. The significant men in a nontraditional relationship usually play it safe by virtually eliminating any discipline from their relationship with the child. Of course, the child is the loser. A child without discipline is like a missile without a guidance system: out of control. Weakening marriage has been and will continue to be a bonanza for mental health professionals and a tragedy for long-term stable relationships.

Deciding to have a child without getting married is a mean and destructive act. The child is the one who will suffer. "Children in one-parent homes are twice as likely as those from two-parent families to develop serious psychiatric problems and addictions later in life."[6] In our permissive society there are few societal pressures to restrict irresponsible choices. The least we can do as a nation is to present the stark evidence. The absence of one or the other parent is well documented as correlated with negative outcomes. Studies of unwed mothers show their children are more likely to do poorly in school, smoke, drink, do drugs, have emotional problems, be sexually promiscuous, be more violent, and commit suicide.[7]

On the other hand, children whose parents remain married reap real advantages, "Adolescents from these families have been found to have better health and are less likely to be depressed, are less likely to repeat a grade in school and have fewer developmental problems."[8]

Marriage is not easy but neither is divorce. Unfortunately the scenario of dysfunctional "blended" (combining of two divorced) families is more common and becoming more so each passing year. Children do not choose their parents; they are born into a family. Since children have no say in the matter of their birth, adults have a responsibility to their future offspring to develop a mature and committed relationship. A relationship that is based on committed traditional vows of honesty, fidelity, mutual respect, and friendship, not on adolescent romantic infatuation. When contemplating marriage, a man and a woman need to consciously consider children before making the plunge. Disagreement on wanting children should be an indicator to place the decision on hold until agreement is reached. The possibility of a child in the future deserves nothing less.

Divorce Is Toxic to Children

Once married, parents have an obligation to their children to do everything possible to create a united marriage. Divorce is not a viable option except in the most extreme cases. Divorce appears to create more problems than it solves. Married couples often think an amicable divorce will eliminate any additional trauma to the child. This is a naïve notion sold lock, stock, and barrel to the American people by the social engineer Smuggers of the 1960s. These anti-establishment intellectuals were far off the mark. Children of divorced parents have to confront new sets of problems including a parent's boy- or girlfriend, stepparents, stepbrothers and sisters, custody, and financial changes. In her book *The Unexpected Legacy of Divorce,* Judith Wallerstein reports in her twenty-five-year-long landmark study that divorce affects children in the following ways:

1. It alters the child's sense of his or her childhood.
2. It makes the child feel different from a child of an intact family.
3. The child experiences multiple losses as divorced parents change partners.
4. The children continue to worry about their parents.
5. Children are hyper-anxious about conflict in their own love relationships.
6. Children have a higher divorce rate than children from intact families.[9]

Neither does divorce solve all the problems for hostile or disengaged husbands and wives. The battle arena moves from the home to the legal system. The bickering continues but changes from money, affection, and spending time together to issues of what time to pick up the children, support money, and the cause for the divorce. Many times there is no one at home to be with the child. "An estimated 7 million (children) are in self care after school."[10] The coldness of disengagement does not become warmer or more engaged nor does the hostile fury become cooler or less engaged in open warfare.

At times spouses can have long periods of disengagement and outbursts of anger. A couple married for nineteen years with two teenage children had lived separate lives for fifteen of the married years. Both had numerous lovers while maintaining a façade of happiness for their children and the community. Truthful communication was nonexistent in their relationship except when in a heated battle. The adolescent children were showered with gifts by both parents attempting to win more loyalty and allegiance than the other. The children had a sense of the infidelity and acted out sexually, obtaining a distorted form of passion in their own lives. After the divorce the parents continued to act as a happy couple in public while continuing to compete materially for the affection of their children. The teenagers continued to act out in a wild lifestyle as confused as ever about a committed relationship.

Sometimes the intense battles appear to be unending. A couple divorced for three years and now both remarried to other people called my office to discuss their elementary-school-aged son and daughter. I announced the ground rules of the session, which would focus on the present, not discussing the past. Each of them agreed. They would attempt to make the adjustment into two separate, blended families less traumatic for the sake of their two children. In what seemed an instant after I began the session, they broke into "you did this, you did that." This was stopped only by bringing them back to the established ground rules. They could not follow the rules established and continued to bicker. I abruptly ended the session after ten minutes and rescheduled separate appointments. Marriage is not a bed of roses but divorce appears to have even more thorny problems.

I Love Him But I Am No Longer in Love with Him

Marriage is not a romance novel, not a bowl of cherries, nor a walk in the park. It is an attempt by two people from two different worlds, two different sexual subcultures, and two different families to come together and merge their lives. Marriage to an immature, naïve person may be seen through romantic lenses but a mature, worldly person understands the magnitude of the endeavor and its potential dividends. Marriage is a rough journey that can end in a wonderful place.

Like going on a vacation, this trip takes effort. Making the arrangements, the airports, the lines, the waiting, the searches are all a hassle. Finally you arrive at your destination and you have to air out the residence, find food, and some means of transportation. There may be things in your residence that have to be fixed or changed to suit you and you still have to plan how to use your time to the best advantage. The reality of a vacation is usually different from what the slick brochure indicates.

In my counseling practice, women have overwhelmingly been the instigators for coming to marriage counseling. I believe since the advent of the women's liberation movement, women have a more comprehensive set of romantic expectations for marriage than men. Over and over again I hear from the wife, "I love him but I am no longer 'in love' with him." What in the world does that mean?

It means that there is a disconnect between the normal experience and the distorted expectations of marriage. Falling out of love is not a sign of a bad marriage; it is a normal stage couples go through. (See the section on stages of marriage.) This is not to say that females should stop being more sensitive to issues in their marriage than the males. What is needed is to identify them and resolve them. It is wrong to interpret the feelings these problems create in both partners to mean the marriage is unsalvageable. Marriages have always taken great effort and realistic expectations and will continue to do so.

Feelings Can and Will Change: Marriage Takes Work

Physical, mental, and sexual abuses justify a divorce, not a feeling of not being "in love." Feelings can and will change depending on what we are doing and thinking. If a person has unrealistic expectations for marriage, he will feel his marriage is a failure. If one has to do all the menial chores while the mate does not share in the responsibilities, there will be feelings of exploitation. However, when a person's thinking about his expectations changes, then his feelings toward his marriage change. When spouses are fairer and more equitable in sharing responsibilities, their feelings change. Feelings change depending on the behavior and the thinking of the spouse. Only through the efforts of the mates will a marriage become a positive experience.

Marriage is an institution that requires effort to make it a positive experience. No one can live up to our idealized expectations, including us. As we mature as individuals, we eventually learn to accept our limitations and our mates'. We learn to appreciate that accomplishments take time and effort. Our small steps inch us ever closer to our dreams. A marriage is a work in progress, until "death do us part."

Modern married couples have been indoctrinated to remain in the perennial dating game of adolescence. After marriage they still maintain their boyfriends and girlfriends, have nights out without the other, spend money without consulting each other, and continue to demand to be the center of attention, even when it offends the partner. When a spouse protests the other's actions, the banner of freedom is raised. Modern couples believe retaining personal freedom and pleasure is paramount just as in our modern sitcom marriages. This appears to be the modern naïve ideal of marriage. The youthful stage of self-indulgence needs to be replaced by maturity for the sake of developing an intimate relationship.

Traditional thought defines the purpose of marriage as raising a family and to this end, the couple grows closer through their efforts of preparing to create the best environment for their children. It is the journey of accomplishing this vision that unifies husband and wife. Spouses negotiate making decisions on what is best for the family, not the individual. The legacy of the family is the major motivation for their marriage. Traditionalists hold the belief that both husband and wife must change to obtain these goals. Gone are the friends whose flirtations interfere with the couple's marriage. Selected friends are kept and new friendships of couples are made who bolster the marriage relationship.

The wife has to make the greatest metamorphosis in the marriage. She has to learn to be supportive of her husband to ensure her husband's success as the main provider. The once-independent woman has to accept her new identity, first as a wife and then as someone's mother. In the traditional marriage women are the center of the family, although they have to go through many changes to earn this status.

In a marriage usually the closest person to us is our spouse. An indicator of a close relationship with another is our ability to self-disclose. Often as the relationship grows we not only share the positive, but upon reaching a certain level of comfort, we begin to share our fears. These fears are often expressed in frustration and anger, quite typically not at the culprit, but at our spouse.

Displaced anger is not enjoyable, though it is a sign of intimacy. Our loved ones help us understand and balance our lives. When we realize how inconsiderately we have treated our spouse, our acceptance of their limitations becomes less of an issue. The three A's of acceptance, approval, and appreciation grow in each spouse. By understanding our own imperfections we better accept our spouse's. This self-approval and approval for loved ones results in an appreciation for our own life.

Our support and delight in the differences between our spouse and ourself brings greater intimacy. This great learning process is naturally fostered in a marriage if each remains in the institution long enough to gain this knowledge. Too many of us have been brainwashed to believe we are entitled to a loving marriage without intense effort. This entitlement to a "great marriage" has real consequences for our children. Unrealistic expectations lead to marital dissatisfaction that can impact the lives of our children.

For the Sake of the Children

John Gottman, PhD, related in a seminar I attended that most couples come to counseling as a last resort to confirm the inevitability of the ending of the relationship. This concept of receiving the blessing of the counselor for the dissolution of the marriage has to change for the mental health of everyone in the family. Couples in a relationship of hope-lessness will suffer from feelings of depression. Parents in constant bat-tle can influence children to "go into a shell" or lash out in aggressive behavior to protect themselves.

A "cold war" disengaged relationship between mother and father can lead to a joyless insecurity for a child or create a compulsive risk taker in search of excitement in a lifeless home. Either extreme of parental hostility or disengagement has a negative impact on the child's devel-opment. Parents have a responsibility to their children to enhance their ability to function in the world.

Years ago many elders advised couples to stay together for the sake of the children. It may be true that many unhappy and joyless marriages are better than the alternative: divorce. The married couple with chil-dren has a lot invested in their union emotionally, financially, and spir-itually for them to just abandon the marriage. Everyone wins, wife, husband, and children, when a couple begins the mature process of negotiation and attempts to limit the immature process of bickering for selfish ego needs. It is the responsibility of parents to their children to work at creating the best relationship possible. The better advice there-fore is to honestly communicate with your spouse and make the rela-tionship a more win-win one.

Traditional Marriage Works

Traditional wisdom is needed to support the institution of marriage to create strong families and to develop and maintain a strong nation. All major religions throughout history sanctify marriage and the family. The Bible says in Ephesians 51:31, "For this reason a man will leave his father and be united with his wife and two will become one flesh." Ephesians 5:33, "However each one of you also must love his wife as he loves himself and the wife must respect her husband."

The deepening love between a husband and wife and their children is the anchor of the family. The love shared by a married couple creates a loving environment for their children. A healthy society evolves as families in communities multiply this shared family love with others. As communities prosper, so does the entire society. The love expressed between spouses has a positive influence on all the lives they touch, including their own. "Moreover, the men who are 'the best marriage bets' are those who are more traditional in their family and religious background."[11]

The positive effect on the wife and husband's lives is well documented. Because of sharing their energies and resources, married couples are better off financially than are single people. The marital relationship gives both members a communication outlet to relieve stress and to maintain a steady course. There is less depression or abuse of alcohol and drugs amongst married couples. In essence, married people are healthier, better functioning, happier, and live longer than single people.[12] Furthermore, married people have greater sexual satisfaction than cohabiting couples.[13]

Marriage is good for society, the couple, and especially the children. The teaching and training of mother as wife and father as husband has a profound influence on the child's ability to successfully negotiate life. Parents will give the love and training necessary for the child to prosper on all levels in life. A child in a functioning family will have the nurturing, character development, and discipline to be strong in most situations. When the child is having difficulty, the parents will be there with advice and needed support. Parents, especially fathers, assist the child in developing inner courage to face the difficulties of the world. Children raised by a healthy mother and father in a strong marriage are indeed fortunate. Evil-intentioned people will bypass a healthy child and look for weaker prey.

A fortunate child has two united parents working toward becoming better and better friends. The parents' efforts in developing a functioning marriage allows the child a front-row seat in learning how to negotiate one of the most, if not the most, difficult task of life. The lessons learned may be mostly on an unconscious level but will shape the attitudes, values, and beliefs in the child's journey through life. The state of the marriage of the children's parents has a direct bearing on the development of the children. A father and mother in constant battle present a warlike picture of intimate relationships, while parents in a more mutually nurturing relationship give entirely different perspectives to their children. Through their relationship parents plant the seeds in a child who will more easily develop inner peace or will gravitate toward more unfair and selfish ways of dealing with others.

The Stages of Marriage Currently Held in Our Culture

No one falls in love by choice, it is by CHANCE.

No one stays in love by chance, it is by WORK.

No one falls out of love by chance, it is by CHOICE.

In the quarter of a century I have had a private counseling practice dealing with marriage, I have found there are six stages in a healthy marriage. There are six fluid, not necessarily sequential, and not mutually exclusive, phases in marriage. A couple travels from one stage to another in order to obtain the highest form of marital love.

A couple probably will enter the infatuation honeymoon stage before or after marriage in our romantically oriented society. This honeymoon stage usually lasts up to two years. After the spell of the honeymoon wears off, most couples will begin the "power struggle." Every couple enters the "power struggle" stage. Well-functioning couples learn to pass on to the "fair negotiation" stage. Even well-functioning couples might waver between the "power struggle" and "fair negotiation" stages. Dysfunctional couples are primarily stuck in the "power struggle" stage and never understand the advantages of the win-win "fair negotiation" stage. With the passing of time the "commitment-loyalty" stage and "faithful-trust" stage grow until culmination in the "uniting in spiritual friendship" stage. Marriage is not as simple as finding a "soul mate" that will insure a loving relationship.

After the selection of the mate, the marriage needs time to "age" like a slab of concrete. Time allows for hardening of the foundation. Though stress cracks on the surface might appear, the cement on the bottom is growing harder and stronger each passing day. A marriage is an evolving process where each phase is present from the beginning and each phase has a period of dominance that leads to the next phase. Marriage is a complicated process that requires time and effort to reach its ultimate goal of love.

When a marriage is evolving toward the spiritual uniting of two people, children unconsciously learn to feel the warmth of a mature, healthy love. Its impact on the health or difficulties of the child should not be underestimated. A functional, loving marriage decreases the risk of children being devastated by negative forces of life.

Stages of Marriage

1. Infatuated honeymoon
2. Power struggle
3. Fair negotiation
4. Committed merger
5. Mutual trust
6. United in spiritual friendship

Infatuated/Honeymoon Stage: Temporary Insanity

Contrary to Hollywood brainwashing, this is not the highest form of love. It is normally the first step and though helpful it is not a necessary step. In modern times infatuation has jump-started most long-term relationships, giving the man and woman emotional motivation and courage to join hands in marriage.

In older cultures, arranged marriages by relatives were the major impetus for the status change of two young adults. The young couple, under strict supervision, was allowed to thoroughly know about the other person's history while having limited exposure to the person. Family well-being and status, not infatuation, were the driving forces in this type of marriage. The couple was expected to develop feelings of attraction during courtship or after beginning the marriage. Infatuation in many ancient societies is considered a form of temporary insanity that needs to be restrained in making long-term marital decisions.

In our Smugger mass media, Hollywood-influenced culture, "love" is superficial infatuation. In this synthetic world a person can fall instantly in love anytime, anywhere with little pertinent knowledge of the person to whom they are attracted. Young people, taking a cue from Hollywood, are always in the most loving relationship that has ever existed on the face of the earth. The first sign of frustration sends them off chasing the latest "hottie."

Infatuation is addictive. Scientists have demonstrated that there are significant chemical changes including heightened endorphins active in the human brain when two people fall in love or fall into temporary insanity. One of my clients who is forty-three years old had been married six times with no relationship lasting more than eight months. She also had many dating relationships with none of them lasting as long as eight months. When the endorphins wore off, so did her relationship.

In historic America, individuals may have initiated a relationship with the opposite sex with significant positive influence from the parents. Courtship was scripted with rules of conduct. The girl's parents met the boy before they allowed their daughter to date. Discussion took place as to the type of family of the suitor. For the most part, young adults took their parents' advice into consideration. The girl's parents

paid for the wedding ceremony. The wedding was a celebration showing the community that the family sanctioned the marriage to the community as much as it was a day for the bride and groom. After the
natural chemical high wore off, the family was there to support the
couple through thick and thin. Adults were wise enough to realize all
young people in the initial state of love believe they have met their perfect mate until their eyes focus on reality and see their mate's imperfections. This moves us on to the next stage of marriage.

Power Struggle: Ego Communication Interference

After the couple comes down from cloud nine, crashing their feet on
firm reality, the battle of the sexes begins. The traditional tendencies
of the woman to nurture and set up a nest and the man's desires for
control over the working and domestic environment have been blurred.
With some effort, the traditional roles are still recognizable. Social engineering beginning in the 1960s by the women's liberation movement
muddied the waters of the different tendencies between males and
females. Though the role reversals are much more common, the battles have not ceased. They have just changed their form. The aggressive career woman and the sensitive, nurturing man may have switched
roles but the need for understanding each other is still evident.

Merging two distinct worlds of a man and a woman is a challenging
undertaking that often takes a half-century of effort. The effort of combining two perspectives is often the cause of great frustration and the
opportunity for greater understanding of self and spouse. It helps the
participants better appreciate the other half of the world's population.
Obviously the emotional, physical, and mental differences of the sexes
have been the source of recurrent themes in art throughout the ages.
The struggle of the two different sexual perspectives of resolving these
human issues is a wonderful impetus for personal growth or a source
of conflict.

Closeness enables couples to hurt each other without any effort. A spouse often blames his mate with a statement the spouse has made in anger as the true feelings of the spouse. It is just as unfair to attribute true feelings to emotional outbursts as to dramatic displays of affection. Genuine feelings are established by meaningful actions over time.

Conflict between spouses is inevitable throughout the relationship. At the beginning of the relationship, couples search for methods to resolve the issue more effectively. The communication skills developed are helpful in putting into perspective selfish ego needs that interfere with developing a meaningful relationship.

Instead of putting effort into clarifying the issues, some couples resort to lying and deception. These couples appear to the community and at times to their immediate family to be a "perfect pair." The truth is a different story. Their relationship is not intimate, they do not merge together. The couple develops superficial relationships with others to maintain their personal emotional needs in their dying marriage.

On the other hand, some people appear to be stuck in conflict without any merging of their worlds taking place. This can be misleading, especially to the children of these couples and to the couples themselves. Not until a separation by illness, death, or divorce does the wife or husband realistically evaluate the significance of their mate to their own lives. Sometimes these separations make them grow fonder and sometimes it leads to regret.

My wife's aunt and uncle did not appear to have a nice word to say to each other for the past twenty years. Bickering over almost everything was their pattern. Yet they remained together for nearly fifty years until the wife died of cancer. As soon as his wife died, all loving memories flooded Uncle Frank's mind. "She was wonderful in this or that," crying as each one reminded him of what he had with his wife. The tragic part is that the fixation on the battle of the sexes prevented them from celebrating their life together and blending their two separate worlds into a fuller life.

This scenario, unfortunately, is a common one. My parents were, and many of my counseling clients are, stuck in the power struggle phase of marriage. It leads many people to shy away from the traditional institution of marriage, believing love cannot endure in a long-term marriage. The reality of the difficulty of this phase of marriage has frightened perhaps the majority of young people into viewing marriage as a romance that can and will be dissolved at the first sign of leaving the honeymoon and entering the power struggle phase of marriage.

This romantic distortion of marriage has opened a Pandora's box of problems resulting in widespread discontent, disillusion, and abuse in marriage. As the head of a domestic violence counseling program for a decade, I learned that abuse takes many forms in the unrealistic world of perpetual honeymoon. All the participants entered the program through the court system after having a disturbance where the police were dispatched. Over the years, I experienced many individuals who came back for group counseling with a new mate, married or unmarried. The unresolved issues remained the same: flirting, money, friends, jealousy, children, time, dominance, and their naïve, adolescent, dogmatic notion of "love." Love was a positive concrete feeling, not a process of two people growing together through treating each other as friends with mutual respect. Each attempted to gain an advantage over the other through some form of deception. There was subtle manipulation or rigid control but there was always an absence of honesty on the part of one or both. My mission was to encourage honest communication. I encouraged the couples to move away from the fear of intimacy and toward beginning the process of fair negotiation. This could give them a glimpse of the long-term process of moving to ultimate love.

Fair Negotiation: Teamwork

This phase is instrumental in getting a couple unstuck from the power struggle stages. Once a couple understands that by being just in their interactions with their mate as well as demanding to be treated fairly, a healthy world of communication opens up to both. Similarly, an honest business transaction only happens when a seller and buyer agree on a mutually satisfying price. This is a win-win situation for both seller and buyer. In the same way, when there is open and honest agreement on how to divvy up resources, each individual realizes the benefits of working together to reach their goals. Even when their individual goals are not mutual, a trade-off takes place. "You meet your particular goal and I will take the next turn to meet my individual objective." Through the process of fair negotiation, both parties see how the long-term vision of being together can work for each of them.

The three A's of a mature relationship begin to emerge: acceptance, approval, and appreciation. The difference between the sexes is accepted as a probable asset in certain situations. Instead of battling, the mate approves and uses the uniqueness of the other person. This utilization turns into appreciation when the desired results are achieved. As couples receive the benefits of the fair negotiation stage, awareness of the next phase of committed loyalty becomes highly probable.

Committed Merger: Shift in Independence, Dependence, and Interdependence

This phase of marriage builds on the successes of fair negotiating. The self-protective urge of being an independent, self-sufficient individual slowly evaporates as a couple resolves daily problems. Over time couples unconsciously merge many aspects of their lives to eliminate unnecessary hassles. As the couple overcomes more and more obstacles, settling on methods to blend their marital vision into a more viable whole, they are drawn together. The outside world defines them more as a definitive couple and the couple becomes more aware of the importance of the relationship to each of them. Children accentuate the importance of the union between husband and wife not only for each other but also for the whole family. The continued merger into the social fabric of the community strengthens the commitment of the couple.

These forces bring the couple to a heightened awareness that any breakdown in their allegiance toward each other will negatively impact themselves as well as the interdependent relationships they have with others. This means their biological families, close friends, and nuclear family provide a support system binding them together. The developing of dependence and interdependence that attracts the two individuals together reverses the independent urge of self-absorption prevalent in the power struggle phase that propels each spouse into a separate world. The need for independence still remains, although in smaller proportion, while the dependence and interdependence become more significant. The committed loyalty of the couple is a response to the evolution of a long-term intimate relationship.

Mutual Trust: Beyond the Fear of Intimacy

As they continue the merging of their lives, the couple increasingly trusts each other. As the journey continues toward a mature friendship, both parties view the growing intimacy less as vulnerability and more as a blessed relationship. The couple moves closer and closer with greater assurance that neither of them would jeopardize their creation by unfaithfulness.

Their fears of intimacy are all but nonexistent now. Each knows the other to almost the point of predictability. Any deviation in the perception of the other is grist for discussion. This couple has come a long way from power struggles. The faithful trust stage allows both to grow closer together through caring about the other. Both husband and wife know their lives are so interwoven that the other would not risk their own future by altering the destiny of the other. There is a continuing refinement of the blending of their goals until neither husband nor wife can envision when they were separate. The accumulating experiences and mutual accomplishments bind them inextricably together for the final years of their lives.

United in Spiritual Friendship: The Merging of Love

Wife and husband, after many years on the path of life together, arrive back into the loving feelings of two hands fitting perfectly together as in a clasp. It is like God provides couples an introductory taste or a coming attraction to the power of love. Instead the final stage of uniting in spiritual friendship is not a tease, it is not an illusion, it is the real thing. It does not go up in smoke when you see the real person you married; instead it grows truer and deeper. The imperfections become their uniqueness. What were once annoyances become fodder for laughter. The trials and tribulations of the past become the landmarks signifying the couple's greatest accomplishments.

This true love is not based on hormonal changes. It is based on spiritual awareness that the husband and wife were blessed by a higher power. As the couple lived a moral life together, each phase helped the couple appreciate the next. No phase was distinct from the other but each phase led to another, leaving behind the selfish concerns of the individual and forging a more selfless relationship. Through the difficult process of uniting with each other in true friendship, both husband and wife become more in spiritual harmony.

Accident, illness, or infirmities of the aging process are not viewed as excuses for shying away from the loved one but an opportunity to assist and show love. Being there in sickness and in health is a sign of mature love. Nancy Reagan's devotion to her husband, President Ronald Reagan, during the ten-year period he was suffering from Alzheimer's disease is a powerful reminder to all of us about the meaning of love. There is no need for excuses, only opportunities for being there for each other.

Finally there is true acceptance, approval, and appreciation. The three A's of a loving relationship are everywhere to be found. The couple better understands they are uniting on every level.

The journey through marriage is not necessarily a smooth one. It has ups and downs. Raising children places great financial, emotional, and social stress on a couple, although the investment for the couple has a potential windfall for them. Through the process of raising children, people learn about themselves and are drawn closer together as husband and wife. The children become the legacy of the parents' relationship. The children often assist their parents as they become aged and infirm.

Traditional Marriage Is a Win-Win for Spouse, Children, and Society

Everyone wins when the institution of marriage is healthy. The couple creates a family together that carries on the legacy of their parents, family, and their nation. Being blessed with healthy children allows parents the opportunity to learn the cyclical nature of life. By naturally evolving through the life cycle of being a child to raising a child to witnessing your children raise their children, we gain a fuller understanding of the meaning of life.

Marriage is a journey that provides us the necessary structure in various segments of our trip to keep us moving forward in meaningful aspects of life. The euphoria of coming together to begin an intimate relationship with another, the awe of giving birth to a child, the gratification of knowing the adulthood successes of your child, the spirituality of experiencing the birth of your grandchild, all shape marriage into a sacred adventure. The cycle of life is our destiny unfolding. The opportunities and responsibilities of each stage of life enhance the meaning of our lives.

Woe to the Smuggers who have not one concrete accomplishment to point to except for their history of pleasure and accumulated wealth. By squandering their lives on illusions of pleasure, no one gains and everyone loses. As their bodies age, their backward glances can only horrify them. There are diminishing numbers of lovers and experiences until they stand alone. There are no children or grandchildren, no family to share their journey. There is only a wasted existence with minimal positive impact on others or any contribution to society.

Marriage is an institution that supports the creation of a healthy family. There is no greater blessing to one's life than to leave a legacy of children grown into responsible citizens. The family provides opportunity to impact others. There is the support and interdependence of two mature adults. Each adult teaches and learns from the person of the opposite sex. The uniting of these two individuals creates an optimal environment for raising a family. The daily decisions of united parents shape highly functioning contributors to society. The ever-expanding network of good deeds that emanates from a healthy family pays dividends to the entire community. The legacy of a traditional family gives the vitality to a nation that allows us to be free. Traditional families are the essential social units of a free nation.

Chapter 6

Demeaning to Elevating Parenthood

You are about to walk out of Wal-Mart. "Code Adam" comes over the loud speakers and the automatic doors do not open. The store is locked down because a mother reported her child missing somewhere in the store. Twenty-five minutes later, you see the mother and child reunited. You and almost everyone else in the store burst into applause.

The only humiliated person in the store is the child's mother. She knows her child was not in danger of being abducted but was just up to her old trick of hiding from her mother. She was found in the toy aisle with a Ken doll to match her Barbie. The child kept on repeating, "Don't hurt me, don't hurt me."

The mother kept her eyes straight ahead, attempting to conceal her embarrassment. The child left the store smiling. She knew she had won again. Since it was her birthday she knew she would still get all the presents and special treats her mother had just purchased even though she had caused a scene in the store. She knew that in one hour her relatives and friends would be gathering at her home and would insure the cooling-off period for her mother. There would be few, if any, consequences for her inappropriate behavior.

The mother did not tell her husband about the incident. She knew he did not want to know. Besides, he would only fly off the handle if he heard what his daughter had done. The mother in this case, like most modern parents, has absorbed the mythology of the child development experts as cultural fact.

Parents have been indoctrinated to be friendly, not strict. Her husband's reactions would be more punitive and her job was to protect her daughter from his becoming upset. This inherent conflict causes the modern parent to become ineffectual. The maternal instinct makes mothers susceptible to being overprotective of their children.

The importance of parenthood has been systematically degraded. Parenting has become a big hassle rather than a blessing. This developmental phase of having a family is rushed for our children and ourselves to be free of even the minimal responsibilities and sacrifices that the Smuggers' permissive and materialistic approach describes.

There Is No Pro-Choice for Children

Even the sanctity of birth has been reduced to a frivolous choice of life or death. Smuggers have been successful in marketing abortion (killing fetuses) as a politically correct concept. There is no pro-choice for the child, only death.

Abortion has been outside my personal radar screen for the past thirty years, as my wife and I were busy raising our four children. Throughout my almost three decades of psychotherapy practice, I was informed by my clients about their personal abortion regrets. I was struck that almost all thought about some aspect of the abortion even when they had their own families. People who were not able to bear other children were often the most preoccupied by "what if the child had been allowed to be born." Men, too, have emotional reactions to abortion. According to Michael Y. Simon, a psychotherapist who counsels men after abortions: "These men often deny themselves the experience of grieving."[1] I knew on an intellectual level that abortion was a personally devastating process for everyone involved.

But it wasn't until our grandson's birth that this issue hit home emotionally. My daughter-in-law had a difficult pregnancy. She had to take large amounts of steroids to keep her food down. We all prayed that the medication would not harm the baby. Never did my son and daughter-in-law contemplate abortion. Thank God, the baby is wonderfully healthy and a great joy to the entire family. My daughter-in-law stated on her son's first birthday that she knew he would be perfect. What incredible faith she has!

My daughter and two daughters-in-law have shown us the sonogram pictures of their new pregnancies. Each couple proudly pointed out details of the pictures. My daughter had an actual video of her eleven-week-old showing the fetus's heart beating, kicking its leg, and sucking its thumb. All three of the women were glowing with the blessing of expectant motherhood. The whole family shared in their excitement. It stunned all of us to see how complete a human being can be at only eleven weeks.

Every fetus deserves the opportunity to pursue a life journey. No selfish concern of the biological parents should be allowed to destroy a life. Many medical institutions have removed the prohibition of abortion from the Hippocratic oath or replaced it with the politically correct document entitled "The Charter on Medical Professionalism,"[2] which does not address abortion.

No moral physician can exterminate a fetus's life for the convenience of sexually irresponsible adults. Our society should hold biological parents and doctor-executioners accountable for their actions instead of legitimizing the death of our youth. The good of our society requires each of us to courageously speak up against the culture of death, breaking our silence of tacit acceptance. Women have a choice in the use of their bodies for sexual activities, not a choice to kill a child to eliminate their sexual indiscretions.

Smugglers have done a wonderful job of dehumanizing the miracle of having children. Young adults of today are desensitized to the impact of abortion on starting their own families. A seventeen-year-old girl came to me for counseling because her parents were concerned with her dating an impulsive, angry young man. She noted that he behaved similarly to all of her peer group. She said she was sexually active and when I asked her what she would do if she became pregnant, she replied without the blink of an eye that she would have an abortion. She did not feel that there was anything morally reprehensible about having an abortion. She believed it would be free of any psychological consequences.

Consumerism and the
Decreasing the Value of Parenthood

Our culture places money, career, personal independence, and entertainment before responsibility for one's family. There is the occasional lip service given by leaders of the community, but the overall cultural message is loud and clear. Raising a healthy family is less important than the car you drive, the numbers in your bank account, or the gated community in which you live. We live in a detached, non-judgmental society. Getting involved with our children is low in our priorities—we have too many other things to do.

Yet children today are more likely to need a longer time to be launched into adulthood. A study from the University of Chicago stated most Americans believe adulthood begins at age twenty-six.[3] The dependence of modern children on the family for their success is much greater today than in the past. But today's parents appear to be oblivious about their impact on teaching their children to make mature judgments. The quality of child-rearing is probably more important today than at any other time in the past.

Parents are making choices every hour of every day about raising their children. Modern parents cannot hide behind ignorance because there are so many available sources of information on raising children. The evidence of our child-rearing practices is readily observable in our homes and communities and is documented daily in the mass media.

Smuggers Advise Too Much Freedom and Too Little Protection

The Smuggers' child-rearing approach of allowing and encouraging the child to be in charge of the family before their diapers are off or bribing them into compliance has been and is an utter disaster.

The advice of the pseudoscientific child development industry is not solving the problem. There is an epidemic of out-of-control children noted in every public setting and officially documented by Steven Hyman, director of the National Institute for Mental Health. "About 13 million children under the age of eighteen, about one in five, have a diagnosable mental disorder, six million children have a serious emotional disturbance."[4]

Deep down, modern parents know the importance of their involvement in their child's life. In a "freedom at any price" society, parents and children are confronted with rampant temptation. Sex and violence are marketing tools aimed at our children by Hollywood, the music industry, merchandizing, and deviant interest groups. The celebrities—gangsta rappers, Hollywood stars, shock jocks, radio, TV, and sports stars—usually take no responsibility for their impact on children by using the ridiculous arguments of freedom of speech: "I'm an artist or entertainer, not a role model," "I'm only doing my thing." When the spokespeople of the celebrities or interest groups are pressed as to their responsibility in corrupting vulnerable youth their voice is united in responding, "It is up to the parents to protect their children."

Modern parents don't make the effort to protect their children from many negative influences, which means children are raising themselves.

Parents will be surprised by their child's abnormal behavior and take a limited amount of their precious time to take him to a specialist. The specialist will take a limited amount of his precious time to label and drug the child to quell the symptom. What could be better? Parents can go back to business as usual and the child can seek out his "virtual media" parents to be further corrupted.

The Wise Man Alternative

The alternative to our laissez-faire approach to raising children is to return to the lost art and knowledge of child-rearing, perfected over centuries. To uncover this lost art and knowledge we would have to seek out a wise man or woman in some hidden mountain range or jungle, unaffected by our global mass media. This wise person would have successfully navigated life's stages and raised a healthy family.

However, the traditional wise man would be a laughingstock in our society if he attempted to assist a parent having problems with his child. The advice of the sage if followed would probably work but would go against all the PC child development psychobabble that has been accepted as cultural fact.

"Yes, wise man, punishing my child would teach him a lesson, but he will no longer like me."

"Yes, wise man, I could give my daughter the cold shoulder until she listens, but she will be psychologically traumatized."

"Yes, wise man, I could not take my son on the trip but I will be punishing myself by missing the trip."

The modern parent would eventually tell the wise man that his traditional methods might be effective but they take too much work and sacrifice. The modern parent would argue that appeasing, ignoring, negotiating, and redirecting may be ineffective, but are much less time-consuming and require less effort.

The reality is that children need parents in any environment—especially in our present day, less-than-moral world. Human infants do not have the instincts to survive without the protection of their parents. Besides physical nurturing, parents in a sophisticated society need to provide systematic discipline to develop positive character traits for the child to successfully survive in an immoral environment. The involvement of both mothers and fathers is necessary to raise an overall healthy child. Anything less than a united team of father and mother working together is placing the child and society at a disadvantage.

Is Two Parents Optimal?

It takes a maternal, loving mother and a strong, demanding father to give the children a well-rounded perception of the world. The children learn they are unique and wonderful people with a great future who are taught they must earn their success. The dual message of love and personal responsibility gives children the character to reach their goals. There are surrogates for single-parent families that can compensate for a missed parent. Optimally it is best for a child to be raised by a loving husband and wife.

A healthy child has parents who act like parents and teach courage and social limits to help their child successfully navigate the complexities of life. A child without parental guidance to modulate his behavior will be out of balance in any world. In a complex society, a child raising himself will either learn to exercise too much or too little aggression in order to survive. It is the responsibility of the parents to fine-tune the genetic tendencies of the individual child. It is the parents' everyday choices that will mold the child into a successful and peaceful child.

This chapter will explain why and how parents should not disregard their responsibilities and obligations to be actively involved in shaping the character of their child. The permissive and materialistic Smugger approach is an abdication of parenthood. Allowing children to raise themselves while the adults focus on making money has been a disaster resulting in an epidemic of mental disorders for children.

I will argue for the return of parents being parents instead of being phony friends. Only through a parent's actually raising a child with strong moral character can the child and society have the ability to be peaceful.

The dividends for the parents will be incredible. Parents will gain wisdom, friendship, and respect from their responsible actions. Raising a child is a spiritual growth process. Children will reap all that the parents provide. Each family member will enrich the lives of all. The so-called sacrifices will nurture their family to blossom into the major asset of their life. They will be a gift to the future generations of their family.

The traditional child-rearing methods I will discuss are addressed in greater depth in my book, *Essential Parenting: Revitalizing and Remoralizing the Family in the 21st Century*.

The Modern Non-Parent: Excuses, Excuses, Excuses

In an airport, the children run in a circle while the parents sit in rows chatting with each other or smiling almost in approval of the children's misbehavior. The few men present ignore the behavior of their children. The two- to four-year-olds run, giggle, crawl, and jump recklessly. The older preteen joins in the chaos and chases the little children around the entire viewing section of the airport. One mother finally gets up to stop her child from squeezing through a second-story guardrail and falling thirty feet. The uncle and father joke with each other while looking nonchalantly at the potential danger.

The scene is repeated in many other settings, not only in the U.S., but all over the world. The above incident took place in the Lima, Peru, international airport. Parents are not enforcing the rules of decency for their children in public places. Children finally stop terrorizing our public spaces only from exhaustion. The new casual philosophy is "let children be children" or "I'm not responsible for my child's actions," or "don't bother me, I am merely the sperm donor or receiver."

Modern parents do not view parenthood as a sacred responsibility. The notion of teaching and training a child to be a responsible and successful adult has been eliminated. It has been replaced by a philosophy that believes children will raise themselves while parents can pursue more self-centered interests. When parents are embarrassed by their child's behavior there are many convenient rationalizations available.

"I don't want her not to love me." This statement is parents' rationalization for not doing their duty. Modern parents have difficulty teaching their children right from wrong because they themselves have been taught the ridiculous notion that a child has to always be happy. When the parents' primary goal is to want the child to always love them, they are paralyzed as disciplinarians. Rather than the child fearing the parents' reaction to a misdeed, the child actually laughs at the parents' weakness.

Parents who want their child to unconditionally love them, even when they are disciplining the child, are more than weak, they are foolish. A child will not like a parent in the short run when they are being disciplined but in the long run the child appreciates it. Afterwards, the young child may try to make up by showing affection to the disciplining parent. The overall evaluation of the parental discipline may not show up until grandchildren are born. That is when the now adult child gives the parent the ultimate, but perhaps left-handed compliment, "I am doing just what you did to me (that I hated as a child) when I discipline my own child." Conscientious parents eventually will reap their just rewards. The only thing necessary is to have patience and live long enough to have grandchildren!

Parents must conditionally give out their rewards, only for the child's appropriate behavior. It is the parents' responsibility to mold the child to have good character. To give rewards to a child irrespective of the quality of his behavior is a prescription for raising a discipline problem. Giving unconditional love to the child and expecting unconditional love in return is utter fantasy and is destructive to both parent and child.

"My child is just like me." This is an indicator of lazy parenting. Usually a parent makes the statement "my child is just like me" as a means of defending the child. When a child has difficulty in math, the parent may respond, "He's just like me, I'm terrible in math, too." A client said about his son's drug addiction, "He is just like me when I was his age." His statement was unfortunately made in front of the sixteen-year-old son. This condones his and his child's self-destructive behavior.

Regardless of the situation, "my child is just like me" is said to emphasize a negative trait of the parent and connecting it to the child is a mean act. It is an easy excuse for the child and becomes a self-fulfilling prophecy. Just because the parent did not compensate for some difficulty does not mean the child should not be encouraged to do so.

"I don't want my child to be traumatized." This means the world is on notice to check with the parents, usually the mother, before doing anything around the child. The precious child should be protected from any discomfort, intentional or otherwise. Parents attempt to make their child the center of other people's worlds. Instead of the child being required to learn to cope with others, the others have to check with the parents before doing anything. This unrealistic expectation on the part of the parents not only creates a frustrating situation of attempting to control other adults but also encourages a whining, tattletale child. Children need to learn what is good and bad from successful elders, not falsely believe the world revolves around them.

"My child is shy." When parents announce this to others it is a warning that the child will not be socially appropriate. The child will not say "hello," shake hands, make eye contact, sit upright, or respond when spoken to by an adult. The child may not be loud or outwardly aggressive but the child is quietly defiant. The child's disregard of the mother's pleas to do the right thing is a sign of ineffectual parenting, not a defective gene.

"My child is very smart." The translation of this statement is "my child is uninhibited and says uncivil and insensitive things, so don't be offended." The parent of a verbally inappropriate child is preparing the adults to the real possibility of verbal abuse while interpreting to the adult the child's obnoxiousness as a sign of intelligence. The truth is the parents have done a poor job teaching and training their child in respectful and appropriate behavior and are making excuses for him. Outrageous, spontaneous expressions by a child do not demonstrate a superior intelligence but do indicate a lack of understanding of the appropriate behavior in social situations.

"How cute he or she is!" Children are not dolls: they are future adults. Whenever a parent attempts to show off her child, it is a bad sign. Usually the child is being called cute when the child is being obnoxious. A three-year-old girl came to my office with her mother and father for a school admission interview. When I asked her what her name was, she smiled and pointed to her dress. She said, "flower" but refused to answer direct questions. She acted "cute," dancing around the room while her parents grinned in delight. Their daughter was told by her parents to sit in the chair. She smiled at them and walked around the room as she pleased. She was disobedient in her passive-aggressive manner. Even if the child's inappropriate behavior tickles us, we have no right to smile or laugh and give him license to do the wrong thing.

"It is easier to do it myself." The reason many children do not pitch in and help their parents is that parents do not take the time and effort to teach their child the necessary steps to complete their chores. Too many children act dumb. Calling the child's bluff means confrontation. In the short run, it is easier for the parent just to do the task. In the long run, everyone loses. The parents wind up being responsible for the child's duties while the child becomes incompetent in another area. The child loses the opportunity to learn organization, time management, and a host of physical skills and instead develops a sense of hopelessness.

I am clinically witnessing a large number of young adults in their twenties who do not want to learn to drive nor become independent from their parents. They are not motivated to grow up. They are not unhappy about the limits of their status or being dependent on others. Their lack of courage to move into a more responsible role stems from the missed opportunities by parents to upgrade their child's duties.

Parenting Is a Sacred Responsibility: Charity Begins at Home

Once you are blessed with a child, parenting becomes a sacred responsibility. If parents do not take this responsibility seriously, they are demeaning this sacred privilege.

When parents raise healthy, productive children, everyone benefits. Parents are essential in developing morally strong people. Adults whose lives are balanced contribute to society instead of requiring others to take care of them. Parents who make the sacrifices necessary to provide their children with a safe, disciplined, and loving environment build a peaceful nation. The parents' sacrifice for their children is the most powerful form of charity. Charity at home pays dividends to the child, community, nation, and especially to the parents.

Parents who do not spend sufficient time preparing themselves for the additional responsibility of being a parent enter this stage of life at a distinct disadvantage. The lack of mental, social, emotional, and financial preparation will negatively influence this privileged and blessed experience. The inability to make an adult commitment to their children is a sign of self-centeredness that can lead to an impulsive action that ends in disaster.

When parents do not nurture and discipline their child properly, they will eventually reach the point of disliking and rejecting the child. A little bit of effort at home with one's children can establish a positive environment for everyone.

Sometime, usually in the twilight of our lives, we contemplate what our existence has meant to others. For most of us our most lasting impact will be on our families. If we did an excellent job as a parent, our children and succeeding generations will follow the traditions we taught.

The Five Generation Rule

Sociologists have defined this phenomenon as the "Five Generation Rule." The research found that the impact of parents on their children lasts for five generations.[5] The way parents raise their children, the love given, the values taught, and the emotional environment created influences not only their children but also the four generations to follow. The blessings of good or sins of bad parenting have long-term consequences on a family. The effect also works in reverse with the family members suffering from the sins of the parents.

Parents using traditional child-rearing methods have a greater chance of raising a well-balanced child. These children are individuals who have time-tested opportunities to develop into well-balanced adults. Children raised traditionally are grounded in a disciplined moral life. This moral discipline gives them inner guidance and fortitude.

They possess the strength to be peaceful, eliminating the vulnerability and insecurity of becoming a bully or wimp.

The "Five Generation Rule" suggests a responsible traditional parent will develop a lasting legacy. By unleashing the wisdom of our ancestors, our nation will continue to prosper. By following our Smugger "experts," we will continue down the path of eliminating the strength of our families. Parents make all the difference in the world in raising a strong, peaceful child or a child out-of-balance. There are no social institutions that can replace the family headed by two involved parents. Alternate lifestyle families are detrimental to the health of children. Two committed parents united in purpose have a greater chance of producing a strong, peaceful child than does a divided home. Parents need to be parents or risk the possibility of developing out-of-balance, weak, and wimpy or overly aggressive, bullying children. Although parents have the most personally at stake in the behavior of their children, it is in the interest of the entire society to support effective parenting and the traditional two-parent family. A healthy functioning American family is an investment our nation can no longer ignore.

Time, Energy, and Keeping One's Word

Being a quality parent requires an investment of time and energy. Any parent who does not keep his word loses the respect of and often creates animosity among those around him. A person known as not keeping his word is untrustworthy. To accept the word of a dubious individual and to discover another deception makes the accepting person feel like a fool. Even a skeptical person will feel uncomfortable around him, for his intentions are not predictable or clear. For example, a parent tells his child that next year they will definitely go on a trip to Europe. Next year and the year after, there is a new excuse and disappointment.

People doing what they say they will is necessary for healthy inter-action. A parent who does not keep his word negatively affects a child. The lack of predictability of the parent forces the child into an unpre-dictable world. Often the child takes control to establish structure. The parent is disregarded or the child acts out to get the parent to perform the expected duties of a parent. In either case, the child is the loser.

Children need a parent who does what he says in order to learn how to behave in the world of the family. A parent who does not keep his word creates a chaotic, dysfunctional environment for the child. A par-ent's effectiveness is as good as his word. The lack of follow-through after a parent says he is going to do a certain thing weakens the credi-bility of the parent and empowers the child to continue these inappro-priate ways. On the other hand, parents who keep their word teach their child that parents mean what they say. The child learns playing games will not work. Parents who follow through and are consistent will produce reasonable children.

The expression "the apple doesn't fall far from the tree" is as true today as it has been in the past. Like it or not, parents have an impact on their children. Just by being there, parents are role models for their child. The child is a sponge and as any parent quickly learns, the child imitates all of their behaviors. As a young parent of four children, I was shocked to see my worst traits reflected in my children's mannerisms and language while the positive behaviors had to be pointed out by fam-ily members and friends.

Children exposed to addictive, abusive, or neglectful parents have a much harder row to hoe in life. I know this is judgmental, but parents who make poor parental decisions are responsible for the outcome of their child's life in the same way that parents who do the right thing will reap the rewards of their efforts. Many self-absorbed parents miss this truth. The truth is, healthy parents who are on the same wave-length produce children headed in the right direction.

United Parents Foster Stability

United parents minimize conflict, while divided parents will soon be seeking family counseling. Parents need to speak with one voice if they want to be effective. Responsible parents will have to get the child to do many things he dislikes to prepare him for adulthood. Good parents will be strict from the child's perspective. They will not be the child's friends. Parents remaining together "on the same page" prevent the child from attempting to divide and conquer the parents by modern-day manipulation techniques.

The opposite of being united is to be divided. Division invites conflict. When one parent sides with the child, the other parent becomes resentful. The child is the victim because he does not receive the necessary teaching and training from his parents. The constant bickering, the counseling couch, and ultimately the divorce court are the end products of a divided house.

Traditional Values and Morals
Are Fertile Ground for Peace

No matter how hard the Smugger "intelligentsia" has tried in socialism, communism, and presently in imposing "new age" values from the top down, it will not be as successful as traditional values. These values were developed over centuries from the grass roots. Traditional values were adopted by nations in the past and are present all over the world because they work. Traditional values of honesty, respect, responsibility, hard work, the Golden Rule, and the Ten Commandments are irreplaceable in developing a peaceful, stable society.

These desired behavior patterns create a predictable and safe world. Conformity in behavior is the expected order while some nonconformity is tolerated as long as it does not severely affect others or threaten the survival of the society. Tolerance of all kinds of behaviors leads to chaos in a family or a nation. A civilization must discriminate between behaviors, assigning them worth or non-worth. Any type of organization needs rules that are followed to successfully function.

Any Civilization Has to Discriminate Between Behaviors

In a world of constant flux, people expend immense energy in rediscovering the wheel. Chaos is a great motivator for people to seek stability, causing most of us to return to our immediate family. In a faddish world of excessive freedom of choice, people lose sight of what is important. When an accumulation of material possessions or experiences becomes the primary focus of the society, the society is losing its spiritual purpose. The family with traditional values being sacrificed at the altar of material wealth is a sign of decadence. Consumerism cannot sustain a society.

It is the mother and father's concern for their children that acts as a gauge to keep priorities in the correct order. A common change in many families will shift the direction of a nation. The health of the family led by parents is the best indicator of a civilization. As families have failed in the great civilizations such as the Incan, Greek, Roman, or Mesopotamian, so have they in this civilization.

The Golden Rule is found throughout the world, in Islam, Hinduism, Christianity, Buddhism, and Judaism, to name just a few locations. The Ten Commandments enjoy universal acceptance as well.

The Incas of Peru greeted each other with, "do not lie, do not steal, and do not be lazy." This message, along with the Incan principles of "to know, to do, and to love," would not alienate any successful culture. If an individual learns about the world around him and uses the knowledge he has gained to the optimal level of his ability, everyone in his community and nation will profit. If a person lies, steals, and is lazy everyone will suffer. The Incas banished the wrongdoer from the community.

Confucius taught about the importance of family ethics for the viability of society. We have lost many of his teachings. In the U.S. we have ever-increasing tolerance for unacceptable behavior. In a PC world we rationalize the most predatory behavior and the perpetrator rarely receives just and swift punishment. *We are weakening our society.*

Morality is naturally taught in the family. The mother sets the tone of morality while the father is the natural enforcer of the rules. Parents working together with discipline can accomplish raising a child with morals. Moral children tend to grow into moral adults. These moral adults establish the foundation for a moral society.

Even with limited guidance from parents, children can learn right from wrong. A child who does something wrong attempts to hide his misdeed. Often the child hides behind a smile while committing his "crime." This means the child understands on some level the incorrectness of his action. An escalation of acting out means the enforcement of the moral code is not being enforced while the de-escalation means parents are doing their job.

The lack of parents enforcing the universally accepted concepts of right and wrong portends problems for the family, community, and nation. A sibling or teacher, a coach or law enforcement officer occasionally might be able to compensate for the parent's dysfunction and the earlier the nonparental intervention takes place, the greater the chances for success. A civilized nation cannot afford to have a large portion of its population lacking good moral training. Conscientious parents are indispensable in making a productive society.

Mothers Need to Be Everywhere

Mothers have lost their elevated status. There is no way a man can replace the role of a maternal woman. For decades the women's liberation movement has systematically ridiculed mothers without careers.

Many women have joined the labor force contrary to their maternal urges. This requires the woman to juggle many of her previous responsibilities while adding additional ones. The increased stress has forced working mothers to look for new approaches to solve the age-old dilemma of finite time and energy. Mothers are the cement that holds the family together. She is the center of the family. She needs to be everywhere for the family to flourish.

Wiping noses, cleaning cuts, feeding, guarding, nurturing, loving, and teaching her children in order to insure everyday survival in life are part of the job description of the mother who needs to be everywhere.

A mother's role is to be everywhere. The sense of security and safety a mother gives a child is irreplaceable. It cannot be given by a host of nannies, daycare workers, or babysitters. Children know the difference. Quality time may make a child exuberant for a short period but the downside is just as great a spike in the opposite direction. The "quantity time" traditional mothers spend with their children is not easily measurable but does not diminish its importance. The National Campaign to Prevent Teen Pregnancy stated, "Teenage girls who are close to their moms are more likely to stay virgins." The recently released research was based on interviews with mothers and their fourteen- and fifteen-year-old children. It found that when families have meals together, when parents (mothers) know where their children are, and when they know their kid's friends it is less likely that a teenager will have sex."[6]

Shortly after Andrea Yates drowned her five children, an attractive thirty-two-year-old mother and client of mine complained of overwhelming anxiety. She related that she attempted to place herself in the frame of mind of Mrs. Yates to understand how she could have killed her own children. She shocked herself when she thought that she might hurt her son under some extreme conditions. As she told her story, it became clear that she was attempting to be Wonder

Woman. She had a thriving small business with her husband. She worked ten to twelve hours a day, seven days a week, focusing on her professional career. Her two children, a fifteen-year-old daughter and a two-year-old son, were cared for by her sister, causing her tremendous guilt, but her "quality time" interaction with her children temporarily alleviated her anxiety. She decided after our first interview that being a mother was not a total waste of a woman's time. She came back for the second counseling session announcing she had bonded with her son. She related that her son used to call her sister "Mommy" but for the past week her son was more affectionate, calling her "Mommy." She informed me she did all the things she wanted to do: playing in the garden, going to the park, and just hugging her children. She made a lifestyle adjustment, balanced her priorities, and regulated her anxiety.

When mothers are not satisfying their maternal instinct, guilt is produced. The women's liberation advocates did most mothers a disservice by demeaning the role of motherhood and glamorizing the usually overwhelmed career woman. Many women have learned the hard way that working outside the home has as much of a mundane repetition as being at home, without the gratification of being a part of your child's life.

Who's Your Daddy

Usually the father has no such inclination to worry about the child's feelings. His commands are meant to be obeyed. He pushes the child to work at his optimal level or gives out the punishment. The father has traditionally, reluctantly or not, been the disciplinarian who knew what behaviors were needed outside the house. The natural fear of the father in the recent past had prevented children from outrageously pushing the envelope.

It is the father's intended or unintended domination of the children that has been the impetus for children growing up on the straight and narrow path and leaving the family nest, usually around eighteen years of age. Dads had been the instructors to success outside the home and put the fear of God into children to extinguish bullying and other evil habits. Where have all the dads gone?

"Who's your daddy?" did not originate with the new millennium beer commercials but has its root in small-town USA. In communities where people know each other, learning about the father of the family meant you would know the character of his offspring. A high-functioning family needs both a mother and father joining together to make a healthy family.

Behind every great man, there is a woman. Behind every great family, there is a strong and disciplined father. "Fatherhood, as any society understands, is the result of training and an act of will. A man who would be a father in name as well as fact must go beyond what is merely natural, a father is a man who follows through."[7] In a traditional family, the father is the head and final decision-maker. The functioning level of the daddy was known in communities to have been directly related to the functioning of the wife and children. An indiscreet philanderer, alcoholic, drug addict, or gambler would eventually take his toll on the other family members. A disciplined, dignified father is the force behind an exemplary family. The immense impact of fathers is obvious to others in stable communities.

"Who's your daddy?" has taken on a different meaning. In our unstable world of divorce, illegitimacy, and absentee fathers, it has come to stand for who is dominating you. Even though young people have no idea of the origin of this expression, they are indirectly giving credit to fathers for setting the family standards. It is a shame that so many children are without active fathers who might have pushed them in developing inner discipline on their journey to excellence.

When the major role of fathers has to be synthetically manufactured by the pop culture, our society is in disarray. Our children, families, and entire nation lose when the media stereotypes fathers as buffoons. This continued disrespect of the sacred function of a father is destroying our families and our children. Too many children are permissively allowed to be out of control. With mothers being naturally protective and husbands absent or emasculated, our children are openly battling for power or are in the dominant position. "Who's your daddy?" sadly has little traditional meaning in our modern world.

The man in a child's life should be the father. The father's role is to give heart, establish standards, and teach reality. Fathers do not have to be everywhere, but wherever they are there has to be intensity. Giving the child the courage to face the unknown is the natural domain of the father. Men are hardwired to be hunters and protectors, not breast feeders of their children. Knowing the skills for survival in the forest, farm, or business world enlightens the father to understand the importance of motivating his child toward certain goals. More aggressive and less sensitive fathers are usually more feared by their offspring. This natural fear of fathers makes most children more responsive to their father's commands.

Disciplining children in the family has historically fallen on the broad shoulders of the father. Having firsthand knowledge of consequences their children will face outside of the home, fathers are aware of the importance of instilling values to guide them. The no-nonsense disposition of most fathers makes them indispensable in the family. The powerful maternal instinct of mothers naturally makes them more protective of their offspring.

In our permissive and materialistic culture, fathers have been stripped of all but one aspect of their role in the family. Fathers today are recognized solely for their position as providers. The absence of fathers who are active in the family is probably the single greatest factor in the explosion of wimpy victims and cowardly, bully-children. When he is present, the final word of the father in the family short-circuits a child's manipulating nonsense. The external discipline given by Dad allows the child to develop self-discipline and to grow into a strong individual with character and a peaceful future. Fathers need to be encouraged to reenter the family with greater recognition of their multifaceted role. Until fathers fulfill all of their responsibilities, "Who's your daddy?" will not regain its significance as a predictor of the success or failure of the child.

Practical Things to Do, Say, and Think When Disciplining

We need to reconnect with our society's conventional wisdom. My father offered me the adage: "It is easier to grow a straight tree than straighten a crooked one," as a form of justification for my pending punishment. Even as a child, when I was about to get punished, I felt my father was doing it for my own good. It helped me focus on my misdeed rather than attempt to talk him out of the punishment. He told me I had to take my punishment "like a man."

My wife often noted what a drill sergeant I was with my children during the time that I worked as a clinical psychologist in a prison. Inmates teach that once the die is cast, it is usually impossible to change a deviant personality. Rehabilitation is a warm, fuzzy concept that is destined to be a naïve dream until space-age microchip insertion becomes a reality.

Daily discipline gradually develops positive habits and eradicates bad ones. The Bible says it best, "He that spareth the rod, hateth his son." A child not trained to be a decent human being is destined to be an adult in serious trouble. Any parent who understands the importance of disciplining her child and does not get off her duff to do it is setting her child up for failure.

When parents use the guidelines of purposeful discipline they realize that their children will not always like them. A parent has to do what is in the best interest of the child, not win a popularity contest. No one likes to receive a punishing consequence, even when it is justified. The benefits of purposeful discipline are a well-adjusted child and a young adult who will be better able to pass on traditional values to his children.

A loving parent does suffer a form of pain when he has to discipline his child. The child might have done something inappropriate but "cute." The child might hit his big brother hard for no good reason, or say an inappropriate adult word that may make a parent chuckle inside but still needs correction. The old saying "this hurts me more than you" is accurate for many incidents. The child is self-centered and does not comprehend this reality. I know as a child I did not. The only thing I knew was I was about to be punished.

When a parent's main priority is to be a friend to his child, he will be handcuffed from acting like a parent. The statement repeated by conscientious parents, "This hurts me more than it hurts you," attempts to address the uneasiness a parent feels when he is inflicting a punishment on his child to teach her a lesson. Yet a dedicated parent with a strong commitment to raising a healthy child has to do his duty: to teach right and wrong. This must be done no matter how emotionally draining or demanding. Following Smugger experts' advice of being a friend to your child sounds nice but has been a major contributor to the ineffective state of child-rearing in today's America.

James Madison put it this way: "Conscience is the most sacred of all property."[8] Parents are entrusted with developing this internal moral compass in each and every offspring.

The following is a "Just Right Moral Consequences Chart." This chart gives the parent the reason for using the consequences, a scripted statement to the child, the results of the consequence, and several examples of the particular consequences.

Types, Examples, Reasons, and Results
of Just Right Moral Consequences

Rewarding Consequences

TYPE	EXAMPLE	MORAL

Reason: Encourages a child to do socially approved behaviors.

| EARNING PRIVILEGES | Drive family car
Watch a movie
Work on a fun activity | "You did a good job contributing to the family so you have earned this privilege." |

Result: Develops the work ethic and promotes contributing to others.

Reason: Allows parents to use the many things
they give their children in an average day.

| DERIVING FROM DAILY LIFE | Trip to the park
Eating a special meal
Visiting a friend
Going to a restaurant | "Your family does many wonderful things with you for doing a good job." |

Result: By pointing out the positive aspects of everyday family
life, parents will not have to continually materially upgrade.

Reason: A way of recognizing long-term positive behavior.

| GIVING GIFTS | Take the family car for your date
Go to a sporting event together
"Let's all go for ice cream" | "Your overall positive attitude and behavior is appreciated." |

Result: Gives the child unexpected boost for continuing to be good.

TYPE	EXAMPLE	MORAL
	Reason: Transfers the parental knowledge to the child.	
TEACHING	Demonstrate how to sew and cook Assist with homework Build a birdhouse	"Your behavior allows your parents to teach you skills necessary to succeed."
	Result: Allows the child to appreciate the knowledge the parent possesses.	
	Reason: Creates a reservoir of good feelings for parents and child.	
PLAYING TOGETHER	Play cards or a board game Practice a sport Make up word games	The child learns that when he is appropriate he and his parents can enjoy each other's company.
	Result: Parents and child enjoy each other.	
	Reason: Marks a special and important event that the parents value.	
CELEBRATING	It is a religious/cultural holiday Did a great performance Received a good report card	"One family member does well everyone profits."
	Result: Family acknowledges the achievements of a family member.	
	Reason: Gives a child a sense of the importance of working together to accomplish a task.	
WORKING TOGETHER	Rake the yard Prepare a meal Paint the house	"Being a team player pays dividends emotionally and materially."
	Result: Child experiences the positive feeling of contributing to family interests.	

TYPE	EXAMPLE	MORAL
	Reason: Encourages child to have quantity time with parent.	
BEING TOGETHER	Watch TV and videos together Drive in the car Eat and pray together Go shopping together	"The atmosphere of belonging is healthy for everyone."
	Result: Gives the child the opportunity to appreciate and observe the parents as role models.	

Punishing Consequences

TYPE	EXAMPLE	MORAL
	Reason: Assists the child in developing good work habits.	
REDOING	You need to redo your homework, composition, report You will redo the yard work You will rewash the dishes, windows	Doing quality work will develop good work habits for the rest of the child's life.
	Result: Helps the child internalize the standards of the parents.	
	Reason: Gives the understanding that something will be detrimental for the child.	
AVOIDING	Should not see that movie, play, video Cannot sleep over at ___'s house. Will not go to that party, dance, game	"I am not comfortable with your safety so I cannot allow you to go there, do that."
	Result: Minimizes the child's exposure to harmful or evil influences.	

TYPE	EXAMPLE	MORAL

Reason: Places a child on notice to improve his behavior.

WITHHOLDING	Cannot watch television or videos Cannot go to gymnastics, dance, soccer Empty child's room Cannot visit friends, have friends visit	"You have lost the privilege to do (something) because you did a misdeed."

Result: The child cannot do a certain activity for a certain period of time until she improves.

Reason: Stops the child from playing self-destructive games.

REVERSING THE GAME	You are not allowed to do your chores You will go to school in your pajamas because you did not get up on time You cannot have this food	"You do not want to do something, now I'm not going to allow you to do it."

Result: Takes the power away from the child and returns it to the parent.

Reason: Forces the child to feel how his behavior impacts others.

DOSE OF OWN MEDICINE	"You hit your sister, she will hit you back." "You called Johnny a name, how do you feel when he calls you a name?" "You won't play with your little brother, now I won't play with you."	"You don't like it when it is done to you so don't do it to others."

Result: Helps child develop sensitivity and empathy for others.

TYPE	EXAMPLE	MORAL

Reason: Pushes a child to reach higher levels of performance.

TYPE	EXAMPLE	MORAL
CHALLENGING/TEASING	"You cannot help me, you're not strong enough." "You can't find that, you are too little." "You aren't old enough to memorize the multiplication tables."	"When you try you can do anything you want."

Result: Motivates a child to reach higher levels of performance.

Reason: An emphatic response to a severe misbehavior.

TYPE	EXAMPLE	MORAL
WITHDRAWING	Cold shoulder Removal from team Sit at table alone instead of with family	Outrageous behavior by child will cause parents to show disapproval by temporarily removing attention.

Result: Forces a child to worry about losing the favor of his parents. Calibrated guilt will be produced.

Reason: This immediately stops a behavior. (Most effective with very young children and needs to be followed by an explanation giving alternative behavior.)

TYPE	EXAMPLE	MORAL
INTIMIDATION	Giving the "evil eye" Standing over child showing bigger size Raising one's voice Spanking, slapping child	Used when the behavior must stop immediately. "Do not do that again."

Result: Inhibits child from hurting self or others.

The sixteen "Just Right Moral Consequences" will only be judicious and correct if parents adhere to the eight steps of purposeful discipline. Parents have to investigate each incident to be "just," to know their child, to choose the right consequence to be effective, and to explain to the child the reason the child earned the consequence and the moral lesson. Through the process of purposeful discipline, children learn to compensate for their shortcomings rather than wallow in being victims.

Adolescents Can Become Adults

Mature individuals realize that life has difficulties for all of us. Adolescents accentuate the imperfections of their lives while romanticizing the lives of others. The realization by an adolescent that there are other people who are much worse off than they is a major step toward becoming an adult. As individuals accept the inevitable difficulties of life for everyone, they apply their energy to resolving problems instead of reciting the pathetic excuses of victimization.

James, a new student in my school, was called into my office for not keeping up with his responsibilities. His defense for being lazy was to recite a litany of problems he has had while living with his parents. After receiving no reaction from me, he began to recite his past encounters with incompetent school personnel. Finally, again getting no reaction, he made an absurd statement to my wife and myself. He stated he wished he had everything like another student, Ray.

My wife and I laughed out loud because Ray has been dealt a life a million times more difficult than James ever thought about. Ray's father was dying from AIDS, his mother virtually abandoned him, and he was behind academically when he was accepted as a student. Ray made incredible advances on every front. He was now a good student, had control of his temper, was well liked by everyone, and even liked himself.

We immediately called Ray to my office to tell him what James had said about him having it all: being a good student, being funny, being super popular, being so confident, and that James wanted to have it easy like he did. Ray smiled knowing James's statement was a compliment. Ray knew that with the help of his grandmother, he had gained control over his life.

Parents who do not encourage their child to be accountable for his actions are doing a great disservice to their child. Feeling sorrow or pity for one's child communicates a debilitating message to the child's emotional development. Anger for not being given what others have or hopelessness for not being willing to change their situation are common reactions by self-centered individuals who have no idea how to gain control over their lives.

It is the responsibility of parents to encourage their child to overcome any shortcoming the child may be dealt. If the child has a physical limitation of being shorter, taller, thinner, or fatter, a mature parent will point out people with the same characteristic who have become successful. A learning problem in school should be dealt with in a similar manner. The parent should encourage the child to use his assets to reach his objective. Through the process of compensation, an individual can use other abilities and deeds to produce the desired results.

Parents need to be responsible to raise a peaceful child. Through systematic discipline training, parents pass on morals and values that will provide direction and guidance to their children. The morals and values provided by their parents' teaching enables the children to have the inner strength to be able to stand up for peace. Parents do matter in developing the character of their children.

Being a friend or part-time parent is abusive to children. Without parental discipline, children are more prone to become bullies or wimps. Children need to be taught moral lessons to understand how their thinking and behavior will affect their future. Ignoring, bullying, or crybaby behavior will become more firmly entrenched in the child's personality. Children with poor conscience development are prone at best to be self-centered and at worst to become full-blown sociopaths.

Being a good parent requires personal sacrifice. You give up the freedom of adolescence for the discipline of adulthood. The long-term benefits are great for the individual family and country. The individual has the important purpose of creating a healthy family. He or she is given back the love of a child, making life meaningful and fulfilling. Healthy families create a vibrant society but not without trials and tribulations. The struggle of being a good parent far outweighs the emptiness of remaining a perennially self-centered person.

Our children, communities, and nation should expect parents to be the best parents they can be. Parenting is not a part-time or low intensity job. By giving our best effort as parents, we receive far more than we can possibly imagine. In a marriage, the birth of a child should not be seen as an interruption of selfish pursuits but seen as a blessing and opportunity to leave one's mark on future generations.

Chapter 7

Disabling to Strengthening Children

The thing that impresses me most about America is the way parents obey their children.

—Edward, Duke of Windsor

The Smugger permissive materialism has wreaked havoc on our families. Smuggers have confused and paralyzed parents. Parents should be involved in the discipline of their children, not be fearful of them. Probably the best method to illustrate the absurdity evident in parenting in the United States is to tell you about a particular family that came in for counseling. For the first session, the twenty-eight-year-old mother arrived with a three-year-old son and ten-month-old daughter. She asked me to help her understand the reason for her son's psychological anger. She related that she and her husband loved both of their children but could not understand why the three-year-old was so angry. She knew it had to be a deep-seated issue even though she could not think of any trauma in her son's life. The birth was uneventful and as she was a stay-at-home mom, he had been under her constant supervision. I asked her to explain how he demonstrates his anger. She told me that at two and a half years old, he used a baseball bat to beat his pet bunny to death. The mother also said that he attacks his younger sister without provocation, making her fear for the safety of her infant, and that he cries hysterically whenever she attempts to punish him. Even with her unconditional loving of her son, this mother could not brush his behavior off as the terrible twos.

As soon as they entered my office, it became apparent that the mother had no control over her son. He did not follow any of her directions but annoyingly clung to her while intently studying me. After ignoring his mother's requests to sit in a chair, I had enough of his nonsense. I commanded him to sit and he readily responded. I asked her how he listened to his father and she said better than to her. I asked her to bring her husband to the next session and gave her explicit instructional materials: a copy of *Essential Parenting*. She could now begin the discipline process to help her son learn to listen better. I told her to share this information with her husband.

Even before being seated for the second session the father blurted out that he knew what was wrong with his son. I asked him to sit down and explain. He said, "My wife never follows through with what she says." He knew his son was testing the limits. He proudly told me his son listens to him when he puts his foot down. The wife said in defense that the boy listens better to her husband but he is rarely home and when he is home he is often preoccupied with other things. The father reluctantly admitted that he rarely interacts with his son. My secretary informed me after the session that the father read a magazine while the son ran around the waiting room.

The father knew his son's problem was not a mysterious abusive event, but rather, poor parenting. He realized through therapy that he needed to unite and support his wife in disciplining their children. The father knew from the beginning the son did not have a traumatic event that altered his development. He understood that his son was never placed on the right track because of weak and inconsistent discipline. He reluctantly admitted he was an absentee and nonsupportive disciplinarian.

The mother was an excellent nurturer who just needed to change her view of discipline. She thought if she gave unconditional love and ignored inappropriate behavior, her child would never develop anger. She learned through therapy that a child appreciated the parent caring through discipline as much as nurturing. A child given a balance of nurturing and discipline is better able to develop frustration tolerance, coping with reality without foolish and dangerous outbursts of anger. She learned that a child is not born with a concept of right and wrong but has to be taught morality by the parents. Punishing a child for hurting another when he is young will prevent him from developing a habit that leads down a path to evil.

A child correctly disciplined develops character, while a child left to his own devices will be, at best, a misfit and at worst, a ticking time bomb. Dylan Klebold, one of the shooters at Columbine High School, had burned his dog to death as his first kill. He came from an upper middle class family. John "Taliban" Walker came from an affluent community in California. John Walker's parents, like the 9/11 terrorist Zacarias Moussaoui's mother, serial killer Ted Bundy's mother, the parents of the Florida teenager who killed a first-grade girl with wrestling moves, and almost every criminal's parents interviewed on television, gave essentially the same three-part defense of their child:

1. He was a good boy.
2. He could not have done such a thing.
3. I love him unconditionally.

The parents of children who commit evil acts are not in any way apologetic for the suffering their child caused others. There is no second-guessing on the part of the parent as to ways they handled past incidents with their child. There is no condemnation of their child's behavior, only the pathetic three-part defense. We can predict what these parents are going to say.

It is an indictment of current child-development practices that parents have been systematically brainwashed to believe they are not ultimately accountable for their children's behavior. Their only responsibility is to follow the prescription for unconditional love by ignoring any bad behavior, no matter how extreme the misdeed, and praising even questionable behavior as positive. The Biblical unconditional love of God to us, imperfect humans, can no longer be used as a smoke screen for parents, abdicating their responsibility to teach and train their children to be civilized human beings.

This socialistic Smugger approach to parenting has been a marketing bonanza. It sells books, but it is not developing a peaceful child. Its virtue for busy modern parents is that it takes little effort. This lazy parenting way of raising children doesn't work. Parents are not insisting their children go to bed at a reasonable hour, are potty trained, eat enough of the proper food, and eat together as a family. Parents are shirking their responsibility. Parents are taking the easy way out of their privileged role. This politically correct approach to child-rearing has and is still producing many out-of-control, angry, and often violent children with little or no conscience development. The major flaw is that it is not based on reality. It is based on ideology, an ideology that insists on methods and concepts that do not produce positive results for children. As long as you follow the Smugger experts' means of raising children you cannot go wrong. Just remember to disregard your child's behavior (ends). This is an ideology that believes the MJE, "means justify the ends." The "means" is following the permissive and materialistic ideology regardless of the results. The "ends" indicate our children are out of control. The "ends" are not working.

The mainstream Smugger experts relentlessly advocate for more freedoms for parents and children and less parental responsibility for disciplining their children. The practical elimination of the call for parental discipline may ease the conscience of today's overwhelmed parents, but does little to shape the character of their child. To appease the child with material goods and allow children to do whatever they want has been and is now a prescription for creating unhealthy children. The means are not working. There appears to be no justification for the continuation of the materialistic permissive approach to child rearing. The permissive materialistic approach failed before and will now.

History does repeat itself. Socrates, a teacher of Plato, once made an observation that could have been said today by any one of our cultural commentators. "Children today are tyrants. They contradict their parents, gobble their food, and tyrannize their teachers."[1]

Amazingly, Socrates's statement powerfully and accurately describes our present culture, even though written four hundred years before Christ. Plato placed the cause of the chaos at the end of the golden age of Greece at the altar of extreme liberty, independence, and tolerance for disrespectful children. The permissive and materialistic approach led to ungrateful children in ancient Greece and is having the same impact in our present society.

Tolerance for abusive behavior is no virtue. It is a sign of shirking our responsibility as authority figures. We need to rethink our extraordinary tolerance of American children's disruptive and inappropriate behavior or continue to produce disabled, second-class citizens. Disrespectful and inappropriate children usually limit their own development in one or more major aspects of life such as developing intimacy with others, doing well in school, or attaining employable skills. We are hurting our children by accepting less than what the child could become.

The immature, self-centered thinking of many children today is a direct result of parental lack of consistent leadership. The entitlement mentality is the result of parents consistently giving in to the demands of the child. In turn these parents impart a victimization mentality on their children, an outgrowth of parents not training their children to be responsible for their own actions. Parents appeasing, ignoring, rationalizing, and redirecting their children does not develop appropriate behavior. But it does create children who are delusional and think they know more than their parents.

Many adults attempt to remain as irresponsible as adolescents. At home, work, and in public, adults are shirking their duties, attempting to dismiss the knowledge gained through life experience, and attempting to disguise themselves as young souls with hats on backwards and the clothing of a seventeen-year-old. Indeed the roles have reversed. Parents and teachers agree, imitate, and fraternize with their dependents while the youth ridicule, lead, and loathe their elders.

America today, like ancient Greece, has taken the admirable ideals of liberalism to a detrimental level. The subversion and overindulgence of liberty cannot be more evident than in the area of spoiling our youth. The cry for greater individual freedom has led parents and teachers to allow children to do their own thing. This laissez-faire attitude of authority figures is effortless, but as mature adults, is an abdication of their responsibilities to the children. This has resulted in children who are selfish, under-socialized bullies or wimps.

The Permissive and Materialist Approach
Promotes the Bully and Wimp Syndrome

Anytime you appease and bribe someone to get them out of your hair, you are creating a monster. It is natural for a young person who has not had a conscience inculcated in him by conscientious parents to attempt to satisfy his selfish desires through any means necessary. When wimpy parents give the demanding and whining child whatever he wants, the child is certainly going to learn bullying and whining pays.

It should be understood that a bully and a wimp are different sides of the same coin. Their manipulation skills are keenly developed, automatically switching them from wimp to bully or bully to wimp mode depending on the circumstances. A wimp, when put in a power position, will use his newfound power in an overly aggressive manner.

For example, an introverted wimpy student who grows up to be a doctor and is treated like a god by the community will suddenly turn into a tyrant. I am not picking on doctors, although I have heard many horror stories from many different nurses in counseling as they relate their interactions with doctors. On the other hand, when an aggressively obnoxious financial broker who is moderately successful loses money in a downturn in the economy, he will move into a self-pity mode, often contemplating suicide.

Bullies and wimps flip-flop depending on the assessment of their rival. A weak opponent brings out the bully, while a strong one brings out the wimp.

The switching from wimp to bully or vice versa can be noted in our interactions with others throughout life. The same conversion of wimp to bully or bully to wimp can be seen in the observation of young children. A little bully amongst one group will kiss up to the leaders of a more powerful group. In the same manner, a subservient child in one group might become an unreasonable dictator in a less powerful group.

The truth is, a bully who attempts to intimidate another and fails will whine for mercy. The reason is simple; a bully is a coward attempting to hide his fears behind a phony exterior of toughness. When the bluff is called, he reverts back to his truly immature, insecure self. Once this is understood, the bullying child or the wimp should no longer be able to easily manipulate the parent.

The child who hides behind a bully or wimp mask is not balanced. The bully/wimp has not been trained by his parents in courage and moral development. By allowing the child to manipulate his parents, he is robbed of the opportunity to learn from the extensive experience of an adult.

The self-centered child remains fragile, immature, and insecure because the child knows the parents really possess the power. The pampered child has limited chances to test his mettle against actual obstacles in life without the parent swooping down and correcting the problem.

A child allowed to bully his parents will not be well-adjusted. His major role models, his parents, have acted like victims instead of mature leaders. The child with wimpy parents knows only the behavior of bullying—or being bullied. This inflexibility of healthy behavioral alternatives makes him vulnerable in peer dominant environments. When the bullying child realizes his tactics do not work outside the home, his anger and frustration turn on his parents. Kids make parents pay for their lack of involvement.

An example of a child punishing her parents is evident in the life of a doctor, his wife, and their daughter. After many years of being permissive with her daughter, the mother told me the daughter said she would not tell her what university she would attend because she does not want her mother to move near her. The truth of the matter is that the daughter is a modern "mama's girl" and is highly dependent on her mother for bailing her out of the situations she creates for herself. She would have great difficulty surviving without her mother and would be the first one to demand her mother be there to solve her problems. The mother allows and excuses her daughter's physically and emotionally abusive bullying behavior. The daughter slaps her mother if the mother attempts to question her about going to a party. The mother is the wimp and the daughter is the bully. I told the mother to tell her daughter that she will have a celebration when she leaves for college. The mother laughed. We both knew she would be a mother who spends the night at her child's college orientation.

American children are experts in manipulating their parents emotionally to get what they want. Children overreact with self-pity and anger for seemingly trivial and ridiculous reasons. "You took me to a crummy barber" or "I hate you for buying the wrong shirt" or even "I am going to commit suicide because I have no friends." The list of things that might provoke their self-pity and anger is endless.

Sometimes children bully their parents by hurting themselves. A mother brought her eight-year-old fraternal-twin son to my office. His mother told me he was placed in "time-out" for not listening in an after-school program while three other boys who caused the problem were allowed to play. He put his head down and started to mumble about hurting himself. The daycare worker was concerned and asked him why he was so upset. He blurted out that his father had attempted to choke him. She knew he was not being truthful. Yet their policy was to rec-ommend the child go to a mental health professional.

The mother knew her son could use self-destructive behavior to get his way whenever he became frustrated. She admitted that her son would do bizarre things to get her attention. She added that he would hurt himself—especially when his aggressive twin brother would attempt to dominate him. The mother related how she would punish his twin brother for causing him to self-mutilate. She said she has had limited faith that he could protect himself against his more assertive brother or anyone else.

The mother was aware that her son's behavior had to change to pro-tect her family. She realized her husband would have been investigated by the state if the teacher was not thorough in her review of the after-school accident. She was open to the idea that her son had to speak up about his grievances directly to the person bothering him. His mother decided her son had to develop the inner strength to overcome his pat-tern of distorting the truth and outright lying or hurting himself to get others to protect him. She realized making her son tougher is prefer-able to self-mutilation and victimization.

Parents accept their child's irrational bullying of them because they feel guilty. Their guilt comes from not being there for their children and doing the things their parents did for them. The child develops a pattern of being a more outrageous bully/wimp and the parent a more confirmed wimp/bully. The entrenching of the child's role as a bully and parent as a victim can appear normal, especially if their friends have a worse situation.

Occasionally, the parent will attempt to lay down the law by screaming and the child will burst out crying. Now the parent becomes the bully and the child the victim only in the heat of the parental outburst. These role reversals quickly return to the child bullying the parent. Parental weakness breeds weakness in their children.

Modern parents have it all wrong. When parents do not exercise their rights and power as parents, they are promoting their children's bullying of them. By providing our children with all the things they want before they even want them and protecting them from any possible pain or hardship we are producing an avalanche of ungrateful bullies/wimps. These ungrateful bullies/wimps begin their antics by pushing us around.

Parents who allow their children to be disrespectful toward them are encouraging the formation of bullying habits in their children. Whenever parents reverse their consequences to protect the child's feelings due to the child's "tear power," the parents are solidifying the manipulative tactic of being a wimp. The child falsely comes to expect the parents to be able to fight all their battles against their peers for them, even when the child instigated the incident. All the child has to do when his bullying of another does not work is whine to his parents as a victim and his parents will fix it for him.

A child being a victim outside the home is not a good policy. As children, victims have learned that crying usually prevents any consequences being given by their parents. The opposite is true in the real world outside the protective confines of the home. They fail to realize that crying in front of bullies only attracts more bullies and abuse. This uncivilized, perverse, and primitive pattern of interaction is far too common wherever children of mixed ages congregate. The older and stronger abuse the younger and weaker unless they have been taught a strong moral code.

Ironically, in this era of the sensitive male, bullying has become cool. Bullies get what they want in terms of power and popularity and the wimps finally receive some form of recognition. The victim gets negative attention from a popular member of an amoral community. The victim comes back for more abuse and the bully basks in his power and popularity. The law of the jungle where the strong prey on the weak was glorified on a national TV show.

ABC's 20/20 show aired an hour-long depiction entitled, "The 'In' Crowd and Social Cruelty." The program showed children being kicked, shoved, or pushed by gangs of usually older and bigger kids on school property while teachers were seen walking around supposedly supervising the playgrounds. A student punched another student (who was perhaps four or five years younger than he) in the face, knocking him out. One six-foot-tall teenager bragged how he had "made someone bulimic, I didn't care." A teenage girl said, "It was fun to me to see people cry." The commentator, John Stossel, who did at times share stories of his own experiences with bullying, appeared to be nonjudgmental toward the self-satisfied, cool bullies. He even appeared to be smiling as he spoke, almost condoning their despicable behavior. There was no apparent remorse for the pain they caused their victims and no moral indignation or condemnation on the part of the narrators.[2]

University of California–Los Angeles psychologist Jaana Juvonen surveyed nearly two thousand sixth graders:

"[I] found that kids who harass other kids typically aren't outcasts with low self-esteem. In fact, they tend to be better adjusted socially than the average middle school student, challenging the common assumption that bullies need ego boosters... No matter how you teach the bullies to see the world differently the rewards of the behavior are still there once they step back into the schoolyard . . . Teaching children not to applaud antagonizers by giving them attention can change social expectations and norms. Empowering them to intervene in bullying situations would be by far the most effective strategy."[3]

In other words, standing up to bullies is the best way to ward them off.

Stossell did not condemn this outrageous behavior but feebly attempted to legitimize it. He related that he was victimized as a geek when he was young, inferring that abuse is not so bad and being a victim can be alright while being brutal to others gives you power and popularity that can last throughout life. The convoluted message of this show is that bullying gives you power and makes you popular without an examination of the liabilities of becoming a sociopath. Instead of bullies being hated by today's children, including their victims, they are almost idolized. Children are not thinking or acting in their own best interest because parents are unable and unwilling to give direction. The Smugger permissive and materialistic approach is the culprit in the epidemic of bullies in our culture.

Bullies should not feel good about themselves, even in a nonjudgmental world. Authority figures and peers need to tell the bully to stop, letting him know that his behavior is wrong. The condemning of the behavior will lower the bully's distorted ego.

Failure of the Permissive and Materialistic Approach

Things were cheap then, but life was valuable. Now life is cheap and things are valuable.

—CAL THOMAS[4]

The permissive and materialistic approach to child-rearing cannot demonstrate positive results in children's behavior. The measurable outcomes of children raised during the era of permissive materialism have been a disaster.

In fewer than fifty years, our Smugger experts have led us far astray from the traditional techniques and values of our ancestors. These social engineers have dismissed the knowledge of many centuries, replacing it with pseudoscientific notions that would free mankind from the psychological problems of the past. The actual results are shockingly opposite.

Children today, for the most part, are out-of-control in their behavior and emotionally unhappy. Today's children are materially and choice rich but spiritually and morally deprived. The lack of moral and spiritual training by parents is evident in a staggering 452 percent increase in our prison population since 1970. Nearly 2 million Americans are in jails or prisons and 4.5 million are on probation or parole. In 1980, the prison and jail population was 500,000.[5]

The ever-increasing number of mental disorders for children presently totals over forty. "Study: More Kids Troubled" cites research that finds the diagnoses of emotional and learning disabilities in children has more than doubled from 1979 to 1996.[6] "Special education enrollment rose twice as fast as overall school enrollment in the past decade."[7] The Columbine-type incidents, shooting another student, gang activities, bullying of children, and open defiance of authority figures are all too common. "The National Education Association estimates that 160,000 kids stay home from school each day because they are afraid of being tormented."[8] We are not raising peaceful nor blissful children.

Parents today have become the newly disabled. The absurd part is they do not even know they are disabled. Modern parents are confused by the contradictory Smugger advice of the experts concluding little to no parenting is the most advantageous way of interacting with children. This permissive and materialistic approach has the benefit to the parents of increasing their personal time and the liability to the children of missing out on traditional expectations of the culture.

In a valueless world, commitment is unnecessary. In a noncommitted world, professional parents go on vacation and leave their kindergarten age child with their secretary. The parents of this untrained adopted child brought her to my school to meet the teacher just before school started. Then they promptly left for a two-week vacation in Hawaii. Their recently hired employee was taking care of the child and was supposed to keep in constant contact with the parents to let them know how she reacted to the first week of school. When an insignificant "wet pants accident" was conveyed to the parents, they overreacted by yelling at their secretary whom the child called "auntie." After the ruckus these parents caused, they continued their vacation for a full two weeks. All of this nonsense over a child wetting her pants opened up the floodgates of parental guilt.

Modern parents frequently overreact to responsible authority figures to protect their children from necessary and legitimate consequences, and yet they act paralyzed when their child is doing something wrong in front of them. Now, parents saying "no" to their children is harder than attacking the credibility of a professional doing his job. The guilt of not functioning as a parent is reversing the behavior pattern of the child and the traditional parent.

Just as the contradictory advice on foods is confusing, so are the contradictions in child-rearing advice. Historically, parents being parents has been effective. Our parents were the king and queen of the home and we could not wait to go out on our own at age eighteen. We were anxious to begin our own journey, away from interference from our directive parents.

The cycle is reversed with modern children who rule the roost, never wanting to leave home, while the parents make any excuse to be out of the house. Often parents allow the young child to rule and then as the child approaches adulthood they try to tighten the reins. "Their sense of entitlement as consumers, together with an inability to let go, leads some parents to want to manage all aspects of their children's college lives, from the quest of admissions to their choice of a major."[9] Parents are not the only ones who are remiss.

Parental guilt for not being there for their children motivates them to overcompensate with material goods and premature social experiences that are detrimental to the child. Children with minimal parental training, limits, and guidance are left to their own self-centered instincts. The result for many children is to be emotionally at war within, to have high anxiety and depression, or to be at war with others by being inappropriately aggressive.

Over the years I have seen an escalation in the incidence of children intimidating their parents and teachers to get what they want. A twelve-year-old boy would fly into a rage to force his parents to change their minds about giving him restrictions. He would throw things until his mother gave in to his demands. As are many children who bully their parents, he was gracious to his friends and was often bullied by strangers. His behavior only changed when his mother put him in a psychiatric residential program overnight. He learned the limits of his power and the reality of his parents' power. The parents learned for the moment that exercising their power curtailed their son's manipulation through his raging and whining.

As soon as their son acted reasonable, the parents reverted back to wimpy parenting. The twelve-year-old tested the limits and the parents backpedaled until the roles returned to their dysfunctional form of child-rearing. The son was bullying the parents and the parents acted helpless.

A fourteen-year-old girl involved with partying, marijuana, and sex would leave her home at night through her second-story window. Her parents were intimidated and paralyzed by her acting out. The rare times she was caught leaving the home was usually because her younger sister informed her parents. She would be contrite as long as restrictions were enforced.

The parents did not believe in causing pain to their children, regardless of how much pain their children gave them. They would drop the consequences for the dangerous behavior, and as soon as the restrictions were lifted, she would go out the window again. The parents screwed the window shut and she went out the back door. In counseling, both parents were bright professionals who came up with good strategies to impact their child's behavior. The parents left enthusiastic to enforce their plan.

The confusing and frustrating thing for me as a counselor was each week without any embarrassment they would report a new excuse for wimping out. Finally they had enough and the next time their daughter ran away the parents reported her missing to law enforcement. She was picked up and held by the police. The parents demonstrated their resolve by waiting before picking her up from the station. Instead of being angry following this incident, this girl came to counseling sessions glowing with a renewed closeness with her parents.

Like other stages of childhood, teenagers understand on some level that discipline is an expression of love. She understood their appeasing her was caused by their lack of parental commitment and their need to pretend to be perfect parents to their equally phony friends.

The Permissive and Materialistic (PM) Approach: "The Means Justify the Ends"

The Smugger permissive and materialistic methods have achieved status as the modern, educated way to raise children. This has become a cultural fact in our society. The media, university professors, and the medical industries have spread this indoctrination. The message boils down to the "means justifies the ends" (MJE). There are fanatical MJE believers. They are taught that as long as you treat a child in a pre-scribed materialistic and permissive manner, you are being a consci-entious parent. The goal of this Smugger strategy is to appear to be a concerned parent, not to produce a child of strong character. Adhering to these socialistically derived means of raising children indicates the quality of one's parenting, not the child's behavior.

Punishment for outrageous behavior has become illegal.

MJE parents are supposed to blindly follow PM-Smugger ideals, dis-regarding what they see. The MJE dogma insists that the parent's methods need to be judged, not the child's behavior. A child's feelings toward the parent are a better indicator of the value of the parenting than the child reaching specific milestones. The focus is on the par-ent's politically correct behavior, not on the child's actions. The high self-concept sect of the MJE believes that as long as you constantly tell your child positive statements, the child will flourish. Parents compul-sively give the enhancing reinforcement even when the child's behav-ior is questionable at best. The belief is that it is better to err on the side of being affirmative, rather than critical.

When a child is being a brat there are tailor-made excuses called stages: "terrible twos," "horrible threes," "tweeners," or adolescent rebel-lion. The parent's function is to shield the child from any pain, self-induced or otherwise. The MJE dogma requires good parents to do anything in their power to protect their child from all forms of suffer-ing, including eliminating any punishment for misbehavior. A MJE par-ent believes she should not give her child pain nor allow anyone else in the world to give pain either. The overindulged child, according to the MJE principles, should be protected from any possible negative choices by the power of governmental laws directly influenced by these parents.

Many modern parents believe that the government should assume traditional parental advisory responsibility. It is for this reason that MJE proponents believe we, as a nation, ought to ban dodge ball, tag, and any other team sport. In dodge ball the MJE thinking is that there might be exhilaration from catching an opponent's ball, but think of the pain of the poor child who was out of the game because his ball was caught. Worse yet, think of the child who was hit by the ball and failed to catch it. There is a double dose of pain. First, the child feels the sting of the ball and, second, has the humiliation of everyone knowing he is out.

The same problem exists for a child who is not talented in a sport such as soccer. Perhaps he is picked last or is not able to be a starter. Some modern parents are using their political clout to stop these incidences of suffering caused by sports inequities. The bullying of school officials and coaches by MJE parents to eliminate sports for everyone is worthless because the MJE parents' main motivation is to show ineffective caring for one's child by shielding him from pain. The greater priority for the MJE parents is to protect their child from pain, outweighing the advantages of allowing him to experience his own strengths and weaknesses.

MJE parents would like others to believe that they are good parents by using the "means" of the court system. Whether the motivation is showing some convoluted caring for their child or a personal political agenda, the MJE parent is less concerned with the ultimate result of his action than the means. A child whose parents are going to prevent other children from enjoying the game of tag or dodge ball will be ostracized from his peer group. The child will suffer more, not less, pain. It appears parents are fighting for their own self-serving reasons, rather than for the child.

The MJE argument always hinges on the appearance of decreasing the pain and suffering of their child. The reality of the end product for their child is often more, rather than less, pain. The case of a self-proclaimed atheist and man who claimed the conception of his daughter was the result of a date rape on him is a bizarre example. Dr. Michael Newdow successfully won a federal district court ruling that the words "under God" be deleted from the Pledge of Allegiance. He did not want his eight-year-old daughter to be forced to say "under God." He claims his daughter is an atheist and should not suffer the pain of being forced to say those words.[10]

The facts seem to be clearly different than his stated fatherly concern for his daughter. A newspaper article headlined "Mom, Girl in Pledge Suit" in the *St. Petersburg Times* states that the girl is a Christian, believes in God, and has no problem saying "under God" during the Pledge of Allegiance.[11] The mother, Mrs. Bennings, never married Dr. Newdow, the father of the third grader, and has full custody of her daughter. Mrs. Bennings says her daughter is proud to salute the flag. It may appear Dr. Newdow has a greater political agenda than a concern for his daughter.

Appearances seem to be more important to the MJE parent than their child's development. If the well-being of the child was the end product and was the ultimate consideration of the MJE parents, they would prepare the child by saying not to play the "unhealthy games on the playground" or would tell them not to say "under God" when reciting the Pledge of Allegiance. The child would learn he has the ability to make choices that would give him control over his life. His parents would have empowered him to stand up to the group if he felt the group was wrong. Would this take courage? Yes, but the child would gain inner strength, a wonderful end product. The child would feel more self-competent in handling difficult social situations.

Instead, the child of an MJE parent is a sacrificial lamb to the ego of a parent who needs the notoriety of being seen by others as a good parent. The child whose parent would prevent other children from having the enjoyment of playing dodge ball or saying "under God" when reciting the Pledge of Allegiance would be shunned or openly attacked. The inevitable result would be the MJE child fighting the parent's battle, not the other way around.

The MJE Parent's Test

Any parent who strongly identifies with the following beliefs and behaviors is a confirmed MJE parent and should scrutinize this book carefully. These unfortunate parents are unaware that the socialistic child-rearing propaganda they follow is destroying the healthy development of their children. A parent who relates with some aspects of these parental characteristics should reconsider some of his or her basic assumptions. The responsible parents who have failed the test are fortunate and will understand the shortsightedness of these beliefs and behaviors. The traditionalists will receive validation for their parenting style.

Please score the MJE Test the following way: 3 highly agree, 2 somewhat agree, 1 disagree.

Providing the Things We Didn't Have

Our children are entitled to everything we did not have as children. This means freedom to do and enjoy whatever they want. Our job as parents is to provide them with the dreams we never obtained. This might mean our children will take advantage of our caring nature by screaming at us, demanding more and more. It may appear to others and even feel as if our own children are abusing us.

At times we may get so upset that we lash out against them. We may go on vacation without the child, even after their pleading. We may demand from their principal or psychologist strong sanctions against their misdeeds. We may restrict the child and even place him in a psychiatric program. These actions may temporarily gain a form of respect and decency at the expense of being an ordinary bully.

When we come to our senses, we realize our child's behavior is only due to the imposition and awe of our power. When we calm down and return to a more permissive, democratic, and friendly approach, the child is empowered by us to display his more pure self-oriented nature. Others might think we are acting submissively but our strategy is to provide a morally unrestricted environment for our child to blossom into a mature adult.

A Responsibility to Protect

To protect their children, modern parents should use their monetary and positional power. Parents have a responsibility to not allow their children to suffer any type of pain. Our increased affluence has brought us greater power to shield our children from the harsh realities they will too soon have to face.

We should allow children to enjoy being children as long as possible. Everyone makes mistakes. A call to the police chief or principal will insure our child has another chance without suffering the capricious consequences of these authority figures. Who can reasonably argue against our compassion? Anyone who has power of position would do the same for any member of his own family.

Children do not need pain, moral lessons, and adversity to learn lessons of life. The connections and money we possess will insure any of their dreams coming true. Our children will inherit our successes as long as we protect them from the harsh consequences inflicted by punitive authority figures. Our children are privileged and shall receive special consideration on their life journey.

Saying "Yes" Instead of "No"

Modern parents should not unnecessarily disappoint or ever anger their child. The best policy to follow when a child has a request is to unequivocally say "yes." Saying "yes" even when you know you have no intention of fulfilling the request, or are uncertain, is smart. This is wiser than saying "no" and getting into the inevitable confrontation.

A child's memory is short and circumstances change with time. The worst thing that can happen is that a parent may have to explain to the child, in a reasonable and friendly manner, that he has changed his mind. The temporary loss of credibility will decrease with time. There will be no anger and disappointment to overcome, only confusion. The child wants to believe in his parents. Time will bring back the child's trust without damaging the friendly democratic environment.

Parenting Made Easy

Children should be free to do what they want. As a child matures, he will naturally learn right from wrong. Given unlimited freedom, the child will learn to regulate himself. Any parental interference by attempting to train and teach the child restricts his development. This often results in a neurotic person. The answer to being an effective parent is to refrain from meddling like your parents did. Sitting back and allowing your child to unfold is the key to healthy children.

If and when a problem surfaces, there are medical and educational specialists to advise us. There are specific mental health designations and drugs to alleviate any symptoms. There is no reason for attempting to be an in-control parent. The only thing it does is to breed resentment. It takes too much time and energy to be responsible for training and teaching one's child. It is best left to the psychiatric and educational experts to resolve any childhood problems. Modern science is much more sophisticated and effective in producing well-rounded children than our time-consuming discipline methods of the past.

An Infant Should Not Impact One's Career or Lifestyle

You can fast-track your career and not sacrifice any quality in raising your child. There can be extended maternity or paternity leave because the co-workers will be glad to pick up the slack. Daycare or nannies will socialize the child until the parents get home from the office. There are always weekends and after-work hours to spend with the child. Juggling time and resources, parents can accomplish excellence in modern life.

Being the best possible parents, having optimal personal growth, and career advancement are shared values in our society. Prioritizing is a limiting concept that has no credence in a progressive world. Parents should not sacrifice their personal freedom for the sake of raising a healthy child. Modern parents can have it all.

Eradicating Male and Female Differences

Modern parents have a responsibility to treat all children equally, regardless of their sex. Any traditional, stereotypical behavior displayed by a child is due to insensitive parenting. Parents need to encourage boys to get in touch with their feminine side, girls to be aggressive, and both to be very concerned about their appearance at an earlier age.

There should be no special activities or toys for boys or girls. Either gender can do anything as well as the other. There is no difference between boys and girls except those instilled by sexist people. Girls and boys have a right to be free to choose who they want to be, not to have it imposed by others through stereotypical expectations.

Being a Unique Parent

Parents are individuals and naturally treat their child differently. There should not be comments like "wait until your father comes home." A wife should never put the husband in the position of being responsible as a disciplinarian. Nor should the husband ever tell the child, "if you don't listen to your mother you will have to deal with me!" The mother needs to develop her own unique relationship with her child.

Parents are totally different in the manner they interact with their child. A child will act out with one parent but not the other. Because the child listens better to one parent than the other, that better-listened-to parent should not jeopardize his friendship with the child by supporting the other parent. A husband and wife should never chime in together and confront the child's assertive behavior.

Parents uniting or sharing power against the child—regardless of his behavior—is an unfair form of bullying. Parents supporting each other would traumatize his sense of security and love. It is better to support the child's inappropriate behavior than to crush his willfulness. Parents should remain neutral in any confrontation with their child and their spouse. An effective parent displays unconditional love for his child. In no way would a loving parent take the side of his spouse against their child. The child's feelings would be hurt when one spouse gangs up and supports the other.

Keep Expectations Minimal

Children should be accepted the way they are, setting high standards leads to frustration and disappointment. We are all different. The position of, "I do not care what other kids are doing, you are my child and you will do what is right" is psychologically damaging. It places too much pressure and stress on the child. It is much wiser to realize there are many other children with poorer grades, who are more disrespectful and abusive than your child. Accepting your child's shortcomings without attempting to push him to compensate will keep his self-esteem high.

Find like-minded authority figures who realize that relaxing standards is the answer to raising a healthy child. There are many coaches, instructors, and teachers who refuse to differentiate between their top and less talented students. Every child is given equal time to participate and to receive the same accolades since all are at the top of the class. Likewise every child has a right to express himself through his appearance. Piercing, tattoos, and dress are means of making a personal statement in a diverse world.

◆ ◆ ◆

A score of 8–12 means you are a traditionalist, 13–20 a confused parent, 21–28 a confirmed modern parent who needs to read the following section for your child's sake.

Critique of MJE

MJE defense of the permissive and materialistic approach is too simplistic and defies logic. As long as people think you are doing a good job as a parent, you are a good parent. It sounds as if we should have polls to determine the merits of a couple's parenting without any examination of their children's behavior or character. Well-intentioned parents are following a socialistic Smugger child-rearing script that sounds humane but is producing dysfunctional children and families.

This makes sense when we understand the father of the permissive and materialistic (PM) approach, Dr. Benjamin Spock, was a pediatrician and socialist who talked about strict and causal discipline in the same breath. He was an expert on medical issues like feeding, illness, and medicines, and did not attempt to deal in a comprehensive manner with the more complex issues of developing character in a child. He had faith that a child would raise himself if you gave him freedom to do what he wanted and met his material needs.[12]

The MJE movement is an attempt to remove any accountability in the permissive and materialistic approach. It has worked well to persuade parents to continue this Smugger practice. It has worked to allow lazy parenting practices to flourish without any negative impact imposed on these parents by others in the community. It has brainwashed us through the media experts to believe you can be an occasionally involved, "quality-time" parent. It has weakened many children, making them bullies or wimps. It has produced cowards in an environment that requires courage.

The MJE parents are shocked and confused by their child's vacillating behavior between being a bully or a wimp. The answer for the vacillating is their lack of being a parent. The role of a conscientious parent is complex. It is much more than allowing your child to do what he wants or to buy him things to keep him happy. It is more than being a friend.

The Smugger permissive and materialistic formula appears to eliminate the headache of being a traditionally responsible parent. It has two simple premises. The first is to be permissive, allowing your children to do whatever they want. The second is to be materialistic and give them the things they want. This prescription frees an MJE parent from the complex responsibility of being a shaper of his child's character.

The permissive and materialistic approach is much simpler in scope, abdicating many objections of child-rearing of the past. There are no issues with punishment, consequences for the children, or need to protect children from evil. Punishment and accountability are illegal while evil does not exist. In the perfect world of the MJE parent, there is no reason to teach and train a child to deal successfully with a harsh and unforgiving reality. The PM mind-set has the affluent environment where everyone is tolerant, good, and forgiving. There is no evil in their perfect world.

The focus of child-rearing does not have to be in preparation for learning to function in a formidable, competitive, and cold world. The modern parent assumes all authority figures are committed to artificially inflate their child's self-esteem, regardless of his behavior. The objective in keeping the child's mood elevated is easy to understand but more difficult to practice.

When a child is given the freedom to do as he wishes and the material goods he desires, he will only be temporarily satisfied. The child is at the beginning stages of "affluenza." This disease progresses rapidly the more the parent attempts to bribe their child through freedom and material goods. The more the child is given these without earning them, the less the child appreciates either. Affluenza in its final stage is seen as depression and bullying.

The MJE's obligatory response is to continue to provide these two ingredients in ever increasing amounts. The child will bully the parents when the parents are not providing them. The parents will act wimpy in front of the child's tantrum, for the parents know they are not 100 percent living up to the two simple dictates of the Smugger child-rearing approach.

The wimpy role of the MJE parents will suddenly change to the bully role after absorbing tremendous amounts of abuse from their spoiled child. Once the parents, now acting like bullies, acknowledge their horrific error of not following the correct MJE dogma, they return to their wimpy selves. The transgression will be appeased by further capitulation of the traditional role of being an in-charge parent. The bullying child will receive more personal freedoms and presents meant to bribe him to be more reasonable.

There is a basic paradox in the PM/MJE Smugger approach. Even though PM/MJE parents want their child to avoid the unpleasantness of reality, these same parents push their child into accelerated social activities without any training in reality. The older we get, the more we realize how difficult life is. MJE parents are supposed to shield children from the harshness and stresses of reality. Children are often nurtured and protected from everyday reality issues and traumatic events as if the parents had the ability to wrap their child in a protective bubble for life. Somehow, these parents believe their child has been selected to live a carefree life. Developing the "too precious child" syndrome in the long run is a mean act. It leaves children vulnerable in dealing with dishonorable or even evil characters.

This is especially true because MJE parents avoid teaching the reality of evil people. They actually allow children to be in inappropriate and potentially harmful social situations such as attending rock concerts, dating, wearing provocative clothing, and having sex before emotionally ready. The reason for the conflicted attitude is that the MJE parent is not only supposed to protect the child from the pain of reality but at the same time supposed to give their children as many social experiences as early as possible. The greater the freedom of choice a child of MJE parents has, the better their parenting even though they have not been prepared to face the dark side of reality.

Parents who restrict the choices of their children can better establish morals and standards. The greater the amount of freedom a child has the less opportunity a parent has to instill morals and standards. Too much freedom of choice for a child creates a vulnerable brat. Having too many choices of objects and experiences spoils the child. They never have time to fully appreciate the thing at hand before reaching for the next. As Plato keenly observed, too much of a good thing, including freedom, has a corrosive effect on society. Excessively liberal ideals have subverted parenting in the United States, leaving children vulnerable to immoral people and ideas.

Many Smuggers refuse to accept that there are evil people in the world. In a speech I gave in San Diego, California, on raising a peaceful child, an educator asked for intellectual clarification. He stated, "You did not mean sex abusers were evil, just people who made wrong choices." I responded that sex abusers are evil because they repeatedly did an evil act. In a nonjudgmental, politically correct world it appeared to him I was making a Biblical reference. The educator could not comprehend that people who choose to do evil acts were considered evil in the past and these same acts make people evil today. No attempt at psychological victimization can whitewash the reality of evil people.

The permissive and materialistic Smugger ideology assumes there is no evil in our world. If there is no evil, you do not have to protect your child from evil. You do not have to teach your child to protect himself from evil or worry about the child himself becoming evil. As long as a parent provides high-quality material goods and experiences, he is being an optimal parent.

In a world without evil, the Smugger approach would make better sense. It is for this reason that modern parents refuse to acknowledge evil in the world. There is no need for the parent to concern himself with lecherous coaches, deviant priests, intruders, too friendly neighbors, or chatroom "friends" on the Internet.

There are times older people may appear to molest children but they were previously victimized and therefore should not be judged. There are no evil people, just people who make wrong choices. Evil may occur in poor, primitive societies, but not in our modern nation. Besides, deviants are not responsible for their evil actions because they are created by society, not by their choices.

In a modern world with its anonymity and overwhelming choices, evil can hide undetected. An individual who swindles someone in one place can relocate somewhere else. A bully can move from one group to another. In a modern world of material wealth, many people believe there is no need for punishment or retribution. Modern psychological techniques can repair the broken spirit. If damage is done to our child at the hands of another person due to our own irresponsibility, we can afford any necessary physical or mental therapy to repair the damage done by a misguided person.

When Smugger intellectuals can argue that a person who abducts from the front of her home, rapes, and kills a five-year-old child is not evil, morality is under attack. The blurring of our values and morals through intellectual rationalization, attempting to prove that they depend on the situation and circumstances, has been labeled "relativist thinking." This anti-reality thinking—where ex-President Bill Clinton can argue, "it depends on the definition of 'is'"—undermines the principles of our country, including how we deal with our children.

Smugger cultural and moral relativism undermines traditional thinking and behavior. In a world that judges people on their material possessions and not on their character, morals become less important. Accumulating wealth becomes the ultimate goal. The manner of achieving this goal is immaterial to the amount accumulated as long as you are liberal in donating part of it to public causes.

The long-range payoff of following the traditional path of raising moral children and living an honorable life is most evident in the latter stages of one's life. When traditional married couples look back and see the successful evolution of their lives and experience the blessings of their children, only then do they receive the benefits of this traditional approach. On the other hand, the modern PM parents can immediately point to their ever-escalating material trophies.

Gradually, traditional parents have been seduced by the almighty dollar to discard the value system handed down to them by their parents. Fathers have become obsolete and mothers are another paycheck to reach an ever-increasing level of affluence. A mountain of material junk has buried the traditional family.

Yet all the money in the world will not bring back the 9/11 victims, or the kidnapped, raped, and murdered children. All the money in the world will not give an adolescent a conscience if it was not developed in early childhood. All the money in the world will not make the sex abuse victims of uncaring priests emotionally and sexually whole. To deny evil may give everyone a sense of security, but it is a false sense of security that puts children in harm's way. Children deserve to have their parents and society give them an opportunity for inner and external peace. We are failing miserably.

Moral Message: Zero Tolerance for Bullies and Wimps

Today's children are as confused as their parents and more confused than children of past generations. Before our politically correct, non-judgmental world, bullies were bad and fighting them, defending yourself, was good. Being a crybaby was not an appropriate method of solving the problem with another child. Parents, teachers, and community leaders were in agreement: Standing up to bullies was a heroic act that was to be applauded.

When I address the topic of bullying, I am not talking about an overly sensitive child making a mountain out of a molehill. No, I am talking about a child intimidating another child to get him to do something against his own self-interest. I am talking about a mean, aggressive, destructive act that has no justification. This self-centered, harmful act must be addressed swiftly and severely by authority figures to teach the child a moral lesson so it is not repeated.

Adults know bullies or wimps are losers. Bullies may have inflated egos in a nonjudgmental environment, but they are still dysfunctional. Emotionally stable people are neither victims nor exploiters. A strong, healthy, and secure adult understands the liability of both extremes of being a bully or a wimp.

Bullying a certain group of individuals will ultimately fail because it is immoral. Someone will eventually rise to stop a brutal act. Being a wimp is not a better solution, as it is a red flag for bullies to enter their world. A person of character will not take advantage of another or allow another to take advantage of him.

A person of character, child or adult, will immediately stand up for a morally weak person being exploited by a morally weak bully. The difference between a healthy person and a bully or wimp is the quality of the parenting invested and the message received from authority figures.

A three-year-old went to a new preschool. For the first three days, he was a model student. Then he began kicking and hitting the teacher whenever he was told to do something he did not want to do. Being the youngest in the family, he used these tactics at home as well. After another incident with a different teacher, he was called into my office. He received a stern reprimand from the principal that this was not allowed in school. His older brother also told him he had to behave in school. His mother was embarrassed enough by his behavior to give him a spanking when he got home. Needless to say, he got the message and his behavior improved.

When children receive precise expectations from united authority figures, their behavior initially conforms. Once again, authority figures need to do their job of investigating questionable behavior. They should take the time to differentiate between bully and victim.

In most of today's schools, the perpetrator and the victim are dealt with equally. Both the bully and the wimp are given an insignificant consequence such as in-school suspension. The rationale is they cannot be certain what happened, which means, "I will not take the time to investigate in order to punish the abuser."

The victims do not have parents who are there when the child gets home to ask what happened. The victims no longer have a majority of peers who have been taught bullying one of their own has to be stopped or they will be the next victims.

The bully should be punished more severely than the victim. The bully has to be humiliated in front of his peers to show him bullying does not pay. The victim should be spoken to in a fatherly manner and told that fighting back against the bully is the morally correct thing to do. The encouragement should be followed by a less severe punishing consequence. Punishment with rational explanation reminds us to avoid repeating specific inappropriate behaviors.

When the majority of society is giving the same moral message, raising peaceful children is much easier. Children understand their role, which is reinforced by authority figures in school, church, law enforcement, and community leaders. The message is loud and clear: No morally conscientious leader will tolerate a bully or a wimp. It needs to be reinforced by authority figures but it has to start at home. Parents establish a peaceful home by being in charge and appropriately using discipline to develop strength of character in their children.

MJE Fantasy To Traditional
Moral Ends Justify The Means

Parenting Manifesto

Responsible parents unite to conquer our bullying and wimpy children. Either they make our lives a living hell or we exert our power to create a peaceful world. Parents are either a part of the problem or the solution. Non-parenting is no longer acceptable. It produces bullies and wimps. In the Smugger world, any parent punishing a child even for inappropriate behavior is being abusive. This is utter nonsense. We need to discipline our children into civilized, productive human beings. Let us have the courage to return to a fundamental, common-sense approach to raising children. As responsible parents we will no longer allow our children to push us around or use tear power to control our lives and ruin theirs.

Traditional parents focus on the child's behavior, not on their feelings. These parents expect the child to be obedient, respectful, honest, helpful, and kind. These parents use physical punishment when a child is young, will give their child the cold shoulder, and say things like "do it because I said so."

Getting the end product of a child who does the right thing is the focus, not being friends or being concerned over the short-term feelings of the child. These parents are more concerned with the child respecting their power of being a parent than being liked by the child. Most modern parents would find them too dominant, or worse, see them as bullying their children. The reality of what works, not the fantasy, is the basis of this approach.

When a child is an infant he can be intimidated (modern parents might view this as a form of bullying) simply by administering a slap on his backside. The infant or toddler knows the score. "My parent can make my life miserable through giving me pain." It is an effective and simple means of disciplining your child to set limits and establish expectations. These love taps are far more humane than allowing the child to waste time and energy on nonproductive tantrums.

As the child gets older and has not been taught obedience, a parent has to abandon the physical "love taps" approach and resort to more sophisticated Mahatma Gandhi-like methods. Gandhi defeated the British Empire through teaching Indian peasants civil disobedience. I have been teaching parents noncooperation with their child's demands to bully them into "crying uncle." ("Crying uncle" was a means adults used to show their superior physical power over children by applying pressure to the child's arm until the child said "uncle.")

My recommendation of noncooperation to parents is to stop taking the child anywhere: to lessons, games, extracurricular activities; they stop doing the child's laundry, giving money, or any of the other things the child expects until the child conforms to the dictates of the parents. The technique is also effective with adolescents.

The only way it fails to bring the older child to her knees is by the parent stopping before the child cries uncle. In my experience, many modern MJE parents do not want to view themselves as "in control" through their power because it makes them responsible. It is too real and harsh for their MJE sensibilities. Besides, most modern parents lack the stamina to outlast their baby bullies. Parents who want to be parents will receive renewed energy through non-cooperation discipline because it works in making children more appreciative.

Parents using the bully pulpit to help their problem child and the family to function better are performing a loving act. By abandoning the wimpy MJE approach and adapting "I do not care how I appear to others, I just want to help my family" approach, a permanent beneficial change will take place.

Parents using their power in punishing their children to develop moral habits are being dedicated parents. Parents pushing their child to conquer fear of pain are instilling courage in the child. Parents who teach and motivate their children to be the strongest they can be will prevent them from becoming bullies and wimps and promote peaceful children.

One major way of promoting strength and courage in a child is to teach him that he can do anything within reason if he puts his mind to it. Parents have the responsibility to refuse to accept the notion "I can't do it" because what it really means is "I won't do it." It is easier for a parent to step in and complete a child's task when the child plays dumb. This is the sign of a lazy, irresponsible parent. It is destructive to the child. It teaches the child that whining will enable him not to be accountable for doing the best he can do. It develops an "I won't try" habit that will eventually result in the child earning a designation as being disabled.

A conscientious parent requires the child to complete the assigned task. The parent tells the child, "Of course you can." By the parent teaching, demanding, and closely monitoring the child until he correctly completes the task, a positive work ethic will develop. This no-nonsense approach of requiring the child to apply his best effort in all endeavors is a positive habit that will encourage his success.

Parents, peers, and the majority of authority figures should applaud anyone who puts a bully in his rightful place as a coward. The role modeling of strength by parents is taught through osmosis to the children. Children unconsciously imitate the full range of their parents' behavior. The ability of their parents to say "no" to their own children's demands, especially when united, is a terrific moral lesson to their children. This strength of character of the parents will enhance their children's ability to say "no" to a bullying peer group or individuals.

I had to learn this lesson growing up in the early 1950s in Brooklyn, New York. In my Italian-American home, treating others with respect was expected and practiced. There was zero tolerance for irresponsible or inappropriate behavior. It was unthinkable for me to be anything but a good boy and listen to my parents. Punishment and fear of the parent were common. When I was seven years old, the streets of New York taught me a profound lesson. I was playing ball with children I had just met from the next block. For no apparent reason, a boy started to push me on the chest, sending me backward. Confused, I did not immediately react, so he continued shoving. Instinctively, I pushed back in anger and, presto, this aggressive child's behavior changed. I realized a paradox: When you stand up and are willing to fight, you often will be left in peace. We must stop asking our children to be mini psychologists in dealing with bullies and encourage them to stand up strong for their right not to be physically abused.[13]

Encouraging Children to Stand Up

This story has been and will be repeated in communities in the past, present, and future worldwide. It is human nature for some people to attempt to take advantage of the weak.

In the seventh grade, the much older juvenile delinquents demanded my lunch money. I refused to give it to them. I was aware that if I gave them my money I would be hassled every day from then on. If I refused and stood my ground, they would leave me alone and go on to someone else. My mother and father encouraged me to defend myself against anyone picking on me.

I was taught it was my moral responsibility not to allow myself to be intimidated by a bully and stand up for my rights, even if it meant fighting. Nurturing behavior in the home was often seen as weakness outside the home. Surviving outside the home is a different matter. The projection of power and confidence, not kindness, is the best antidote for repelling uncalled-for aggression in any environment. A morally strong person's toughness may hide his kindness but does nothing to extinguish it.

The strong and secure are more likely to give a helping hand than the weak and insecure, though with less fanfare and without self-serving motives.

When I was a young teenager coming home on the West End subway three teenage hoodlums entered the car I was riding in. They wore black leather jackets and carried knives in their hands. The ringleader went up to an old man and spat directly in his face. The elderly man said nothing and no one else spoke. Everyone on the crowded car was in stunned silence. The two other accomplices ridiculed the other passengers.

I was about the same age as these juvenile delinquents and they made my blood boil. As soon as I realized not one adult was going to react, I blew up. I screamed at the ringleader and started toward him. The train started slowing down, the doors opened, and the three punks ran out of the door. Moral outrage does repel evil.

Societies Need Strong Fathers

In all honesty, the major reason I had the courage to be tough was that I was unwilling to face my father. He taught me I had to do what I had to do. In other words, he disciplined me to be more concerned about his reactions than of anyone trying to bully me.

Our society needs fathers to be fathers, not wimps. The father's focus is on disciplining the child to prepare him to be successful in the world outside the home. A Mayan proverb expresses this concept very well. "In the baby lies the future of the world. . . . his father must take him to the highest hill to see what the world is like." Ken Cannon, a Cherokee chief, says this in another way. "The father creates the child's heart. The father gives the child courage and a more realistic perspective of the world." Fathers are essential in teaching children to use their own internal strength to prevent others from intimidating them.

Children need to be taught that courage gets better results than cowardice. Victims do not have fathers who say, "You need to fight back to defend yourself or more bullies will whip you." Fathers that say "If you do not fight back, I will hurt you worse than the bully" have been silenced in this "sensitive male" era. The only way to stop the victimization of our children is to bring back morality where abuse is punished and defending yourself is rewarded.

A clearer understanding of right and wrong will end much of the confusion for parents and children. There is a wonderful anonymous saying: "If God wanted to be more permissive, instead of the Ten Commandments, he would have given us the Ten Suggestions." Fighting for what is morally right gives us strength that repels evil.

Discipline your child before it is too late. The lesson learned by observing human nature is simple: Either your child attempts to control you or you control him. When a child knows a parent, teacher, policeman, judge, other authority figure, or even a peer will use his power, the child will conform and stop testing the limits.

Many modern Smugger parents reading this book would be horrified to think they have ever intimidated their child. This is utter nonsense. These parents don't want their child to ever fear them. Yet any child perceives a parent as a giant. The incredible size difference, strength, and power are undeniable to even the most friendly oriented parent. Whenever a parent forcefully emphasizes a behavior or a thought, he will unconsciously intimidate the child. It is only through conscious dedication to be a playmate that a parent can eliminate the normal fear a child has for a parent.

However, there are parents who have not been brainwashed by the Smuggers. They are not ashamed to be old-fashioned parents. They give commands and follow through with what they say. These effective parents expect children to listen and do not care whether their children are temporarily upset with them when disciplined. There is no fear in the parents' minds about traumatizing the child. This parent believes children are resilient and appreciate caring demonstrated by discipline.

Parents shifting to a reasonable, yet higher behavior standard will enhance the future of their children. An impossible-to-reach standard creates a neurotic personality and a standard of tolerance or a standard set too low will create a misfit, a misfit who does not have the necessary ability to succeed in the world. It is time for American parents to become more balanced. It is time for American parents to become more intolerant of their children's negative behavior for the sake of their children's future. It is time American parents return to traditional moral methods of raising children where children receive punishment for their transgressions and earn privileges for their responsible behavior.

As early as possible, consciously command your child to do things. In other words, command your children; establish who is boss. If you do not, your authority will be tested until the child perceives you as a wimp. Once your power is firmly established, you can back off and be a firm, strong, and loving mother or father. This power can be corked like a genie's bottle for the next needed performance. Children, like everyone else, understand raw power, responding to it or using it to their own advantage. The choice is either to be a parent, to be abused, or worse, to be disregarded.

Parents have to realize that they are responsible to teach their children how to act. The parents need to demand appropriate behavior and expectations from their children. When the child acts out, the parents have to use their power to put him back on track. This calculated intimidation by parents is in the best interest of the child, inoculating him against becoming a bully or a wimp.

Our children deserve parents who will give them a foundation for future success. It is unconscionable for modern parents to continue to follow child-development Smuggers' contradictory advice primarily because it is easier and less time-consuming than time-tested, more traditional methods. Creating a peaceful, emotionally healthy, and inquisitive child is not an automatic genetic process like a blossoming flower. It is hard work, but the payoff is huge.

Throughout the history of man, parents have passed down the culture of society to the children in the family. No amount of cultural engineering by Smuggers is going to replace the role of morally disciplined parents in creating a civilized and peaceful child. Only through the sacrificing of the parents to live an exemplary life can their children receive the gift of a strong foundation. The moral role modeling of parents and other significant adults is essential in developing the character of a child. Our nation needs to talk the talk and walk the walk of a moral life. The Smugger PM/MJE mentality has to be recognized and rejected to give our children the opportunity to be healthy and successful adults.

Chapter 8

Living Right, Living Disciplined: Winning the Culture War

Watch your thoughts; they become words.
Watch your words; they become actions.
Watch your actions; they become habits.
Watch your habits; they become character.
Watch your character; it becomes your destiny.

— FRANK OUTLAW

The above quote clearly shows how personal discipline adds to the value and quality of your life. Aristotle went into great depth about the effect of habits on the overall character of the individual. This book emphasizes that the purposeful discipline of children by their parents, by establishing positive and moral habits, creates a conscience in the child, which culminates in a strong moral character. This strong moral character is naturally attracted to the spiritual aspects of life.

Living right means being disciplined. America's form of government requires moral citizens.

We are currently in the midst of a culture civil war. The damage from this war is evident on an interpersonal basis with an explosion of out-of-control bullying and whining behavior on a personal level and on a national level with the assault on our values, institutions, and morals. Peace requires discipline, while a lack of discipline leads to internal turmoil and external war. We are off track. Marriages are dissolving. Violence, drugs, sexual abuse, and corporate and political corruption are widespread. Our religious institutions are lacking integrity. We are in a culture meltdown that will lead to an implosion of our civilization.

The sides in this war seem to be firmly entrenched. On one side are the modern people who worship materialism, the self, pleasure, government control of everything except when it interferes with them, the woman's right to be sexually irresponsible, and the power to change the law in the middle of the game to alter the culture. On the other side are the traditionalists who believe in God, family, discipline, limited government, the sanctity of life, and the rule of law. If Americans want to continue to be the leaders of the free world, we have to choose the more arduous path of traditional discipline or lose the America we know and love. We need to reject the cancerous utopian illusions and temptations of hedonistic bliss. We must remain on the path of righteousness for ourselves, our families, our country, and world peace. The foundation for that journey is the strong family.

To establish and maintain a fulfilling life and a peaceful, strong nation requires discipline. The training starts in the family and continues throughout our institutions. Our institutions of marriage, school, religion, law enforcement, business, and politics have to follow the disciplined moral path and have the same consistent message the child receives at home.

Our children have to be prepared to confront the inevitability of adversity and the existence of evil. Strong moral character helps us to negotiate the pitfalls and temptations of life. Strong moral character is necessary to be successful in life. Strong moral character leads to spirituality and peaceful, loving people. In a moral society, peaceful people will be leading the country on all levels of society toward the historical middle of the political spectrum. This is the legacy of our forefathers.

Our founding fathers worked very hard to create this wonderful country and we are throwing it away. Our founding families were wise men and women of strong moral character who willingly sacrificed their status, prosperity, and lives in the making of our nation. Their gift to future generations was to place our nation on a firm road to peace. Abraham Lincoln used this road during the Civil War. "In a time of change and danger he sought wisdom from generations gone before. The ideals of the founding fathers have been his beacon in the storm."[1]

Our Constitution is based on rational principles based on human nature, not on intellectual fantasy. Our forefathers knew the limits of laws and the importance of the character of their families and individuals of a nation to remain a free people. They understood that a free republic relies ultimately on the family to teach, discipline, and develop the character of its people. A nation based on freedom needs honorable citizens who will hold those freedoms dear and not attempt wholesale abuse of their liberties. Our society relies on committed parents to teach the fundamentals of morality by example.

Our nation was based on what actually worked, not on an intellectual theory. George Washington said, "To be prepared for war is the most effectual means of preserving peace." He knew, as a student of history, that strength repelled people of evil intent while weakness attracted them.

Our founding fathers left a blueprint that has guided our nation to become the most economically, militarily, and morally powerful country in the world. A plan based on morals and values was passed down and proved time after time to lead to peace, prosperity, and happiness. It is a formula that requires many personal sacrifices and pain but it has paid great dividends to our nation and made America the light of freedom and the envy of the entire world.

From God to Hedonism

In the arrogance of the 1960s we rejected history and embraced hedonism. By discarding traditional thought, many naïve individuals believed they would shield themselves from the pain of reality and experience pure pleasure. The traditional values and morals established by our fore-fathers are diametrically opposed to the values of the current self-absorbed "me generation" that has infiltrated into positions of power throughout our society.

During the 1960s, many young people believed they deserved power. In institutions of higher education, these youths were propagandized about the limitations and inequities of their culture. Many baby boomers were swept off their feet by the antiestablishment, hippie movement. This immature, self-serving movement ridiculed everything traditional and replaced it with the worship of youthful pleasure. Any-thing so-called "old-fashioned" was out and anything new and radical (sex, drugs, and rock and roll) hedonism was in.

The wholesale, emphatic rejection of traditionalism was a very self-serving method of anointing the baby boomers as the chic, new wise ones of the end of the twentieth century. In little over forty years, the traditional morals and values on which our nation was established became as foreign as hieroglyphics to many of the new generation.

In our youth-oriented culture, living a balanced life is ridiculed as boring and uneventful. Being in a spiritual place is incomprehensible to a culture that focuses on open glorification of the grotesque in the unnatural light of night, in a drug- or alcohol-induced altered state. The "youth culture" walks on the wild side where the perverse is glorified and embraced.

The present, self-absorbed culture is all about creating a fantasy life. It is based on short-term hedonistic benefits. The beauty of nature, a sparkling beach, or snowcapped mountain is shunned for a man-made lifestyle of wild, all-night parties where lying, drinking, and drugging are at a premium. Daytime is for resting, for the action they crave is in the flashing strobe lights and unrelenting flow of alcohol and drugs that takes place at night. This is a long way from a spiritual path.

In a phony fantasy world there is little light of truth, only the impressing of each other through distortion. The process is to build oneself up and tell others what you think they want to hear, rather than what you know to be true. Lie begets lie until the truth is as foreign as reality. What is real vanishes into the smoke, mirrors, and slight-of-hand of the next con.

Logical and disciplined thinking has no roots in a world of darkness and pathetic wishful thinking. Fantasy is a much easier and more pleasurable path in the short run than following the difficult traditional path proscribed by our elders. Piercing, tattoos, promiscuous sex, drugs, and alcohol give a person an immediate identity and acceptance into a social group. The immediate euphoria is pleasurable, but the reality hangover is inevitable and undeniable. To delay the pain of life the answer is simple: Do more addictive actions and reinvent yourself by changing your image and groups.

The celebrity addicts of our present youth-worshipping culture are unable to go beyond the adolescent stage. The new and never-ending assortment of crude and rude perennial acting teenagers in music, sports, and television are thrust upon our children as gods. The youth-worshipping media asks not an accomplished dignified member of society to speak. No, instead the media markets a major interview with a youth-worshipping babbling person whose personal life is a perpetual disaster. Ridiculous as it seems, these people who are unable to live a functional life are telling the rest of us in America how to run the country.

The disastrous personal lives of celebrities are a result of their lack of morals. These celebrities of hedonism do possess an attribute, ability, or talent that is real and undeniably superior to the average person. Most, if not all, have conquered some form of adversity increasing their self-confidence in facing the painful stress necessary to rise to a position of prominence in any field. Without a firm foundation in morals to guide them, they will use their ability to dominate others for their own personal gain. Lying, deceiving, and thrill-seeking escalate into more graphic forms of abuse. Retaining power regardless of the consequences to others moves the person further into the realm of evil.

Great moral leaders like Washington, Lincoln, and Gandhi did what was best for their countrymen while suffering immense personal sacrifice. Their strong willfulness was used for the greatest good to obtain a state of peace. On the other hand, strong-willed people without basic morals appreciate little of the beauty of the world around them—except perhaps to use it to gain more and more control over others.

This greed for power through money can be seen in corporate corruption where executives "cook the books" to gain huge bonuses or sell tainted products to the unaware consumer. It could be seen in deceitful political behavior that betrays the interests of others and uses power to avoid any consequences for unlawful behavior.

When the purpose of a person's life is solely for his own self-interest with outright contempt for the rights and good of others, he will perform evil acts. When President Clinton had oral sex with Monica Lewinsky in the Oval Office there was little moral indignation from our leaders. Yet a message was sent to many young girls who were given the green light to have oral sex with boys. Frightfully they heard the message from the president of the United States that oral sex is not sex.

The sad truth is we as a society have lowered our expectations of our leaders to the point where there is no moral outrage for their corrupt practices. We have become cosmopolitan or jaded depending on the side you have fallen in the culture civil war.

Our secular Smugger elite is obsessed with convincing America that immature and deviant sexual behavior is normal. Their incessant message of sex is spread on sitcoms on television, and through the media in advertising, news, and entertainment. All types of sex have been rammed and manipulated into the minds of all of us. We are supposed to accept any sex act as normal. Nothing is sacred and no one seems to be immune from this invasion. Without sexual boundaries a nation slides into a hedonistic existence. When a civilization has no higher purpose than individual pleasure, vital forces are sapped, creating a vulnerability to decay and decline.

Sexual acts are best kept behind closed doors for a society to flourish. Public sex—whether heterosexual or homosexual—contaminates everyone, especially our children. To expose emotionally immature children to explicit fornication or sodomy is to foster an unbalanced world prone to deviant addiction. The worshipping of promiscuous celebrity sluts is a prescription for hedonism.

The homosexual marriage campaign is an attempt to equate and legitimize homosexual with heterosexual behavior. It will un-define marriage. Without a true definition of marriage between a man and a woman, all types of sexual involvement will become equivalent. Polygamy, bestiality, bisexuality, or homosexuality will have the same status as a marriage of a man and a woman. This would open a Pandora's box, unleashing a barrage of people further pushing the envelope of normality. The advocacy for same-sex marriage is a smokescreen for a more formidable and devious agenda.

Even if we agreed to homosexual marriage, it would not be the end of the demands. A nation's choice through laws and norms creates the stability or instability of a society. According to Al Randell, a homosexual talk-show host and guest on the Bill O'Reilly television show February 16, 2004, same-sex marriage is not a priority of the homosexual community. He noted civil contracts can insure property rights. Mr. Randell indicated that the homosexual marriage issue is a stepping-stone to a more ambitious amoral agenda. Patrick Moore in *Beyond Shame: Reclaiming the Abandoned History of Radical Gay Sexuality* calls for a nonmonogamous radical homosexual right of expression. In-your-face homosexuality is a plague on the spiritual and mental health of our nation.

Homosexuality is a choice, not a right. It has been practiced by a small segment of the population throughout history. It should not be promoted.

Political correctness cannot redefine nature and morality. Debauchery may be more pleasurable in the short term but will have disastrous effects for individuals in the long run. Hedonistic practices by a large segment of any nation have and will destroy that nation.

Marriage is defined by God and nature as a union between a man and a woman.

This clear definition of marriage is essential to a civilization's survival. The sanctioning and rewarding of marriage between a male and a female emphasizes the importance of propagation for the continuation of the society. Marriage and its rational extension of a family is the cornerstone of all dynamic civilizations.

All sex should be a private matter. It ought to be kept behind closed doors for the sake of our children and nation. Hedonism will destroy our civilization as it has others throughout history.

Crossroads: Smugger Permissive/
Materialism or Traditional Discipline?

He who passively accepts evil is as much involved in it as he who helps
to perpetrate it.

—MARTIN LUTHER KING JR.

In our PC, permissive, and materialistic world, evil is not acknowledged, pain is anesthetized, punishment is banned, and God is dead. People are not accountable for their actions. Punishment is illegal in a world where there is no right and wrong. All behaviors are equally sanctioned in the world of equality. A permissive world requires no sacrifice of time and energy to teach and enforce the societal expectations. The violence of the bully and the fighting back of the self-defender are seen as morally equivalent. It is as if these people do not make distinctions of behavior so they will not have to face the fact that evil exists.

The Smugger revolution has converted many to believe it is important to make no mental judgments of others. Being judgmental is divisive but being tolerant is enlightened. A non-judgmental person does not have to take sides on issues. There is no reason to get angry or stigmatize an action in a world of equal values or said in another way, valueless world. One of the slogans of this counter-movement that sums up the valueless "Brave New World" is "Why can't we all just get along?" Too many of us have bought this sentiment at great cost to our values and morals.

Thank God there are people with moral character.

We are not all getting along. Conscientious people cannot morally accept parents not doing what they need to do. Many parents choose to do "their own thing" with little regard for their children.

Nonparenting causes responsible people to have to carry the burden created by the parent's neglect or abuse. More and more responsible grandparents are attempting to salvage their grandchildren from their self-absorbed sons and daughters. Schools and churches have attempted to teach courses on responsibility, sexual decision-making, and value clarification along with group therapy to fill the gap created by parents not doing their job. Politicians in our local communities have passed curfew laws. The abuse and neglect laws attempt to force parents to be better, but to little avail.

The truth of the matter is no other social institution can duplicate the dedication and effort of two committed parents working together to share their knowledge, morals, and values to make their children's lives better than theirs. The importance of the family has lost its priority in our present greedy materialistic era.

All behaviors are equal in a Smugger's world. The bully and victim, taking personal pride or being lazy, nuclear family and non-family, maintaining high standards and "getting over," our founding fathers and deviant celebrities, drug-free and druggies, law-abiding citizens and criminals are already treated equally without discrimination. In the first phase of the culture civil war all behaviors are acceptable.

The society becomes unsettled when a vacuum is created. The Smuggers' propaganda established a new set of values. The second phase of the counterrevolution reveals the agenda of one world government based on rational scientific thought where pain, poverty, and evil are extinct and are replaced by material abundance and personal pleasure equally accessible to all as paradise on earth. In other words, it is the same worldview I was taught forty years ago in undergraduate school, yes, the Marxist Utopia!

Everything was turned upside-down. The Smuggers have been incredibly effective in shifting the perceptions and values of most educated Americans through universities, media and politics. Thanks to these "situational ethical thinkers," the commonsense approach to dealing with issues has been contaminated to render it useless.

In this Smugger counterrevolution, a slap on an infant's backside is the equivalent to a brutal beating or a child crying after the death of a loved one is the equivalent to a child crying to manipulate. A youngster fighting back after being attacked is the equivalent to bullying a helpless younger child. A parent preparing a nutritional meal is equivalent to a parent giving her child a nutritionally useless junk food such as a "lunchable."

Since all behaviors are relative, we tolerate them equally. Marriage between a man and a woman should be treated the same as a homosexual relationship. A change in Florida adoption rules gives no preference to a married couple over a single person adopting a child. "Gay rights activists also support the change because they think it undermines the twenty-six-year-old state law that prohibits gay people from adopting."[2] Our culture is being attacked.

This counterrevolution of the past fifty years has reaped a culture full of absurdity and hypocrisy. This movement was supposed to free females from being sex objects. Today even elementary school girls are wearing thong underwear and short tops showing their navels and acting like streetwalkers. This was a significant accomplishment for the feminists. They have enabled females to equally treat males as sex objects. Many modern sensitive males are hypervigilant about their appearance. They are so compassionate they weep in public, shave their body hair, and wear earrings, yet have the lack of ability to maintain intimacy in long-term relationships.

Smuggers ridicule the institution of marriage while pushing for homosexual marriage announcements in the newspapers. They argue for more money for education while lobbying and passing laws against home schooling in California. They are fervently for affirmative action while being against any form of discrimination. They advocated against corporal punishment though they advocate through NAMBLA for adults having sex with children. They feel it is unfair for children to assist parents financially but it is the responsibility of parents to furnish their adult children money until they die.

Smuggers fight against any form of sexual harassment of females though it is allowed if the perpetrator has the right political persuasion. Crimes against minorities and homosexuals are hate crimes, while the same crimes against whites and heterosexuals are lesser crimes or not crimes at all. The same people who fervently support girls having their all-girl leagues not to be overwhelmed physically by the opposite sex are the same people to demand the right of a 115-pound high-school girl to play football on the same field with male football players double her weight.[3]

The Smugger-Marxist secularists argue for total freedom of speech then hypocritically censor facts that go against their belief system. The American media's unwillingness to highlight the United Nations "Oil

For Food" scandal, America's successes in Iraq, and the human rights abuses that are occurring in communist or socialist countries is an example of this selective reporting.

The Smuggers have selectively used the First Amendment to continually alter our culture. Their success is undeniable. Using mass persuasion methods devised in Nazi Germany's enlightenment and propaganda ministry, these leaders have reshaped the way we view everything from marriage to education, to community, to religion, to family. Unlike the Nazi German's propaganda, it is not part of the government but is external to it. During President Clinton's eight years potentially negative stories were suppressed as the media attempted to shield his administration and immediately praised the positive claims of this presidency. On the other hand, George W. Bush's administration has been attacked on every front and is given no credit for obvious successes. Are the media showing a cultural bias against traditional beliefs?

The primary Smugger objective in America is not to maintain one particular administration. Its goal is to dismantle the culture until it is sufficiently weakened to allow for a bloodless coup from within. Our cultural perceptions are under assault by the clever use of systematic brainwashing. The Smuggers are cleansing us of our traditional morals, knowledge, and beliefs, and are inserting failed communist notions in their place.

The First Amendment to our Constitution exists for only the Smuggers, not for anyone expressing traditional values, morals, and beliefs. A perfect example is Mel Gibson's spiritual movie, *The Passion of Christ*. It was treated by Hollywood and the media as a horribly violent, senseless production. The attempt of the Smuggers to deny the production and promotion of this movie was an attempt at censorship. The removal of Ray Moore from the Alabama Supreme Court for displaying the Ten Commandments in the Montgomery courthouse lobby was a clever Smugger victory in selective censorship.

Our culture has been turned upside down by Smuggers. This has been accomplished by using a process of double standards expressed through selection to bolster their agenda and indignation aimed at what is counter to it. Sex, violence, and deviancy are relentlessly forced on the public as long as there is no moral lesson to be learned.

Any moral message is condemned as divisively harmful. Sexual abstinence (virginity), manly resolve, heterosexuality, being pro-life, stay-at-home-moms, faithfulness, manners, righteousness, and patriotism are rejected and ridiculed.

By exaggerations of their human frailty, even historical heroes are attacked. These tactics render them as flawed characters, denying them recognition of their accomplishments while promiscuity, abortion, intellectual babble, homosexuality, careerism, profanity, gangsterism, and anti-Americanism are venerated and glorified. The dregs of the traditional America are paraded on Hollywood's award extravaganzas. Madonna, Britney Spears, Snoop Dogg, and Michael Jackson remain on top not for the quality of their performance but for their clever exhibitionism.

The morally bankrupt national media is touting self-promoting opportunists as humanitarian idealists. Fidel Castro, Jesse Jackson, Jane Fonda, Kofi Annan, Ted Kennedy, and Ted Turner are lauded for their hypocritical compassion for the downtrodden. A clear distinction between good and evil is not tolerated and immediately censored as politically incorrect.

The Smuggers' control of the media has been a powerful weapon in reshaping our culture. The selective use of the First Amendment has been a smoke screen for subverting our society. The double standard and inherent inconsistencies of their argument are becoming more evident. The propaganda of the Smuggers will self-destruct under the light of truth. Let us all have the courage to shrug off political correctness and self-censorship and be honest and truthful to ourselves and others. Truthfulness will expose and quiet the Smuggers' distortion of the first amendment.

Media Entertainment Antipathy

To win this culture war we must become discriminating readers of the news. We must notice who has written which article from what news source to better recognize the hidden agenda of the reporter. Many "news" articles are commentaries, not factual reporting of information. This bashing of traditionalism by the Smuggers has been well documented by Bernard Goldberg in his book *Bias*.

Celebrities are poisoning our minds against our leaders who are extolling traditional values. Hollywood and the media appear to be unanimous in their hatred of the stable middle-class, working Americans who are the backbone of the country. The non-enterprising, unemployed, and the privileged elite are the focus of their adoration and attention, in sharp contrast to their often-antagonistic dealings with productive people.

Not only does the media inappropriately use its power to push its disdain for traditional values, the entertainment industry is coming out of the closet with a vengeance. Hollywood celebrities believe they have a right to use the entertainment forum to influence the public politically. "Why does it have to be unpatriotic to do something that is our inherent right, which is to debate issues?" asked Tom Fontana, creator of shows such as *OZ* and *Homicide*. Whoopie Goldberg's show, *Whoopie*, referred to a G. W. Bush character by saying, "I can't believe he's doing to my bathroom (flushing) what he is doing to my economy." A *Law and Order* character played by Jesse Martin referred to President Bush as "the dude who lied to us." Jerry Orbach, who plays his partner on the show, stated, "Saddam Hussein did have such weapons because the president's daddy sold them to a certain someone who

Living Right, Living Disciplined: Winning the Culture War   265

used to live in Baghdad." Ms. Goldberg was asked if she would be pleased if her show could contribute to the defeat of President Bush. She answered, "I would like that."[4] There is little doubt of the hidden agenda of the entertainment industry.

The use of public airwaves to demean our elected leaders is certainly unethical, if not illegal. The strongest message we can send these inflated ego "stars" is to stop viewing their shows and films. Loss of income and fame, not morals, appears to direct these crass self-promoting Hollywood types.

We as a nation are at a turning point in the road. As we continue down the road of self-absorbed materialistic hedonism, we will sacrifice our individual inner peace through the sins of our immoral lifestyles. This loss of our morality will accentuate our lack of spirituality, leading to personal dissatisfaction, and eventually weakening the vitality of the nation. Each additional evil convert will further contaminate our country, making us ripe for internal or external conflict.

Internally as a nation we are in the midst of an explosion of deviant behavior ranging from cheating, lying, and bullying to random child rape and murder for pleasure. At the same time, our unwillingness or inability to apprehend and punish these internal terrorists of peaceful communities makes our nation appear weak to foreign terrorists. Our nation will continue down the moral relativist path of the last fifty years or choose to move to the center, back to the moral roots that nurtured our nation to greatness.

Making no choice will cause our loss of moral resolve and our surrender to the terrorists. Making no choice to change our national direction is a choice.

The easiest path, and the most devastating for the citizens of our nation, is to ignore the cultural and moral civil war taking place in all our sacred institutions. This noninvolvement will insure the clear victory of the immoral, permissive materialistic society: The Culture War would end in defeat. If we do not decide to change the direction of our country, it will result in a weak, decadent society vulnerable to attack by foreign powers.

Let's face it; it is easier to live in fantasy than in reality. Spending money is easy. Paying the bills is hard. Permissiveness with children is easy. Correcting the ramifications of their misdeeds is difficult. Lying, cheating, and stealing are easy. Suffering the consequences of being apprehended is hard. Tolerating evil is easy. Facing the anguish of an evil act is horrific. It may be effortless not to change directions, but expending energy to avoid a pending disaster is an action we cannot disregard.

A Bitter Pill to Swallow: Pain Builds Courage, Character, and a Disciplined Life

Life is a series of often-painful challenges on the road to the destiny we create. The expressions seen all over our country several years ago on bumper stickers and T-shirts saying, "life's a bitch" or "shit happens" infuriated me. Anyone who has the audacity to believe life will follow his or her desires is living a delusion. Children die, people lose their "secure" jobs, wars break out, unimaginable terrorist acts happen, accidents befall people we love, and illness strikes, as well as many other unfortunate possibilities that are beyond our control. This is life, folks. To attempt to deny or to feel no one else has faced similar suffering is a prescription for a life as a loser. To confront and conquer a significant setback is a sign of a winner. The old saying "adversity builds character" is as true today as ever.

In the modern culture all pain, physical and psychological, is dealt with a pill instead of the power of the mind. Reality cannot be wished away through alcohol, drugs, or a life of virtual reality fantasy. The pain encountered in living needs to be accepted and experienced to learn from the lessons of life. One cannot appreciate or learn from life while taking Prozac, Zoloft, Ritalin, Ecstasy, crack, or any other mind-altering substance. Yet many powerful segments of society, medicine, education, psychology, youth culture, and the media act as pushers for the "magic pill" solution of dealing with life.

There are natural tragedies brought into our homes every night via television. Pictures of forest fires, earthquakes, hurricanes, and floods occur usually with a statement from an affected person or two. The reactions vary from anguish "that my life will never be the same" to the other extreme of "this incident will give me an opportunity to rebuild a better life." The difference in mental attitude says it all. When adversity hits, some people wallow in self-pity and others fight back using the setback as an impetus to move forward with a stronger and clearer vision. Pain exists in every phase of the life cycle.

An individual has to confront pain to learn how to successfully manage it. People gain strength from perseverance. The infant pushes his body in various motions until he is able to lift his head, arms, and legs. First he crawls, then masters wobbly walking, and soon is exploring his world inside and outside his home. The skills and knowledge learned from those around him are soon expanded to the neighborhood and school. The lessons from appropriate authority figures he meets builds on the foundation provided in the home.

Upon reaching a level of maturity with the assistance of parents and other role models we are able to overcome many major obstacles in life. As each problem is resolved we learn a lesson. Maybe the lesson is as simple as the fact we need to switch hands when we are shoveling to prevent hurting our backs or as complex as why someone who you thought cared about you rejects you. All pain has a way of focusing one's attention on a particular problem. It is one's prerogative whether to not to do anything about the issue or to confront it and find a solution to the problem. The successful person searches for the answer to the problem. The way we resolve a significant problem can shape our future.

During our lives, we have personal contact with people who experience traumatic events or we experience them ourselves. Some of us fall into a hole of depression while others become an inspiration. A sixteen-year-old student of mine was in a car accident and lost movement from the chest down. His attitude toward his condition never seemed to affect his sense of humor or view of the world. He continually cheered up those around him as soon as he came out of the intensive care unit. The incident seemed to give him greater maturity. He put 100 percent effort into his rehabilitation and has become a very conscientious student and citizen.

Conquering the pain of failure or misfortune by overcoming it produces increased courage. Traditionally, Father was the one who instilled courage in children. By a father demanding more and more responsible behavior from his child, the child increased his or her tolerance of pain and lost the fear of confronting the challenges of life. "You will learn to ride the big bike, pick yourself up and try again." The pain of falling is immaterial to reaching your goal. When a person realizes he can obtain his objectives if he is willing to pay the price through his efforts, he is on track to become an independent, mature adult in control of his life.

Courage to face the short-run pain is the answer to having a successful existence. Any successful business owner will tell you about the initial sacrifices necessary to get the enterprise on a strong footing. Starting over again after a tragedy like a serious accident or a loss of a loved one takes immense courage, first to deal with the emotional pain of the loss, and then to deal with the pain of getting yourself back to where you were before the loss. George Washington lost more battles in the American Revolution than he won. Abraham Lincoln lost many elections and business ventures before he became president. Thomas

Edison failed one thousand times before inventing the electric light bulb. A winner has to learn to deal with the pain of failure.

The possession of a strong will without a conscience is a powerful combination for evil. The absence of a conscience makes it easier for a person to con his way to the top. His strong will enables him to absorb greater dosages of painful stress than the average person. This hedonistic lifestyle leads to excesses that may delay the pain without resolving the problem that is causing the pain. Eventually the pain will be felt at higher levels than even the strong personality can manage. A hedonistic lifestyle of only relying on pleasure eventually swings the powerfully appearing person out of balance.

Excessive gratification in one area causes us to be out of balance in others. Being out of balance is stressful until it is corrected. The most rapid means of returning a person to balance is administering corrective discipline. The only reason we accepted our mothers giving us bitter medicine when we were sick was to get better. Illness is painful and we learned that a bitter pill puts us back on the road to health. We learned eating right, sleeping enough, and exercising prevents us from getting ill in the first place. The best method of minimizing acute and chronic pain is to avoid excesses through living a disciplined life. Our traditional wisdom is based on common experiences of many individuals over time that teaches us what works and what does not.

Mankind often has a short memory. Overindulgence has been known throughout history to cause imbalance. The ancient Greeks and Romans spoke about the virtue of moderation. They knew anything taken to excess, even a good thing, could have adverse effects. Too much food, drink, sex, work, or entertainment will unbalance anyone. The list of ways of being excessive is endless. I spoke of Plato's observation that excessive freedom without responsibility will produce a decadent society. It leads to wasting more time and energy running from problems than solving them. The accumulation of the unresolved issues and the attached pain results in the person's downfall. Historically the ideology of hedonism has led to chaos and the eventual collapse of civilization.

Our society needs to accept pain as a natural part of life. It teaches us to live a more healthy and balanced life. For our society to survive and prosper we must awaken from our dream state of self-absorption. We must accept pain's ability to teach us many life lessons. Parenting may be a painful sacrifice, but if done correctly it pays great benefits. Many parents do not train their children in moral choices because it is painful to the parents to administer punishment to the child. By parents' unwillingness to deal with the initial pain of training their children, they leave the child vulnerable to evil forces. These parents expose themselves to their children's unguided choices that will hurt the child, the family, the community, and the nation.

Purposeful Disciplining of Children Is Essential for Peace

We as a nation owe an incredible amount to parents who are willing to be traditional parents: parents who live disciplined and virtuous lives. These parents sacrifice their selfish pursuits for the betterment of their family. These mature parents follow the Golden Rule: "Do unto others as you would have them do unto you" in all aspects of their lives. Traditional parents know from their own childhoods, by observing their children, and by listening to adults who have raised healthy children what needs to be done.

There is no greater moral principle to generate a world of peace than the Golden Rule. If most parents were able to instill the Golden Rule in their children's consciences the nation would be a much safer and decent place to live. The foundation of this path is formed by the aggregate of parents in our nation functioning as parents, not friends to their children, minus the aggregate of parents who are not doing their job. When the majority of parents are being responsible parents, teaching their children right from wrong, we are developing a base of strong future citizens. If we follow the Golden Rule we would not offend others by our actions. We would be respectful, industrious, responsible, kind, generous, and honest, all traditional values.

Parents teach their values through role modeling. By role modeling moral behaviors parents demonstrate to their children that morals and values do matter. When a parent stands up to any person attempting to bully him into some form of submission the child learns a real lesson much more powerful than a lecture.

Honesty and obedience are characteristics of a functioning family. These virtues are role modeled and practiced daily with great impact on the child's value system.

Even abstract values such as time management are more effectively taught by role modeling than by lecturing. Parents teach the importance of time by their decisions. In a harried lifestyle time is at a premium. Parents can make better use of family time by demanding everyone pitch in for the sake of the family. Children learn valuable skills by contributing to the daily chores. This gives parents time to relax and be better parents by spending time alone with their spouse. Children who are occupied with chores and homework have less time to be bored. After finishing their duties they are more appreciative of their time to do the things of their choosing. Every family member benefits when all members act responsibly.

Effective parents closely supervise and monitor their child's time. These parents teach their children which particular television shows and behaviors are acceptable and which are not. The children of a functioning family are programmed directly by the parents. There is no need for a V-chip or censorship filter because parents have lovingly taught their children the wisdom of following their advice or suffering the pain of the judicious use of moral consequences.

Parents Are Obliged to Teach About Evil

Bullies are everywhere. We must learn to deal with them. A schoolyard bully, teacher, coach, or bureaucratic bully, even a nation attempting to bully another, all fear the same thing: being exposed for what they truly are, cowards. Bullying in any form does not respond to kindness or rational thinking. It only seems to respond to power through strength. Thus we must have our child, students, citizens, communities, and nation develop mental, emotional, and physical attributes to the fullest. By developing strength on all levels we are fostering a peaceful society. To create a peaceful society we must start with the children.

The child is "evil-proofed" by traditional moral and value training, making him or her less vulnerable to the seduction of the self-absorbed life style. Morals and values ingrained in one's being act like warning lights for us, indicating something is not right. When a dishonorable person does things to others you would not like done to you it is time to be judgmental and move on to safer company. Lying, stealing, cheating, committing adultery, disrespecting, neglecting, and abusing are immoral acts that cannot be excused by the situational circumstances of the individual. Our children have a right to know right from wrong. It is the responsibility primarily of the parent to forewarn the children of the many forms of evil.

An individual with moral character has the courage to stand up to anyone with evil intentions attempting to unjustly hurt another. Bullies see this resolve of character and turn away looking for easier prey. Strength of character is a natural deterrent to all types of abusers. A person of strong character will at times unknowingly protect other close people through the power of his character. Parents are responsible to teach their children character development. Political correctness has to be subverted for the sake of our children.

Parents need to be brutally honest about the consequences of deviant behavior exhibited by any members of the family, community, or media. This will conflict with the propaganda spread by Smugger proponents. As the debate becomes more evident and intense it will open up the eyes of these potential victims of this war: our children. Children need to be protected by parents who are willing to be parents.

Besides role modeling and monitoring their child's actions parents need to pass on their religious training and personal wisdom. Parents need to tell their children when someone is doing something wrong. Pointing out the long-range negative consequences of an immoral act and then the positive consequences of the flipside, an honorable act, teaches the child that a person's moral choices do matter. As a child matures, experiencing more things outside the home in school, church, and neighborhood, he will be given opportunities to better evaluate the actions of others if he starts with a strong traditional moral and value system. The parental discipline that is the basis of forming the foundation of the child's character will continue to crystallize as the child is exposed to more of the outside world.

Higher Education Indoctrinates, Not Educates

As a professor for a decade I learned firsthand of the fantasy world of the university. Established campuses are ivory tower oases isolated from the daily problems of everyday life. These professors who are shielded from practical issues pontificate about making the world more perfect. Their thinking is based on failed Marxist ideology where one is rewarded according to their need rather than their merit, where everybody is equal regardless of their effort. The Marxist assumptions and rhetoric are convincing if you disregard history. The campus lifestyle and biased messages throughout the higher educational experience is no less intense than the reprogramming centers used by the communists to indoctrinate their subjects.

Of course the university experience should encourage students to question the traditional wisdom that is the basis of our nation. By only presenting the negative side of our system and lifestyle, our institutions of higher learning are not educating but propagandizing. Only students coming from families that have taught traditional strong values and morals have the foundation to make informed decisions. Parents who provide their children with core values are insulating them against the brainwashing often present in gangs and religious, political, and social cults. These core values will keep the maturing person on track to live a productive and peaceful life. As the person reaches the status of a dignified elder, his moral power and wisdom will act to keep our nation on the right track. We as elders have failed. We have allowed the cycle of morality to be in disrepair.

Responsible adults need to assume the role of moral leaders. Our nation has had the longest exposure to self-absorbed consumerism. Elders should take steps to modify the negative impact on children. Authority figures united with parents can persuade adolescents to boycott the hedonistic media programs. Adolescents have a right to learn values and morals that will guide them to be good and productive people.

Mature emotional and academic expectations produce positive, confident, and disciplined children. By community leaders uniting to develop a healthy community, children will have time to spend on real interactions with peers and adults and less with media indoctrination. Then children will become more mature and less emotionally depressed and self-absorbed. By concentrating on academic excellence schools will strengthen the thinking processes and discipline of the child.

Parents need to insist that community leaders adhere to socially approved thinking and behavior. Many adolescents in the U.S. are inundated by the continuous barrage of anti-traditional social messages and are in emotional turmoil about the direction they should take.

Adolescent rebellion began in the U.S. as soon as the mass media was able to reach this segment of society through television, radio, and video. The messages are blatantly anti-traditional values. When community leaders are reinforcing the same morals and values as the families who live in the community, minimal conflicts will exist for the children.

We need to begin again to venerate the wisdom of older citizens who have learned the truth from living over time. Our conscientious parents or our retired grandparents are great community resources who need to be heard by our children. Perhaps it is time for the silent backbone of our country to begin to be heard. Whenever I speak to civil groups, I urge the "Greatest Generation" to become involved in schools, youth groups, and to communicate with the children and grandchildren. The Greatest Generation has overcome a great depression, a world war, and a host of individual adversities. These are the people who have grown wiser through experiencing the challenges of life. Our ancestors throughout history as well as older citizens with character have the keys to peace.

The moral silent majority has the responsibility to break their silence and expose the Smuggers' agenda. We as a nation need to listen.

Social Institutions Do Matter in Raising a Peaceful Child and a Peaceful Nation

"Peace is not only better than war but infinitely more arduous."

—GEORGE BERNARD SHAW

Each social institution plays a key role in creating a peaceful child. Even if the child comes from a home where he has learned the beginnings of good character, the world outside the home will reinforce or corrupt the character of the child.

Our society has an impact on each and every one of us. No matter how wonderful a job parents do in creating an idyllic environment for their child, the world outside the home has a profound impact on a child. Any peaceful child confronted by the horrors of unprovoked violence will lose his sense of security. A child is snatched from the front of her house by a sexual predator. A drug-crazed mother in suburban America beats her child senseless. A child witnesses a drive-by shooting in the neighborhood. A child in Bosnia goes out to buy food down the village road while bullets fly from two directions. A Palestinian child is accidentally fired on, or an Israeli child is unable to walk the street in front of his home for fear of a homicidal bomber. All these children are experiencing the emotional scars of war. We as a society have a responsibility to our children to insure a sane and secure world for our children to grow up without unnecessary trauma. Nothing should stand in the way of our national resolve to provide a peaceful nation. A breakdown in social institutions leads to violence.

Peace can start with raising peaceful children with strong moral character but does not end there. Other social institutions like marriage, school, local communities, the media, and national military need to support each other to create a world of peace. When a society develops a strong social institutional infrastructure the nation is investing in peace. It is like a boxer who puts great effort into physical training: does pushups, runs long distances, and weightlifts to increase his stamina even though he hopes to win each fight in the early rounds. The professional fighter has prepared himself to have the stamina to be the victor even in a long, grueling fight. Things in life do not always go as planned. We have to prepare for the worst possible scenario. Peace takes long-term investment and preparation to be ready at any time to respond to unprovoked aggression.

Defense of its people is a primary function of a nation. Through strong political leadership and a level of discipline, our military and national leaders can keep our awareness of the importance of strength in deterring a civil or foreign attack. The demise of the military is the final indicator of the fall of a civilization. All social institutions need to work on an optimal moral level to foster continuing peace.

A healthy, functioning marriage provides an everyday example to the children of peaceful co-existence. A dysfunctional marriage, either hostile or disengaged, will disillusion the child towards marriage and rob him of an optimal atmosphere for personal growth. The stress a child faces in a violent school removes the focus from learning to surviving. A community of random shootings, open exposure to sex and drugs, is not a peaceful environment. It is a war zone that breaks down rather than builds up the united effort essential for establishing and maintaining peace. The ultimate solution to unprovoked violence is prevention. Morality-based social institutions retard the growth of evil.

Dividends of Traditional Values and Morals

History has taught us that traditional values and morals work together to create a peaceful society. It is a more difficult approach than the Permissive/Materialistic approach to life but it pays greater dividends to the overall society.

- ▶ If we want evil to decrease we need to teach and train our children in traditional morals and values.
- ▶ If we want corruption in our institutions to decrease we need to abide by our code of ethics or be punished.
- ▶ If we want to live in peace we need to move forward to a more value- and moral-laden society.

Our traditional values teach us the importance of discipline. It is "easy come, easy go," as we see with lottery winners and instant celebrities who quickly find themselves penniless. We learn people are responsible for their choices and their actions, which is a value under attack in our present culture by the victimization and entitlement movements. Our choices of overeating and becoming obese, drinking too much and becoming an alcoholic, wasting money on gambling and going broke, taking drugs and becoming addicted are currently said to be genetically determined instead of being choices. When people make terrible choices in spending their money on expensive addictive behaviors, these "bums" are bailed out by federal programs because somehow they are entitled to the same material benefits as someone who has been careful with his money.

Our society has to reject the phony excuses of immoral irresponsibility to maintain our national strength.

Our traditional morals and values are anchored in the best of human nature. These traditions work because they always have worked throughout history in whatever civilization had people wise enough to employ them. We must give great respect to people of impeccable character living good and fruitful lives, the wise men of the families, communities, and nations. We must refrain from continuing to listen to silver-tongued "Ponzi schemers" who have used immoral means to accumulate wealth and fame while living lives littered with self-made personal tragedies.

Functioning Families Are the Concrete that Binds the Civilization

Being a strong parent is a loving act. To be a conscientious parent by using the fear of punishment and love to shape a successful citizen is not abusive or bullying. Being an appeasing parent instead of disciplining one's child is neither laudable nor loving. As the adult we must teach and train the child as a true loving act instead of attempting to be a friend and surrender to the self-interest of the child, which is a lazy, cruel, and possibly abusive act.

Every citizen has a vested interest in our children. Children are the future of any society. We need our society to do everything possible to stabilize our world for our children.

The research is conclusive, everything being equal; two-parent households are superior to any other family circumstance. It is a difficult task for two united parents to raise healthy children. Single parenthood is like fighting with one hand tied behind your back. We need to disregard the narcissistic celebrities who advocate having children without a spouse or adopt a child who is dropped like a "hot potato" as soon as the novelty wears off.

Being a parent is a sacred responsibility that should be honored and sanctioned by our nation. The unique roles and perspectives of fathers and mothers provide children with an optimal environment in which to develop into healthy people.

We cannot throw away the family without giving away the nation. Traditional families are the backbone of any vibrant civilization. It meets everyone's individual needs while giving everyone a sense of belonging. The family is a wonderful social unit where members can share love, fun, knowledge, power, and purpose. It allows all members to have roles that enhance the development of each particular person. Parents learn how to be good leaders and children good followers. It is an environment where children are given an opportunity to learn to be parents, where parents learn to be grandparents and grandparents have the opportunity to pass on their wisdom to all the younger generations.

Humans are social beings who all possess the need to belong. All mental illness can be traced to poor or nonexistent interpersonal relationships. This is the reason that isolated people to seek out groups regardless of the cost. Teenagers join gangs, take drugs, engage in promiscuity, or do other activities to be part of a group. "Chat rooms" on the Internet have become so important that people will share their most personal feelings with total strangers.

The family provides a meaningful, safe, and loving environment to meet all our basic needs. When a disaster like 9/11 or personal tragedy like a death of a loved one strikes, people turn first to their families. The family gives real meaning to our lives. Our significant family members cannot be fully replaced by artificial relationships or any other contrived institutions. The family is essential for a healthy civilization.

What We Must Do To Win the Culture War

Victory in the Culture War will require that patriots "take care of business." I am not necessarily talking about taking up arms. It will be how we prioritize our daily lives that will ultimately decide the survival of our civilization. Each choice will create our destiny as a people and a nation.

Our daily priorities should be based on traditional principles and values, not on the "want lust" (consumerism) created by the self-indulgent secular-Smugger agenda.

Traditional principles are:

▶ Meeting family needs

▶ Thanking God for our blessings

▶ Doing the right thing: living a moral life

Prioritizing the traditional way gives citizens a proven means of maximizing beneficial choices for family community, nation, and self. In a modern world of many choices, these principles will direct our choices. At any given time it will become self-evident as to what needs to be put on the top of the priority list.

The family is society's best social unit for meeting basic needs, training, and disciplining its members. Loved ones watch out for each other better than the most dedicated government social worker. Strong families produce healthy, successful and satisfied members.

Citizens who thank God for their blessings are less vulnerable to "want lust" than citizens who follow the secular materialistic path. Counting our blessings makes us appreciate the important natural and spiritual aspects of life. Acknowledging the wondrous gifts of love, freedom, health, and nature inoculates us against the temptations of evil.

Doing the right thing guides our priorities, creating stronger moral convictions. The level of morality of our people will determine the strength of our institutions and thus of our nation.

Responsible people have to be proactive to win the culture war. The reestablishing of our superior traditional values and morals takes responsible action by all citizens.

The following twenty values will enable us to win the Culture War. There is no free ride. We must all contribute to earn the prize of peace, freedom, and prosperity. The traditional path takes consistent and constant perseverance. The efforts of a united, God-loving people result in the dividend of living a free and peaceful existence, a life with moral courage, fighting wrong in all its forms. Make the daily choices that will defeat the Smugger cultural relativists' invasion.

Be proud to live a stable, loving, and "boring" existence.

A stable life creates a wholesome environment for everyone to thrive. The counter-revolutionaries have equated an honest, hard working individual with a "boring" loser. Nothing could be further from the truth. We all need predictability, structure, and well-defined values and morals to have security and trust. Do not accept the putdown of being boring for fulfilling your responsibilities. Conscientious citizens are the backbone and true heroes of a highly functioning society.

Enhance your personal discipline.

By each of us developing our inner discipline to the fullest we are strengthening our nation and ourselves. A disciplined life makes us less vulnerable to the seduction by a hedonistic culture. Good morals and physical and mental health give us the personal power to resist temptation. Overextending our finances through binge spending keeps us tethered to the materialistic treadmill. Freedom from hedonistic materialism will come from gaining control by preserving our time and money. True freedom to become a traditional cultural warrior starts with personal discipline.

Teach and appreciate patriotism for the ideals of America.

Emphasizing our mistakes and imperfections while ignoring our exceptional accomplishments is not a heroic act. It is a deceitful and at times treasonous one.

Americans have a right and an obligation to express their patriotic feelings for the great accomplishments of our country. The true history of the great sacrifices that resulted in the spiritual strength of America should be taught to our children. The reason for the greatness of our country can be traced in the knowledge found in the development of civilized man. By teaching historical fact our children will gain enlightened, not blind, patriotism. Our national ideals of freedom and the inherent responsibilities are worth defending and communicating to enlighten other cultures.

Fight against self-censorship of thought by being judgmental and politically incorrect to protect all of us.

We need to fight against self-censorship and fear by being honest with others and ourselves. We should expect the best from our children, teachers, police officers, politicians, and especially from ourselves. By setting a high standard for others and ourselves we can improve the entire society. To evaluate whether our standards have been met we need to be judgmental. Being non-judgmental and tolerant of inappropriate or evil behavior is un-American and will lead to the demise of our civilization.

Pray to God; have faith.

A godless society leads to hopelessness, self-destruction, and moral decay. We need to thank God for giving us the opportunity to live in a free nation. It is wise to pray to God to protect our nation from evil forces. We need to be a God-loving nation to remain on the course of good.

Say "no" to abortion and zero population growth.

Babies are little miracles that are assets to everyone. The zero population growth movement will mean the demise of our nations that all need people to survive. We need children so we can pass on the torch. We need to reward parents for having children, not for killing their babies. Even most glib Smuggers cannot rationally make the abortion holocaust a moral act. Our nation has to have population growth in order to survive and prosper. There is no reason for communities, local or national, to support anything but the most effective functioning environment for our children: the family. Alternative lifestyles do not have procreation as a natural function. A society moving away from the natural order of things is undermining its moral authority and sacrificing its resources to lifestyles that do nothing to perpetuate the society. These are dysfunctional lifestyles for the nation. Communities have the responsibility and right to promote the traditional family for the sake of our children and the entire society. Our tax structure should give incentives, not disincentives, for raising families.

Stop watching trash on television.

Send a message to media Smuggers. Stop watching the movies, sitcoms, and even news shows that are propaganda for immorality, deviance, and anti-Americanism. We need to protect our minds as well as our bodies. We will change the culture by our daily choices, not allowing the counterculture to destroy our values, morals, and beliefs.

Keep sex in the bedroom.

We need to object to public sexual displays, be they heterosexual or homosexual. Sexual involvement ought to be private. Sex is only one element of life. Sex in music videos, television programming, advertising, and politics is polluting the minds and spirit of our children. There are a myriad of issues that our children have to confront and resolve to be mature and healthy adults. Allow our children the opportunity to be normal by keeping sex behind the closed doors of our bedrooms. This gift of God should remain out of sight until the person is sufficiently mature to handle the responsibility as well as the pleasure.

Teach that reputation does matter.

George Washington and other dignified men worked hard at maintaining their reputations. He realized his reputation had profound impact on everyone around him, especially on the birth of our nation. Our children need to learn this truth that a reputation does follow a person.

Good choices create a healthy reputation while bad choices create a negative reputation. Over time a positive reputation becomes a moral pillar of our society and a role model, strengthening the entire society for a peaceful existence.

Be a parent, not a friend.

Parents are supposed to parent the children, not the other way around. Obviously, parents, with their long-term experience and adult responsibilities are best able to lead the family. When parents abdicate their responsibilities as parents, fantasizing children are raising themselves. Parents, teachers, and other authority figures have to ignore it when a child acts hurt or angry when disciplined. Mature adults have a responsibility to teach, train, and prepare a child for the future, not attempt to win a popularity contest or merely chauffeur from one activity to another. It is better for society for children to resent adults who teach moral lessons than to like or tolerate adults who abdicate their leadership responsibilities. As the child matures into an adult the resentment towards the adult's strictness melts into a higher level of awareness that turns into respect. The payoff may be delayed but it is worth the wait for the adult and the society as a whole.

Promote self-defense for the sake of our children and the nation.

Children should be encouraged to defend themselves. Children should no longer be taught to be ashamed to use force in defense against an unprovoked attack. Using self-defense does not mean a person must become a bully. A victim defending himself is not equivalent to being a bully. Bullying and other forms of evil seek out and strike the vulnerable and innocent. They want to intimidate and control others for their own pleasure. Any hesitation to fight by their victim is seen by an evil person as weakness. Whining, crying, begging, or even talking is like putting a red flag in front of a bull.

Young people who demonstrate the courage to fight are being kind to bullies. A show of strength against a bully gives the bully another chance to reconsider his immoral act. We as parents and community leaders need to encourage a child to fight to protect himself. The child has the right to protect himself and has a responsibility to other children to show them that standing up to bullies unveils the bully as a coward. Adults need to understand that acquiescing to bullies leads the bullies to become full-blown sociopaths.

Teach the moral of the story.

Parents, teachers, ministers, and other authority figures should be judgmental. They should use every opportunity to point out the long run consequences of particular behaviors. Children do not have sufficient time on earth to know the ultimate outcome of their behavior. From the simple physical impact of smoking, drinking, drugging, or overeating to the more complex moral implications of stealing, promiscuity, lying, or being lazy, behaviors have to be continually discussed to help children understand the consequences of their choices. By the use of real examples, children will be given vivid understanding of life. When adults share their wisdom the children will have a better opportunity to make the right decisions in life, avoiding personal disaster.

Fathers need to be fathers.

The role of a father cannot be eliminated without creating havoc in the family. Fathers are relentlessly resented and ridiculed in the media as the traditional head of the family. The strong disciplinarian role of the father is necessary to keep children on the right path. The absence of fathers in the family is correlated with high drug use, school dropout, unwanted pregnancy, and crime. Fathers with all their dominating shortcomings are better for the family than not having a father at all.

Family comes before friends, work, or pleasurable experiences.

Our future happiness hinges on our family more than on anything else. Friends come and go, especially in our mobile society. At retirement the "symbolic watch" can tell time but will not love us. Manmade pleasurable experiences are short-lived and frequently have hangovers. The power and importance of the family members grow with time. By developing a united family all members feel a sense of belonging, power, purpose, and the experience of happiness. Our nurtured family is a sanctuary for its members.

Accept punishment, fear, and calibrated guilt as essential for discipline.

Modern parents, by setting high behavioral expectations, have to demand that their children be good. When the child is acting badly he has to receive an appropriate punishment. Because corporal punishment has been restricted, psychological administration of pain is necessary to foster a conscience. When parents show disapproval by turning a cold shoulder towards the child, or say that he is a disappointment to the parents, he learns to avoid these consequences by being more appropriate. Fearing parents is natural for children, helping to motivate them to be the best they can be. Teaching a child to have appropriate guilt for misdeeds is the basis of a healthy conscience.

Parents unite with responsible authority figures.

To correct the Smuggers' message to children that they disregard or even disobey the dictates of other authority figures, parents must evaluate the integrity of these community leaders to protect the community. When the leader does not meet the parents' criteria for integrity the parents must fight to remove the person from his or her position of power to protect their child. When the leader demonstrates his or her goodness the parent must support this authority without falling prey to the child's attempt to weasel out of appropriate consequences. Parents should unite with dedicated teachers instead of defending their child against the indefensible. The issue is to teach the child to do the right thing. No longer can we accept the anti-establishment message that our children should automatically disobey and disrespect authority figures.

Educate our children in the concept of normalcy.

"Normal" has to exist for a society to flourish. America's strength has been to define "normal" as that which complies with the natural order of things. We need to hold up the traditional virtues of the "all-American" family as our role model of normal behavior. The normal order of things is healthy for the nation. Attempting to tolerate all deviant behavior will bring us to ruination. Our role models should be normal people who have lived extraordinary lives, not celebrities who continually self-destruct.

Require by voting that our schools be small enough to teach academics, moral character, and the greatness of America.

Neighborhood schools where teachers know all the students and the students know all the teachers create a family atmosphere. Parents, teachers, and administrators have to be on the same wavelength in order to establish and maintain high standards. This is conducive to establishing a strong academic and moral program. Our schools are the primary institution in which one generation passes on the culture to the next. Small, intimate schools are best able to provide a safe, secure, and manageable environment. These schools communicate the skills, morals, and ideals of the society. Our educational institutions need to teach our traditional culture to all our citizens.

Take control of your family's mental and physical health through self-study.

Do not run to the doctor for every little trifle. God has provided us with the natural ingredients for good health. Like maintaining peace, staying healthy takes discipline and effort. Proper parenting, diet, meditation, relaxation, sleep, and exercise are indispensable in creating a healthy body, mind, and spirit. Learn what you can do to keep healthy and how to cure life's little ailments. Gaining control of our family's health will free us from the escalating medical industry's prescription drug cycle of illness. To win the culture civil war we must free ourselves from the servitude of the oppressive medical, psychological, and educational industries.

Train children in common sense.

Common sense is not very common any more. It has to be taught by adults or through "hard knocks." When adults share their knowledge of everyday life with a youngster it helps to set the groundwork for common sense. As meaningful long-term relationships dwindle, sense is replaced by ignorance. Elders have a responsibility to communicate their wisdom to others by teaching the moral of their story. Our nation is a stronger place when citizens' common sense is elevated.

The answer is evident: To preserve our peaceful and productive civilization, we must move towards the cultural center. This is the same center our forefathers selected for the course of our nation. The traditional position is where freedoms are balanced with responsibilities. This is where individual needs do not exceed family and national commitments. Our traditional values and morals have been perfected over time with a proven track record. The discipline required for a traditional lifestyle takes effort but produces peaceful results. Long-term peace for our nation has been and will be obtained by following the central path defined by our traditions.

The culture invasion is attempting to fragment our society. The continued movement towards the radical Marxist left will lead to an implosion that will inevitably result in chaos. This chaos will incur the need for a sharp correction to the far right: a dictatorship, a form of government that will eliminate our individual rights and the traditions we have built over a 250-year period. An attack from an outside power is the other alternative, a war that a hedonistic/materialistic society cannot win.

What will remain is a stark choice between peace and war. The traditional path down the cultural middle is a difficult one to follow because it requires that we think and make moral, disciplined choices. It recognizes that evil and good, pain and pleasure, punishment and reward, and self and family are realities that cannot be disregarded or wished away without becoming perilously out of balance. In order to save our national peace we must make disciplined choices to keep on the right course and not move the wheel too far to the left or too far to the right.

◈   ◈   ◈

We know for sure that institutions led by authority figures must be moral in their actions. Parents must be disciplined people.

Citizens must vote, act, and speak up, breaking the Smugger bonds of PC culture control so that we can remain free.

If all citizens live a disciplined life and make the right moral choices, the exceptionalism of our nation will be preserved.

Notes

Introduction
Choosing Sides in the Culture War

1. Barry Goldwater, speech (accepting party nomination for president, 1964).
2. Thomas Paine, *Parent Country*, 206.
3. Plato, *The Republic*, 335–36.
4. Matthew Spaulding, ed., *The Enduring Principles of the American Founding* (Washington, D.C.: The Heritage Foundation, 2001), 25.

Chapter 1
Defeating the Enemy: Smuggers

1. George J. Marlin, ed. *The Quotations of Fulton Sheen*, (New York: Doubleday, 1989), 97.
2. William Safire, "Sixteen Truthful Words," *Tampa Tribune*, July 20, 2004, 11.
3. Connie Bruck, "The World According to Soros," *The New Yorker*, January 1995, 57.
4. Ibid., 70.
5. Rachel Zabarkes Friedman, "Lawyer of Jihad," *National Review*, August 23, 2004, 31.
6. Julius Caesar, *Commentarii de bello Gallico*.
7. John Fonte, "Why There Is A Culture War: Gramsci and Tocqueville in America," *Policy Review*, 104 (2000).

8. "Students Partying Might Be Genetic," *Tampa Tribune*, August 31, 2003.
9. Mike Bates, "More People get their Biased News from ABC," *Oaklawn Reporter*, October 14, 2004.
10. Congressional Record, U.S. Senate, July 15, 1994, 59106.
11. Frank Ahrens, "Sinclair Flip-flops on Broadcasting anti-Kerry Film," *Tampa Tribune*, October 20, 2004, 7.
12. Associated Press, Thursday, August 12, 2004.

Chapter 2
Moving from Mythology to Wisdom

1. Judith Wallerstein, *The Unexpected Legacy of Divorce: The 25-Year Landmark Study* (New York: Hyperion, 2001).
2. Ann Landers, "Hitting a Child is Never Acceptable," *New York Times*, August 1, 2000, national edition.
3. Kirk Kichlight, "Occasional Spanking Doesn't Hurt, Study Says," *Tampa Tribune*, September 6, 2001.
4. John Rosemond, *To Spank or Not to Spank* (Kansas City: Andrew McMeel, 1994), 8.
5. Jill Lawless, "Britain Says No to Child Abuse; Yes to Spanking within Reason," Associated Press, November 9, 2001.
6. Leonard Pitts, "No Spanking May Be What Hurts Kids," *Tampa Tribune*, February 9, 2001.
7. "Quality Time in Eye of Beholder," Associated Press, July 18, 2002.
8. Sharon Begley Wall, "Esteem Builds on Achievement Not Praise for Slackers," *Wall Street Journal*, April 18, 2003.
9. Jeff Dohn, "Lying One Key To Social Acceptance Among Teenagers, Study Suggests," Associated Press, December 17, 1999.
10. Lauren Slater, "The Trouble with Self-Esteem," *St. Petersburg Times*, May 5, 2002.

Chapter 3
Dismantling to Building Community

1. Jack Dunphy, "Cowardice Masking as Courage," *National Review Online*, January 13, 2003.

2. Benjamin Franklin, *The Autobiography of Benjamin Franklin* (New York: Dover, 1996), 64–65.

3. Richard Brookhiser, *Founding Father: Rediscovering George Washington* (New York: Free Press, 1996), 121.

4. Libby Copeland, "Cuddle Parties Put Strangers in Touch," *Tampa Tribune*, September 3, 2004.

5. David Crary, "Youth Gambling a Growing Trend, Research Reveals," *Tampa Tribune*, July 14, 2003.

6. Amy Harmon, "CU Online: The New Type of Bully Tells Classmates," *Tampa Tribune*, Saturday, August 28, 2004.

7. "Massachusetts Father Pleads Innocent in Hockey Rink Killing," www.cnn.com, July 10, 2000.

8. Plato, *The Laws* (London: Penguin, 1970), 339.

9. Judith Levine, *Harmful to Minors: The Perils of Protecting Children from Sex* (New York: Thunder's Mouth Press, 2002).

10. Lisa Sutherland, "Operation Obesity," *Tampa Tribune*, December 7, 2002.

11. J. Michael Kennedy, "Levine Wins Times Award for Powerful 'Harmful to Minors,'" *Los Angeles Times*, April 27, 2003.

12. Christopher Gould, "Believers Have a Right to Speak Up," *Tampa Tribune*, May 2, 2004.

13. Robert Spitzer, "Psychiatry and Homosexuality," *Wall Street Journal*, May 23, 2001.

14. Franklin, *The Autobiography of Benjamin Franklin*, 45, 53, 74, 81, 91, 92, 119.

Chapter 4
Indoctrinating to Educating Students

1. Ben Feller, "Sexual Misconduct in Schools Tabulated," *Tampa Tribune*, July 1, 2004, 12.

2. Rebecca Adler, "Better Grades Don't Mean Freshmen Are Smarter," *Tampa Tribune*, February 1, 2003.

3. Cal Thomas, "Education Plus Money Does Not Equal Achievement," *Tampa Tribune*, July 6, 2004, 15.

4. Michele Meyer, "Should Your Child Really Be on Ritalin?" *Better Homes and Gardens*, September 2003.

5. "ADHD Diagnosis in Children up 90 Percent since '89," *The Florida Catholic*, January 27, 2000.

6. Robert Holland and Don Soifer, "Drug Alternatives," *Tampa Tribune*, January 18, 2003.

7. Susan Brink, "Doing Ritalin Right," *US News and World Report*, November 23, 1998, and Paul Recer, "ADD Difficult to Diagnose, Treat," *Tampa Tribune*, November 20, 1998.

8. Peter K. Breggin, *Reclaiming Our Children: A Healing Solution for a Nation in Crisis* (New York: Perseus, 2002).

9. Bill Hendrick, "Adult ADHD Gains More Attention from Doctors and Drug Makers," Cox News Service, September 2003.

10. Erica Goode, "Zoloft Does Well in Study," *New York Times*, August 27, 2003.

11. George F. Will, "Colorado Takes a Measured Step Back From Mass Medication of School Children," *Tampa Tribune*, December 2, 1999.

12. Kenneth Gilpin, "New York Sues Maker of Antidepressant Drug Paxil," *New York Times*, June 2, 2004.

13. "Stigma of Laziness Threatened," *Tampa Tribune*, February 29, 2004.

14. Jim Adams, "Bullies Are Everyone's Problem," *Junior Scholastic*, 105 (2002): 7.

15. Marty Reimer, "Beating Bullies," *Psychology Today* (February 2003): 79.

16. Mahatma Gandhi

17. Rowland Nethaway, "Smaller Classes May Sound Good, But the Evidence Isn't There," *Tampa Tribune*, June 17, 2003.

18. Darby Saxby, "Bye-Bye Junior High School," *Psychology Today* (August 2003): 22.

Chapter 5
Battling to Uniting the Sexes

1. Louis Fischer, *Gandhi: His Life and Message for the World* (New York: Mentor, 1954), 11.

2. Ibid., 20.

3. Ibid., 29.

4. Robert H. Knight, Family Research Council, www.taconic.net

5. Emma Rose, "Single Parent Children More Troubled, Study Shows," *Tampa Tribune*, February 2, 2000.

6. www.fatherhood.org

7. David Boldt, "A New Look at Unwed Births," *Philadelphia Inquirer*, September 24,1999.

8. Patrick Fagan and Robert E. Rector, *"The Positive Effects of Marriage: A Book of Charts,"* (Washington, D.C.: Heritage Foundation).

9. Judith Wallerstein, *The Unexpected Legacy of Divorce: The 25-Year Landmark Study* (New York: Hyperion, 2001).

10. Liz Trotta, "Author Decries an Abbreviated Childhood," *Washington Times*, October 19, 1999.

11. This quote is from the National Marriage Project at Rutgers University. David Crary, "Marital Attitudes of Men Studied," *Tampa Tribune*, June 25, 2004, 15.

12. Cal Thomas, "More than Politics are Needed if the Traditional Family is to be Restored," *Tampa Tribune*, May 20, 2000.

13. John Gottman, *Clinical Manual for Marital Therapy* (Indiana: The Gottman Institute, 2002): 513, and Linda Waite and Kara Joyner, *Journal of Marriage and the Family*, February 2001.

Chapter 6
Demeaning to Elevating Parenthood

1. Stacy Kalish, "Lingering Thoughts About Abortion," *Psychology Today* (June 2004), 14.

2. B. Forrest Clayton, *Suppressed History: Obliterating Politically Correct Orthodoxies* (Cincinnati: Armistead, 2003), 15.

3. Martha Irvine, "Keys to Adulthood: Finish School, Get a Job, Raise a Family," *Tampa Tribune*, May 9, 2000.

4. Steven Hyman, "America's Out-of-Control Children," *Psychology Today*, (May–June 2000), 30.

5. Laura Sessons Stepp, "Infant Homicide on Rise, Researchers Debate Diagnoses," *Tampa Tribune*, December 11, 2002.

6. "Mothers are the Ultimate Security Blanket of the Child," Associated Press, September 16, 2002.

7. Richard Brookhiser, *Founding Father: Rediscovering George Washington* (New York: Free Press, 1996), 161.

8. James Madison, Essay on Property, March 29, 1792.

Chapter 7
Disabling to Strengthening Children

1. Socrates
2. "The In Crowd," *The John Stossel Show*, February 15, 2002.
3. "Everybody Loves a Bully," *Psychology Today* (April 2004).
4. Cal Thomas, *The Wit and Wisdom of Cal Thomas* (Ohio: Promise Press), 75.
5. William Bennett, *Index of Leading Cultural Indicators, Updated and Expanded* (New York: Broadway Books, 2000), 27.
6. "Study: More Kids Troubled," Associated Press, June 6, 2000.
7. "Census Shows 1 Out of 12 Youngsters Suffers From Disability," *St. Petersburg Times*, July 6, 2002.
8. Mark Brown, "Bully Proof Your School," *Today's School*, Vol. 3, No. 5 (2003).
9. Judith Shapiro, "Lessons in Letting Go for Parents," *St. Petersburg Times*, August 24, 2002.
10. Ellen Goodman's, "New 'Separation' Questions Arise From Pledge Case", *Tampa Tribune*, June 23, 2004, 9.
11. "Mom, Girl in Pledge Suit," *St. Petersburg Times*, July 12, 2002.
12. Benjamin Spock, *Baby and Child Care* (New York: Dutton Books, 1992).
13. Elin McCoy, "What to do . . . When Kids are Mean to Your Child," *Readers Digest* (1997).

Chapter 8
Living Right, Living Disciplined: Winning the Culture War

1. Benjamin Thomas, *Abraham Lincoln* (New York: Alfred Knopf, 1951), 500.
2. Maya Bell, "Couples, Singles Now On Equal Footing For Adopting," *Tampa Tribune*, October 19, 2003.
3. "My Dream: A Time to Punt," *St. Petersburg Times*, September 7, 2000.
4. Jim Rutenberg, "Shows Speak their Creators Dissatisfaction with Bush," *Tampa Tribune*, April 4, 2004.

Acknowledgments

First and foremost I want to thank my wife for her loving support, hard work, insight, and technical skills that helped in producing this manuscript. My son, Rocco, his wife, Julie, and my brother, Larry, were always there to give assistance and invaluable feedback throughout this lengthy project. My friend, Tony D'Alessandro, sent voluminous emails on the Culture War. My other three children and their spouses helped whenever they were asked.

I want to give special thanks to my editor, Anne Sorock, for her enthusiasm, encouragement, and expertise in helping with this project. I would also like to thank Alex Novak, director of marketing, and the whole Regnery team, for their guidance through the entire publishing process.

Index

Britain, xi, xxi
British Broadcasting Corporation
   (BBC), 17
Brokaw, Tom, 22
Buddhism, 195
bullying: Internet and, 77; parenting
   and, 216–22; in public schools,
   103–4; self-defense and, 137–40,
   285–86; tolerance and, 243–50
Bundy, Ted, 213
Burke, Edmund, 26
Bush, George W., 5, 13, 22, 264
Butler, Lord, 5

Caesar, Julius, 15
California, University of, Berkeley,
   32
California, University of, Los Angeles, 221
Cannon, Ken, 247
capitalism, 24
capital punishment. See death
   penalty
Caplan, Arthur, 130
Castro, Fidel, 10, 263
The Cathy Fountain Show, 84–85
Cato Institute, 106
CBS, 21
character: adversity and, 266–70;
   discipline and, 144–45, 251;
   divorce and, 213; evil and, 24–26
"The Charter on Medical Professionalism," 181
Chicago, University of, 182
child-rearing. See parenting
children: community and, 74;
   courage and, 246–47, 248; depression in, 131; divorce and, 29–31,
   154, 159–61; entitlement and, 43,

215, 230–31; family and, 193;
   freedom and, 79–80, 232; honesty
   and, 37–39; Internet and, 77–78;
   marriage and, 156–61, 277; nor-
   malcy and, 146–48, 288; parent
   micromanagement and, 121–23;
   protection of, 40–43; quantity vs.
   fantasy time and, 74–75; same-sex
   marriage and, 87–88; self-defense
   and, 137–40; self-esteem and,
   49–50; sexual abuse of, 81–86.
   See also parenting
choice, freedom of, xvi, xxiii, 64–65,
   87
Christianity, 195
Churchill, Winston, 94
Cicero, xxii, 153
Clinton, Bill, 2–3, 240, 256
Clinton, Hillary, 2–3
colleges. See universities
Columbine shootings, 138, 223
Common Sense (Paine), xxiv
communism, xx, 24
community: American Dream and,
   72–73; artificial relationships and,
   78–81; dissolution of, 67–68; gay
   issues and, 86–90; Internet and,
   91–93; materialism and, 73–76;
   media and, 67, 77–78; necessity
   of, 93–94; parenting and, 95–96;
   protection of innocent in, 69–71;
   responsibility and, 73, 94–97;
   restoring, 97–100; role models
   for, 68–69; television and, 90–91;
   virtual, 90–93; virtue and, 71–72;
   voluntary association and,
   100–102
Conduct Disorder, 55
Confucius, 196